CONVERSATIONS OF THE MIND

The Uses of Journal Writing
for Second-Language Learners

CONVERSATIONS OF THE MIND

The Uses of Journal Writing
for Second-Language Learners

Rebecca Williams Mlynarczyk
*Kingsborough Community College
of the City University of New York*

LEA LAWRENCE ERLBAUM ASSOCIATES, PUBLISHERS
1998 Mahwah, New Jersey   London

Lawrence Erlbaum Associates, Inc., Publishers
10 Industrial Avenue
Mahwah, New Jersey 07430

Cover design by Kathryn Houghtaling Lacey

Library of Congress Cataloging-in-Publication-Data

Mlynarczyk, Rebecca.
    Conversations of the mind : the uses of journal writing for
second-language learners / Rebecca Williams Mlynarczyk.
        p. cm.
    Includes bibliographical references and index.
    ISBN 0-8058-2317-4 (acid-free paper). — ISBN 0-8058-2318-2
(pbk. acid-free paper)
    1. English language—Study and teaching—Foreign speakers.
2. English language—Composition and exercises.   3. Diaries—Authorship—Study and teaching.   4. Report writing—Study and teaching.   I. Title.
    PE1128.A2M554   1997
    428'.007—dc21   97-30927
                                                     CIP

Printed in the United States of America
10   9   8   7   6   5   4   3   2   1

In memory of my father,

Bert Williams

Contents

Foreword

It is with great pride and pleasure that I welcome you to *Conversations of the Mind: The Uses of Journal Writing for Second-Language Learners*—pride because I had the good fortune to sponsor the original version of this text as a New York University dissertation, and pleasure because I have just had the chance to renew acquaintance with Rebecca Mlynarczyk and her students by means of a powerfully revised and extended version of that original text.

Chief among those pleasures is the power and clarity of the voice I hear, which reminds me of the many hours I have spent both discussing teaching and learning with Rebecca and reading her learning logs. As she points out in the beginning of *Conversations of the Mind*, her interest in student journals was sparked by her experience of their power as learning tools for her. The ongoing transformation of her teaching that she reports in this book began with a transformation of her learning experiences in our doctoral program. She had proved herself to be both an exemplary learner/teacher and extraordinarily gifted at sharing her explorations, her struggles, and her successes. Those of you who have not yet met Rebecca have a treat in store as you join these *Conversations*.

In addition to meeting Rebecca, you'll also get a chance to meet her students and watch them learn and grow as speakers/writers of English, and as people. Their stories are individual, of course, but they resonate with those of other students in this class, and other students Rebecca has taught before and since. The portraits are so finely and engagingly drawn that they also enable teacher/readers to compare them to our own, which in turn allows us to use them to reflect on our teaching while Rebecca is reflecting on hers.

This is profoundly a book about teaching and learning, but it is not a collection of lesson plans or even a method as such. It is, rather, the description of a reflective practitioner in action as she tries to understand how what she does as a teacher affects—and effects—her students. Equally, she is trying to get beneath the surface of the polite ESL class to see how her students are learning as they experiment with a kind of writing which is new to all of them and which "works" in different ways for each of them—powerfully for some, minimally for others. And, most impressively of all, the final chapter opens up each of Rebecca's tentative conclusions by questioning in turn the role of gender in personal writing, the role of culture in journal writing, the virtues and defects of freewriting, the effect of journal writing on connected knowing, and the issues of privacy and audience in journal writing. The chapter is appropriately entitled "The Conversation Continues," and it shows a thoughtful teacher reflecting on her practice in a way that invites us to similarly reconsider our own assumptions and thereby be part of the ongoing dialogue.

In addition to their usefulness for teachers and teacher educators, these *Conversations of the Mind* provide a model of the power and utility of qualitative inquiry for deeply understanding teaching and learning transactions. Teacher/researchers would do well to emulate the care with which Rebecca has gathered her data as well as her procedurally cautious but ultimately conceptually bold interpretation of these "cases" within the context of this class and of her teaching as a whole. This boldness comes across most clearly in the last chapter, where she uses the cases to question her own stereotypes and prior beliefs as well as those held by some of the most respected teacher/scholars in our field.

In spite of the large number of people with whom teachers work every day, teaching is a surprisingly lonely profession in terms of the amount of collegial talk most teachers engage in about their teaching, and visiting another teacher's classroom is even rarer. One of the great joys of this book, therefore, is a chance to visit with a teacher whose merit does not derive from great performances at the chalkboard, but from a deep commitment to understanding how students learn and to bending her efforts toward strengthening their learning. All good teachers learn more from their students than they teach them, so it is my pleasure to invite you to learn with and from one of my students as you join these *Conversations of the Mind*.

—John S. Mayher
New York University

Preface

This book grew out of my desire to know more about the uses of journal writing for second-language learners. As a teacher of writing to college English as a Second Language (ESL) students, I had often noticed that when I asked my students to write about their attitude toward writing, or the difficulties of writing in English, or their thoughts about and reactions to the books we were reading, they responded with a freshness and direct-ness—and often, it seemed, with fluency and correctness—that were miss-ing from their formal essays.

Although there have been many informative studies of ESL student journal writing (Peyton, 1990; Peyton & Staton, 1993; Root, 1979; Spack & Sadow, 1983; Staton, 1980; Staton, Shuy, & Kreeft, 1982; Zamel, 1992), none of them adequately addressed the questions in which I was most interested:

- Why do some students welcome the chance to keep a journal while others resist it or refuse to do it altogether?
- Why do students use their journals in such different ways, some writing creatively or reflectively while others limit their responses to summarizing the assigned course readings?
- Is there something inherent in journal writing that encourages students to write reflectively?
- What psycholinguistic or cognitive theories help to explain the power of journal writing for some second-language writers?
- Why do some journal entries strike teachers as so much more interesting and rewarding than others?
- How do teachers' responses to their students' journals affect the students as writers and thinkers?

Eventually, my interest in exploring such questions and in learning more about the complex processes involved in second-language journal writing led to the research described in this book.

Conversations of the Mind is based on a teacher-research study of journal writing in a course I taught at a large urban college—a pre-freshman composition writing course for ESL students. Realizing that the journals themselves, the words on the page, were only one of many pieces of the puzzle, I decided to interview several students after the semester ended in order to learn more about their personal and academic backgrounds and about their perceptions of the role of journal writing in their learning.

My decision to study students within the context of my own classroom was based in part on my awareness of the limitations of much of the existing research on student writing. Too many otherwise exemplary studies have been conducted outside the writing classroom (see, for example, Emig, 1971; Perl, 1975; Sommers, 1979). The research described in this book portrays the students' journal writing as it occurred in the larger contexts of a specific class at a specific institution. Moreover, it focuses not only on the learning experiences of the students, but on the teacher's learning as well.

The focus on the teacher as learner is important because teachers comprise the primary audience for *Conversations of the Mind*. Because of the book's concern with second-language writers, it will be especially useful in programs that prepare teachers to work with students for whom English is a second language. For graduate students enrolled in Ph.D., M.A., or certificate programs in TESOL (Teaching English to Speakers of Other Languages), this book provides a deeper understanding of the writing and thinking processes of the students they plan to teach.

The book is also intended for teachers who work with native speakers of English, especially students at the secondary or college levels. Based on my experience as a teacher of writing to both native speakers and ESL students, as well as a significant body of research in second-language writing (Leki, 1992; Raimes, 1983, 1985; Zamel, 1976, 1983), I believe that although writing in a second language is more difficult than writing in a first language, the thought processes are similar. Much of the research on first-language writing provides insight into second-language writing, and the reverse is often true as well. Thus, it is possible to learn a great deal about journal writing in general from the specific experiences of the second-language writers in this study.

With its close look at the processes and products of student journal writing, this book is relevant to students in graduate programs in composition and rhetoric. Even if these teachers in training do not intend to work exclusively with second-language students, the changing demographics of student populations in the United States make it likely that their classes will at times include ESL writers. For the few teachers who will work only with native speakers of English, the book provides a deeper understanding of the complexities of student journal writing, regardless of the native language of the students.

The book is also intended to serve as a valuable resource for use in qualitative research courses or in education courses for preservice or in-service teachers that rely on "teaching cases" for study and analysis. By providing an extended "case" based on actual teaching practice, the book supplies authentic material for intensive discussion and critique.

Finally, the book is relevant for general readers including teachers, scholars, and others who would like to learn more about the fascinating phenomenon of student journal writing.

OVERVIEW OF THE BOOK

Chapter 1 introduces the research questions and methods that guided the study of student journal writing. Chapter 2 examines the reading that informed my investigation of the mental processes involved in journal writing. Particularly helpful in my emerging understanding of these processes were the linguistic theories of Lev Vygotsky (1978, 1986) and James Britton (1970, 1982) and the concept of connected knowing as articulated by Belenky, Clinchy, Goldberger, and Tarule (1986). Chapter 3 moves from the realm of theory into the practical world of the classroom, with descriptions of the context in which the students' journal writing took place. Chapters 4, 5, 6, and 7 are detailed case studies of the journal-writing experiences of five of these students. Chapter 4 is the story of Roberto, a student from Colombia and an enthusiastic journal writer who used the journal to reflect on his own experiences in light of his reading. Chapter 5 focuses on Cliff, a student from Ethiopia, another prolific and reflective journal writer. In addition to exploring personal issues in his own life, Cliff used the journal to provide detailed answers to my questions about his past history as a reader and writer of English. Chapter 6 chronicles the experiences of Maribel, a student from the Dominican Republic, who used her journal primarily for summaries of the reading that I judged to be largely "unreflective." Chapter 7 contrasts the experiences of Lan, from the People's Republic of China, and Kiyoko, from Japan—two young women who outwardly appeared to have many things in common but who had very different reactions to freewriting and journal keeping. Chapter 8, the concluding chapter, discusses the larger implications of the case studies, particularly the ways in which they often belie common assumptions about writing and culture. This final chapter is a reminder of the constant need for teachers to reexamine their practice and learn from their students. Appendixes A through E include unedited samples of student journal entries and my response letters.

A NOTE ABOUT THE STYLE OF THIS BOOK

The impact of any ethnographic study depends largely on the researcher's skill and sensitivity in writing, for as Geertz has pointed out, "The ethnographer 'inscribes' social discourse, *he* [or she] *writes it down*. In so doing, [s]he turns it from a passing event, which exists only in its own moment of occurrence, into an account, which exists in its inscription and can be reconsulted" (1973, p. 19).

My goal in writing this book was to describe the essence of what I learned about journal writing from the students in my own classes. However, in relating what I learned, it seemed inappropriate to use the cool and dispassionate language of the scientific observer. It was more fitting and more honest to acknowledge my own involvement with the students I was not only studying, but also teaching.

As I pondered the different ways to present my findings in writing, I eventually came to think of this book as a conversation among many different voices. There are the voices of the scholars whose work has influenced my thinking. There are my own voices—the experienced teacher, the self-assured researcher, the overwhelmed data collector. Most important in the pages that follow are the voices of the students on whose experiences this book is based. And like me, each student has many voices as heard in the journals, in classroom discussions and conferences in my office, and in the more relaxed and expansive atmosphere of the ethnographic interviews.

As I worked at combining the various voices to reveal what I learned, I was reminded of my grandmother, Minnie Stamps, piecing together scraps of gingham and calico into beautiful patchwork quilts. Most often I found myself remembering the "flower garden" quilt, under which I slept for most of my childhood. Many mornings after my best friend Patty had slept over, we would sit on the bed and talk about where the different patches had come from, sources that ranged from feed sacks from Uncle Edward's store to the dress I had proudly worn in second grade.

This book is, in some ways, a quilt made of words. As with my grandmother's quilts, the materials were gathered from many different sources, but they have been carefully arranged and held together by one person's judgment and sensibility. And like the flower garden quilt that sparked so many early morning talks between my friend Patty and me, this book will, I hope, mark not the end but the beginning of the conversation.

ACKNOWLEDGMENTS

Throughout my career as a teacher of developmental reading and writing, I have never ceased to be inspired by the resourcefulness, intelligence, and creativity of the students with whom I work. The students who participated in this study earned my deepest respect and appreciation for so openly sharing their thoughts and experiences. I offer them my heartfelt thanks.

The study on which this book is based was conducted for my Ph.D. dissertation in New York University's School of Education. I am deeply grateful to the three professors on my doctoral committee, John Mayher, Margot Ely, and Barbara Danish.

I also wish to thank the members of my writing group—Susan Babinski, Jane Isenberg, and Pat Juell—for the support and encouragement, the conversation and critique they so generously provided over the years in which this project came to fruition.

My interest in student journal writing developed during the years in which I taught in the English Department at Hunter College. Many in that department offered their collegiality and support. I thank especially Allan Brick, who was then the Department Chair; Richard Barickman, the current Chair; and Louise DeSalvo, Karen Greenberg, John Holm, Kate Parry, Ann Raimes, and Trudy Smoke, colleagues who shared my interest in journals and the teaching of writing.

I also wish to thank my current colleagues in the Department of English at Kingsborough Community College for their encouragement of this project and for their own commitment to sound writing pedagogy. I am particularly indebted to Stephen Weidenborder, Chair; Bonne August, Director of Freshman English; Robert Viscount, formerly Director of ESL; Marcia Babbitt, with whom I now codirect the ESL program; and Kate Garretson.

During the spring of 1996, I participated in the CUNY Faculty Development Seminar on Balancing the Curriculum for Gender, Race, Ethnicity, and Class. This seminar, under the adept leadership of Dorothy Helly of Hunter College and Marina Heung of Baruch College, was an important influence on my thinking, particularly in regard to issues related to language and gender.

In the summer of 1996 I served as codirector of New York University's Study Abroad Program for teachers, located at Trinity College, Oxford. This program offered me the opportunity to work with outstanding British and American writers and educators. I would like to express my appreciation to the other codirectors, Marlene Barron and Jane Isenberg, as well as the NYU students, who inspired me with their energy and creativity.

Many people at Lawrence Erlbaum Associates have earned my thanks for helping to make the publication of this book such a satisfying experience. I got to know Naomi Silverman, my editor, while working on my first book, and in working with her again, I have benefitted even more from her wisdom and editorial experience. One way in which Naomi demonstrated her expertise was in her choice of reviewers. I would like to thank Joy Kreeft Peyton of the Center for Applied Linguistics and Ruth Spack of Tufts University, who read the manuscript carefully and provided many insightful suggestions. I also wish to thank Debbie Ruel, Senior Production Editor, for guiding the book through the publication process with efficiency and good humor.

Finally, I would like to thank my family, without whose love and support I could not have written this book. My husband, Frank, enthusiastically supported the project from start to finish. My daughter, Susanna, sustained me with her interest and incisive reader response. My son, Alex, kept me balanced with his belief in the power of perseverance interspersed with timely reminders to "take a break." My sister, Carol, and her partner, Robert Asher, were steadfast in their belief that I should seek publication. My mother, Ruth Adams, now in her eighties, is one of those rare individuals who has never stopped learning and growing. She provides a worthy model for my life as a teacher and an intellectual. My father, Bert Williams, who died when I was nine, provided inspiration through his journals and letters, which my mother shared with me while I was working on the book. He was a man of great integrity and kindness, a dedicated teacher, and a prolific and eloquent journal writer. This book is dedicated to his memory.

—Rebecca Williams Mlynarczyk

1

Introduction:
The Teacher, the Study, the Students

THE TEACHER

The idea for this book originated on the evening of September 11, 1989, when I attended the first meeting of the doctoral seminar in English education at New York University, the first course I had taken since receiving my master's degree in 1968. As I left the class that night, I felt excited to be a student again after 15 years as a teacher of developmental writing at the City University of New York. The requirements for the course seemed simple enough: Read a book a week and respond by writing a learning log, or journal, to be shared with the professor and a student partner. The reading list looked demanding but the learning logs would not be graded.

Not many weeks had passed before I realized that the type of writing elicited by these learning logs was different from anything I had produced before. The strong, clear voice that began to emerge in my learning logs seemed to have an opinion on just about everything and wasn't afraid to enter into dialogue and occasionally into disagreement with the likes of Louise Rosenblatt, Howard Gardner, and Jerome Bruner. Although this voice belonged to me, it surprised me with its intensity. It had remained steadfastly silent during my previous academic writing as an undergraduate and master's student in literature. Where did this voice come from? And what could I learn from listening to it?

When I tried to analyze how the learning logs were different from the many formal papers I had written previously, one obvious difference was that the logs were not graded or held up to some unreachable ideal. All my previous academic papers had been evaluated by the professor, who responded with a letter grade and a brief note, usually devoted to justifying the grade. Often, the grades I got on these papers seemed more a reflection of my ability to echo the professor's opinions than a reward for original thinking.

Another difference between the learning logs and my previous academic papers was that in the doctoral seminar, writing and learning were seen as social activities. As a college student in the 1960s I wrote all of my academic papers strictly on my own. In those days collaboration on academic work was akin to cheating. Thus, my papers were written in isolation from my peers and read only by my professors, never by my friends or other students in the class. In contrast, the learning logs I wrote when I returned to graduate school in 1989 were read not only by the professor, but also by one or more student partners. In effect, the logs served as the beginnings of compelling conversations about the books we were reading; the professor and student partners wrote responses in the margins of the logs, which were left wide for that purpose. Ironically, the time pressure of having to respond to a book a week helped me relax. My professors and my partners couldn't expect these weekly logs to be polished and perfect. What was more important, neither could I.

The increased involvement I felt in writing the learning logs was not only because of the heightened social dimension. Much of the excitement I felt in these early logs had to do with my own interaction with the books. I found myself grappling with difficult concepts by expressing them in my own words, making connections between ideas in the books and previous reading, testing out the authors' ideas by drawing comparisons with my own experience. I particularly remember a log about Howard Gardner's *Frames of Mind* (1983) in which I related several of Gardner's proposed types of intelligence to people in my own life. As a result of this active processing of the reading, I still clearly remember Gardner's theory. His notion of musical intelligence is now inextricably linked with my musician friend Jack. The concept of spatial intelligence is intertwined with memories of the artistic development of my daughter, Susanna.

As I progressed from one course to the next, journal writing remained a consistent feature of my learning. In a linguistics course I took at another college, in which students were graded on the basis of a midterm and final examination, I was struck by how much my workload and my learning were reduced when no journal was required.

Not only was I intrigued by the power of what Britton (1970) referred to as "expressive writing" in my own learning, but I had also noticed that when I asked the ESL students I taught to keep journals about their reading or to write informally about their writing processes, many of them seemed to write with more power and directness than when they were composing formal essays. I wondered whether this impressionistic judgment would hold up if I investigated student journal writing in a more systematic way. Eventually, my curiosity about the uses of journal writing for second-language writers led to the research described in this book.

THE STUDY

Conversations of the Mind reports the results of a teacher-research study in which I observed and analyzed the journal writing of students in my own classroom. These students were enrolled in two sections of an ESL writing course I taught at a large, urban public university in the spring of 1992. This course was the last one in the ESL sequence before the students took freshman composition, which offered credit toward graduation and in which ESL students were mainstreamed with native speakers of English.

In developing the research design, I wanted to understand the students' experiences with journal writing within the larger context of the writing classroom, for as Mayher (1990) has pointed out, it is important to situate research on writing within the complex social world of the classroom. Besides attending to the classroom context, I also wanted to learn as much as possible about the students' educational backgrounds and previous life experiences. In an influential article focused on the need for research on bilingual writers, Valdes explained why this is important:

> Writing researchers must be aware that any research done on writing alone that is not directly grounded in the academic and personal experiences of the minority students in question will contribute little to our understanding of the actual value of writing for these students, of the other factors that influence their academic success, and of the approaches that could be taken to break long-established patterns and expectations. (1992, p. 119)

Because I was attempting to understand the students' journal writing within broader societal and educational contexts, qualitative research methods were most appropriate. The methodology I selected as offering the best way of capturing this complex interplay is classified by Tesch (1990) as educational ethnography. The primary "instrument" in this type of research is the human observer (Lincoln & Guba, 1985), and the goal is to discern patterns through recursive processes of close observation, rich description in a field log, and ongoing analysis of data (Tesch, 1990).

By choosing to focus on the students in my classes, I also chose to be an active participant in the research process. This is consistent with Schön's notion of research on the process of reflection (1983). As I set up a learning environment and observed the students' experiences with journal writing, I too was constantly reflecting—not only on their learning, but on my own as well.

The decision to conduct the study in my own classroom placed it within the tradition of teacher research, defined by Cochran-Smith and Lytle as "systematic and intentional inquiry carried out by teachers" (1993, p. 7). Teacher research is much more context-specific than is university research, which usually begins with already existing theoretical or empirical information. As Cochran-Smith and Lytle have pointed out: "Embedded within the particular questions of teacher researchers are many other implicit questions about the relationships of concrete, particular cases to more general and abstract theories of learning and teaching" (1993, p. 15).

In my study I soon discovered that serving as teacher and researcher created certain challenges. Balancing these two roles required tremendous effort, and at times the roles were in conflict. One example that comes to mind occurred during an individual conference with a student near the end of the semester, when I was torn between wanting to spend the conference time discussing the student's journal and feeling obligated to concentrate on helping him to prepare for the final exam. I opted to do the latter.

The students, too, were undoubtedly influenced by my dual roles as teacher and researcher. They were surely aware that I thought journal writing was an important activity, which may have influenced what they chose to tell me during conferences and interviews. I tried to set the tone by explaining the importance of honest answers and probing to find out how the students really felt about journal writing—not how they thought I wanted them to feel. In conducting interviews with students, I attempted to relinquish the role of teacher, thus allowing the students to teach me about their experiences with the journals. And when this role reversal occurred, it was one of the most rewarding aspects of the entire research project.

In addition to the risks involved in conducting the study within my own classroom, there were some significant advantages as well. Most important was my intense interest in and involvement with these students and their journals. Lofland and Lofland referred to this as "starting where you are" (1984, p. 10). Another important advantage was having automatic access to "the richest possible data" (Lofland & Lofland, 1984, p. 11). Only as the teacher could I have had such complete access to the total context. Erickson (1993) stressed the advantages of this "insider" position when he said that reports of teacher research "portray the teacher as agent in a way that cannot be portrayed in research conducted by intermittent visitors to the classroom, however sensitive they may be as observers and reporters. The teacher comes to know teaching from within the action of it, and a fundamentally important aspect of that action is the teacher's own intentionality" (p. viii).

The knowledge of the students as individuals that I built up during the semester provided a significant advantage when conducting the subsequent ethnographic interviews. This knowledge continued to be extremely helpful in the final stages of analysis when I attempted to make meaning from diverse data sources. Often, as I was pondering the meaning of a particular journal entry or interview segment, the student's face would appear in my mind and help me to determine the significance of what this individual was trying to say.

The experience I have acquired in my many years of teaching developmental writing was also useful in interpreting and analyzing data. This advantage was counterbalanced, however, by the effort to suspend my existing theories and let the data talk to me directly (Ely, Anzul, Friedman, Gardner, & Steinmetz, 1991; Lofland & Lofland, 1984). Phenomenologists refer to this suspension as "bracketing" (Hycner, 1985, p. 281, quoted in Tesch, 1990, p. 92). Although it is impossible to suspend one's preconceptions totally, it is possible to reduce their interference in the research by openly attempting to articulate what they are (see the section entitled "Stance of the Teacher-Researcher" in chapter 3).

Like most ethnographic research, this study of student journal writing relied on multiple research techniques and a variety of data sources (Goetz & LeCompte, 1984). These included the students' journal entries and my own written responses, classroom interactions and individual writing conferences as recorded in an extensive field log, audiotapes and transcriptions of relevant class segments and conferences with students, and ethnographic interviews with five student participants selected from these classes after the semester ended.

Journals

Because journal writing was the focus of this study, the principal sources of data were the students' journals (samples of student journal entries appear in the appendixes). From the beginning of the semester each student was asked to keep a journal, which included in-class freewriting on prompts I devised as well as out-of-class entries about the assigned reading, *A Place for Us*, an autobiographical account of a Greek immigrant's assimilation into U.S. culture (Gage, 1989). The guidelines for the journal (see p. 42), which

I distributed during the second week of class, suggested that students use their journals to write about themselves and their reactions as readers and writers. The guidelines went on to state: "Of course, readers and writers are also people. So if there are personal things you would like to discuss in your journal, that's fine too." Students were asked to write in the journal about five times a week and to produce at least five pages of writing. They were also reminded to add all of the 10-minute, in-class freewrites to their journals.

I collected and read the journals every 2 to 3 weeks, responding either in individual letters to the student writers or, toward the end of the semester, in letters written to the class as a whole (samples of these varying types of response appear in the appendixes). In the excerpts from student journal entries reproduced in later chapters, I have not made corrections in spelling, grammar, and usage. In the rare cases where I felt a correction was necessary to ensure clarity, I supplied it within brackets.

Field Log

The field log was the running account through which I attempted to make meaning of the students' journal writing within the context of the class. As I read and responded to each set of student journals, I recorded my impressions in the log, commenting on patterns I noted in different students' journals and recording my own reactions. Also included in the log were my observations of and thoughts about what was happening in the classes, which met twice a week. Often I took notes during class while the students were writing and later added these observations to the log.

Interviews

Because of my desire to study not just the texts of the journals but the students' experiences in keeping them, interviews were an essential component of the study. Because of the open-ended nature of my research, I decided to conduct ethnographic interviews rather than more structured interviews using a predetermined "schedule" of questions. Spradley explained why the ethnographic interview is an essential tool for qualitative researchers:

> … when we merely observe behavior without also treating people as informants, their cultural knowledge becomes distorted. For human beings, what an act means is never self-evident. Two persons can interpret the same event in completely different ways. (1979, pp. 32–33)

Despite the free-flowing nature of ethnographic interviews, they differ from everyday conversation in two significant respects: The interviewer makes the purpose of the talk explicit and encourages the participant to repeat or expand on statements made earlier.

I decided to conduct the interviews 2 to 3 weeks after the course was over, reasoning that the students would be more open and honest with me after my official role as the evaluator and grader of their writing had ended. This meant, of course, that some time had elapsed since the students actually wrote the journal entries we discussed during the interviews. There were advantages as well as disadvantages to the retrospective nature of these discussions. A possible disadvantage was that the students' memories might be incomplete or inaccurate on some points. For the purposes of this study, however, it was beneficial that the students had had several weeks to put their experiences with journal writing into perspective and to assess the meaning of the journals in their learning. And even if I had interviewed the students regularly throughout the semester, their accounts of journal writing would still have been retrospective in the sense that the entries would have been written before the interviews.

I held two interviews with each of the five participants. To prepare for these interviews, I reviewed the field log and the student's journal entries in order to develop a broad plan of questioning. The second interview with each participant provided opportunities to clarify and expand on material that had emerged in the first interview and to obtain additional information. The interviews were conducted in a conference room at the college and lasted approximately 1 hour each. I audiotaped and transcribed each of the interviews in its entirety. Quotations from the transcripts, which appear in later chapters, are reproduced verbatim except for the deletion of false starts ("I think, I think that ... ") and fillers such as "uh" or "mmm." Words or phrases that were emphasized by the speaker appear in italics. When one speaker abruptly interrupted another, this is indicated with slash marks at the end and beginning of both utterances ("She didn't, you know,/" "/She didn't say which one should be longer or anything?"). Because participants were assured of anonymity, pseudonyms are used throughout the book.

THE STUDENTS

In choosing student participants, I used "purposive sampling" (Lincoln & Guba, 1985) to select students from a variety of linguistic and cultural backgrounds. Even more important, I wanted to interview students who had

had different experiences with journal writing, ranging from those who wrote prolifically and reflectively to those who seemed to struggle to eke out a few words each week. During the last class session, I approached five students and asked if they would be willing to come in for interviews after the semester ended. All five agreed to participate.

Roberto, an 18-year-old college freshman who had emigrated from Colombia with his family 4 years earlier, responded positively to journal writing from the beginning of the semester. He wrote engaging journal entries about many different subjects of his own choosing. I hoped to learn more about what factors contributed to Roberto's effective uses of the journal.

Cliff, who had been born in Ethiopia and was a native speaker of Amharic, also moved to the United States when he was 14. At the time of the study, Cliff was 21 years old and in his third semester of college. Like Roberto, Cliff enjoyed keeping a journal and often used it to reflect on important personal issues. But his journal was more formal and more tightly organized than Roberto's. I wanted to know why Cliff chose to approach his journal as a series of personal essays rather than the freer exploration of ideas Roberto used in his journal.

Maribel, an 18-year-old freshman born in the Dominican Republic, had also immigrated to the United States at age 14. Unlike Cliff and Roberto, Maribel used her journal almost entirely for summaries of the reading, and her journal appeared to me to contain few examples of reflective writing. During the interviews and analysis, I hoped to learn more about why Maribel did not use her journal for written reflection and how, in future courses, I could encourage students to use their journals more reflectively.

Lan was a woman in her early 20s who had been born and educated in the People's Republic of China. I selected her as a participant because she, like many other students in the ESL writing course, was having difficulty passing the final writing exam. During the semester in which the study was conducted, Lan was taking the writing course for the third time. I wondered whether the increased fluency she developed through journal writing had been a significant factor in the language growth that enabled her to pass the exam at the end of the semester.

Kiyoko, also in her early 20s, had completed several years of university work in her native Japan before deciding to continue her studies in the United States. In her journal Kiyoko wrote primarily about the course reading or other topics I suggested, and I judged many of her entries to be reflective as she analyzed the book and her own responses to it. Kiyoko had demonstrated tremendous language improvement during the semester, and

I hoped to learn more about whether the journal played a role in her improvement as a writer of English.

GUIDING QUESTIONS

The questions that guide teacher research often arise out of teachers' day-to-day classroom concerns. Why does a particular teaching method work so well for one student but not for another? Why does the writing assignment that was so successful last semester fall flat the following term? Despite the tendency of teacher research to deal with specific cases or particular situations, however, it also often relates to more abstract and theoretical concerns. In the words of Cochran-Smith and Lytle: "The unique feature of the questions that prompt teacher research is that they emanate from neither theory nor practice alone but from critical reflection on the intersection of the two" (1993, p. 15).

In the study described in this book, it was my intention to look closely at the experiences of individual students as they kept a reading/writing journal over the course of one 14-week semester. What would they choose to write in their journals? What different writing processes would they employ, and what might account for these differences? How would keeping the journals affect the students' acquisition of English and their growth as thinkers and writers? I was particularly interested in whether the students would use their journals in reflective ways—writing thoughtfully about such topics as themes and issues in the book we were reading, their own writing processes, or their progress in acquiring a second language. Finally, I was interested in investigating my sense that there were important differences between journal writing and more formal types of writing such as essays and reports. Would the students be aware of the same kinds of differences I had noticed while keeping learning logs during my doctoral studies?

What I offer to readers in the following pages is not a definitive set of answers to these questions. Nor is it an unqualified endorsement of the value of journal writing for second-language students. Rather, I provide a glimpse at how journals worked or failed to work in one classroom. This goal is consistent with the expressed aim of ethnographic research in education, which does not attempt so much to solve problems as to open up new ways of looking at educational experiences. As North expressed it:

> The aim of Ethnographic inquiry ... is to enlarge "the universe of human discourse," in Geertz' phrase—not to describe it, or to account for it, or to

codify it, but to *enlarge* it, make it bigger. Its power as a mode of inquiry, and hence the authority of the knowledge it produces, derives from its ability to keep one imaginative universe bumping into another. (1987, p. 284)

It is my hope that by giving readers a close look at the uses of journal writing for a particular group of students and their teacher, this book will encourage other teachers, writers, and researchers to reflect on the problems and possibilities of student journal writing.

2

Textual Explorations: Thinking and Writing in Journals

When I began reading to gain insight into my questions about journal writing, I embarked on an adventure in which there were occasional frustrations as well as unexpected discoveries. In one sense, all the literature on writing as a mode of thinking was related to my questions about the mental processes involved in journal writing. Yet none of the existing literature adequately explained these processes. As I continued to read, there were times when I felt as if I had set out on a journey without a roadmap. Although it is now possible to conceptualize my emerging understanding in a neat, linear way, there were times when the process was anything but neat as I groped my way along, gaining insight, sometimes from unexpected sources, as my questions about journal writing grew and changed.

RESEARCH ON JOURNALS AND DIARIES

I began this journey by familiarizing myself with sources devoted exclusively to journal writing. Personal diaries have been studied by, among others, Baldwin (1977), Gannett (1992), Progoff (1975), and Rainer (1978). A continuously expanding literature relates to the uses of writing to learn and teacher-assigned journals (see, e.g., Fulwiler, 1987; Gere, 1985; Johnstone, 1994; Mayher, Lester, & Pradl, 1983). Dialogue journals involving native speakers of English as well as second-language learners have been analyzed in depth (Peyton, 1990; Peyton & Staton, 1993, 1996; Staton, 1980; Staton, Shuy, & Kreeft, 1982; Staton, Shuy, Peyton, & Reed, 1988).

However, very little of this research deals with the psycholinguistic processes involved in journal writing. The question of whether journal writing is conducive to reflection is largely ignored by these studies.

The researcher who comes closest to studying journal writing as reflection (although she uses the term *introspection* rather than *reflection*) is Marilyn Sternglass. In *The Presence of Thought: Introspective Accounts of Reading and Writing* (1988), Sternglass carefully documented the experiences of graduate students in English and language education as they kept introspective journals exploring their reading and writing experiences during a one-semester course. She described introspection as "thinking about one's processes and then describing those thoughts in the language that gave form to them" (1988, p. 43). Thus defined, introspection is closely related to reflection, which includes, but is not limited to, thinking about thinking; one can reflect about problems and processes outside the self. Sternglass emphasized the need for additional ethnographic studies of introspective writing set in different writing communities and particularly stressed the need for a study of "less proficient language users" (p. 203). Such a study, she felt, could determine what writing and thinking strategies these "less-skilled" writers use and how their approaches differ from those employed by the graduate students in her study. Sternglass emphasized that only through naturalistic studies that take place over extended time periods will students be able "to reveal as much as they can of the factors that influenced their interpretations of [reading and writing] tasks and the shape of the outcomes" (p. 204).

STUDIES OF SECOND-LANGUAGE WRITING

All of the sources mentioned so far deal with writers who are using their first language for journal writing. In my study, the students would be writing in a second language. A question that naturally arises is how the journal writing process differs under these conditions.

A review of research in the area of second-language (L2) writing reveals that very little can be stated unequivocally about the differences between writing in a first and a second language. However, there is an emerging consensus that the individual writing processes of ESL students differ considerably and that these individual variations should be taken into account in studies of L2 writing (Raimes, 1991). Research supports the popularly accepted belief that people who begin to learn a second language in childhood, particularly before adolescence, usually have a better chance of acquiring a native-like facility (Larsen-Freeman, 1991; Leki, 1992). Not surprisingly, second-language writers often experience frustration caused by lack of appropriate vocabulary and interference from grammatical features of the first language (Zamel, 1983). However, the native language can also be an important resource when writing in a second language and not just an impediment (Cumming, 1989). In any case, variation among individual language learners is enormous (Larsen-Freeman, 1991; Leki, 1992). Thus, it seems likely that the thinking and writing processes employed when students are writing journal entries in a second language will vary greatly from one individual to another. In broadening my understanding of the processes involved in L2 writing, the work of Vivian Zamel has been particularly valuable.

Writing to Make Meaning

As early as 1976, Zamel suggested that much could be learned about teaching writing to ESL students from examining research with native speakers. In a subsequent study, Zamel (1983) observed that "skilled" ESL writers showed writing behaviors that were strikingly similar to those of skilled native-speaker writers in other studies (see also Raimes, 1983, 1985). These skilled writers engaged in recursive processes of planning, writing, and revising, and they delayed concern with grammar and correctness until the editing of the final draft. Before that stage the writers used a variety of strategies to deal with linguistic difficulties, for example, circling words they were not sure of, leaving a blank space, or writing the words in the native language. In contrast, the student whom Zamel (1983) categorized as "the least skilled writer" seemed to be preoccupied by matters of form and correctness from the very beginning, which seemed to short-circuit the writing process, limiting her revisions to changes of words or phrases but rarely changes of meaning. This type of premature fixation on editing has often been noted in studies of native speakers with inadequate writing skills as well (Perl, 1975; Scardamalia, Bereiter, & Steinbach, 1984; Sommers, 1979). But these studies leave certain questions unanswered: In journal writing, where the explicit purpose is to express meaning without worrying about form, do "skilled" and "less skilled" bilingual writers still use different approaches? A related question is whether journal writing might free less skilled writers from worries about form and correctness, enabling them to explore their ideas more fully.

A theme that runs through all of Zamel's work is the need for ESL students to experience writing as a way of making meaning. She believes that "while it is certainly true that language allows for the expression of ideas, it is also true that a search for and commitment to ideas can generate language" (Zamel, 1991, p. 12). And she suggested that an effective way to encourage this generative use of language is to ask ESL students to be interactive readers by writing during all stages of the reading process (Zamel, 1992). In my study I hoped to look closely at students' informal writing about their reading for signs of such generative language use.

Zamel's belief that it is important for ESL students to use English to generate meaning is related to the notion of "comprehensible output." In a summary of research on second-language acquisition, Larsen-Freeman (1991) pointed out that Krashen's (1982) view of the critical importance of comprehensible input for language learners may be an oversimplification. Swain (1985) suggested that students' fluency in a second language does not develop solely as a result of exposure to the language. It is also essential for the second-language learner to use the language, to generate "comprehensible output." Extensive journal writing in a second language is one way of getting this practice.

The recognition of the crucial importance of meaning making in language learning is manifested in the increasing trend, toward communicative language teaching (CLT) among second-language educators (Savignon, 1991). However, Tarvin and Al-Arishi (1991) suggested that, contrary to what one might expect, reflection is not encouraged by many of the practices of communicative language teaching. True reflection requires time whereas many CLT activities call for "conspicuous action and spontaneous response" (1991, p. 9). After examining certain practices used in CLT classrooms—for example, one activity requires second-language students working in pairs to respond orally and immediately to the question, "If you were President of the United States, what is the first thing you would try to do?" (1991, p. 14)—Tarvin and Al-Arishi concluded that instructors who stress CLT should also find ways to give students the time and space needed to engage in genuine reflection. Asking them to write regularly in a journal is one obvious way of implementing this suggestion. And many ESL teachers have in fact been experimenting with journals (see Root, 1979; Spack & Sadow, 1983). The second-language journals that have been most widely studied are dialogue journals, a sort of conversation conducted in writing.

Dialogue Journals

Dialogue journals were first studied intensively beginning in 1979 in connection with the work of Leslee Reed, a teacher in Los Angeles who at the time had a class of sixth graders who were native speakers of English. During Reed's long teaching career, she has developed a system in which each of her 25 or so students writes daily in a journal, to which she responds every evening. These written conversations have been studied by linguists at Georgetown University and the Center for Applied Linguistics in Washington, DC (Peyton, 1990; Staton, 1980; Staton, Shuy, & Kreeft, 1982; Staton, Shuy, Peyton, & Reed, 1988). When, in 1980–1981, Reed began teaching a class of second-language students, many of whom were recent immigrants, she continued her use of dialogue journals, providing a new dimension for the research on journal writing. And, partly as a result of this research, journals are now widely used in many second-language classrooms (Peyton & Staton, 1993). The potential of journal writing to facilitate the learning of adult ESL students has also received attention in recent years (Peyton & Staton, 1996).

Dialogue journals differ in significant ways from those in which students write solely about academic work. They consist essentially of written interactions conducted over an extended time period, with each writer having regular turns for writing and the ability to choose his or her own topics, which may relate to personal or academic issues (Staton, Shuy, Peyton, & Reed, 1988).

Because of the conversational nature of dialogue journals, the partner is extremely important. Some teachers ask their students to write to other students. But Leslee Reed chooses to be the sole reader for her students because she wants them to use their journals to discuss classroom issues with her and to work through personal problems that affect their work in the class. In responding to the journals, Reed tries to avoid typical teacher behaviors such as evaluating, correcting, or giving generic encouragements such as "nice description." Rather she attempts to move the conversation along by asking for clarifications, talking about her own feelings, and introducing new topics.

According to Staton (1988), the distinguishing feature of dialogue journals is not the informality of style, or the students' ability to set the agenda, or even the interactivity of the writing. All of these features occur in elementary classrooms where teachers encourage students to write about personally significant subjects and then respond in meaningful ways to that writing. What distinguishes the dialogue journals in Leslee Reed's teaching is the use of writing to get things done: "The power and interest in these dialogues comes from the fact that the students and teacher are taking action when they write, and by their speech 'acts' their relationship and often the classroom situation changes from day to day" (p. 28).

In analyzing how Reed's journals differ from most writing done in schools, Shuy (1988) focused on language registers. According to Joos (1961), speakers have access to five "styles," or registers: (a) intimate—exchanges with lovers or close friends; (b) casual—the chatty style used when speaking with friends; (c) consultative—the style used to exchange information in school or work situations; (d) formal—the monologic style used when giving a formal speech; and (e) frozen—literary, archaic, or legal expressions such as "all in favor say aye" (Shuy, 1988, p. 75). All children enter school with competence in the intimate and casual registers of the spoken language. Yet when they are taught to write, many are not encouraged or even allowed to use the resources of their oral language competence.[1] Instead, even beginning writers are expected to produce the written equivalent of (d): the traditional school essay, which is comparable to a formal speech, an oral form with which young children are not familiar:

> Writing begins, as far as the schools are concerned, with monologue writing—the formal essay styles (even though this is sometimes referred to as "informal"). One can only wonder why we have been so blind to the fact that this pattern is in direct violation of the developmental sequence of the other kind of language used frequently and often successfully by all children—their oral language. (Shuy, 1988, p. 77)

A key difference between the way that children learn to speak and the way they are taught to write in many classrooms relates to the presence or absence of a responsive listener/reader. In Shuy's words: "Speech implies a listener, and listening involves absorbing that talk and then speaking back to the other person" (1988, p. 74). Most school writing, however, takes place in a conversational vacuum, with students expected to write on a topic selected by the teacher and to fulfill the teacher's, not their own, goals. This type of writing is basically a monologue, with the teacher's response occurring in the form of evaluation rather than meaningful communication.

In studying the dialogue journals of Reed and her students, Shuy discovered a type of school writing that was truly interactive and self-motivated and thus much closer to oral language: "It is two people talking to each other in writing, exchanging hopes and fears, evaluating, assuring, questioning, and clarifying" (1988, p. 81). Shuy's discussion of the oral language basis of dialogue journals is an important one for writing teachers. And a rigorous

---

[1]It's important to note that this description of the sorry state of school writing instruction is not true of many of today's preschool and elementary classrooms (including those in the public school where my own children learned to write). Teacher-researchers like Donald Graves (1983) and Lucy Calkins (1983) have developed and disseminated effective and exciting ways of teaching children to write that emphasize meaning making and writing as genuine communication. However, in many U.S. classrooms writing is still equated with essay writing, with negative results that Shuy (1988) described.

linguistic analysis of the journal exchanges between Reed and her sixth graders convincingly attests to the fact that these students are drawing on their oral speech resources in ways that will eventually help them become more resourceful and more effective writers (Staton, Shuy, Peyton, & Reed, 1988).

COGNITIVE AND LINGUISTIC THEORY

In order to gain insight into a possible connection between journal writing and reflection, I consulted relevant sources in cognitive and linguistic theory. Reflection has long been studied by philosophers, cognitive psychologists, and scholars interested in composition (see, e.g., Dewey, 1933; Higgins, Flower, & Petraglia, 1992; Scardamalia & Bereiter, 1985; Scardamalia, Bereiter, & Steinbach, 1984; Smith, 1991). Since the publication of Donald Schön's influential book *The Reflective Practitioner* in 1983, educators have devoted a great deal of attention to the role of reflection in schooling and professional life (Cruickshank, 1987; Schön, 1983, 1987, 1991; Tarvin & Al-Arishi, 1991). Surprisingly, however, none of these studies of reflection has investigated writing—particularly journal writing—as a form of reflection.

In examining cognitive and linguistic theory for insights into the mental processes involved in reflection, I found the work of the Soviet psychologist Lev Vygotsky and the British linguist and educator James Britton to be especially useful.

Inner Speech

Vygotsky's concept of inner speech is first elaborated in *Thought and Language* (1986), which was originally published in Russian in 1934. This concept is of key importance in understanding the freedom and power many writers experience in journal writing. Vygotsky elaborated his theory of inner speech in reaction to the concepts of Piaget. According to Piaget, children progress from nonverbal autistic (individualistic) thought to egocentric thought and speech and finally to directed (social and logical) thought (Vygotsky, 1986). Vygotsky rejected Piaget's notion that the child's thought is initially autistic and looked for another explanation of what Piaget referred to as egocentric speech, in other words, speech in which the child is not attempting to communicate with another person but is in effect talking to himself or herself.

Vygotsky and his research team conducted variations on Piaget's experiments to try to learn more about the egocentric speech of the child. They found that when they introduced a difficulty into an experiment (for example, asking the child to draw but not giving him a pencil), the occurrence of egocentric speech increased dramatically. Vygotsky thus concluded: " ... egocentric speech does not long remain a mere accompaniment to the child's activity. Besides being a means of expression and of release of tension, it soon becomes an instrument of thought in the proper sense—in seeking and planning the solution of a problem" (1986, p. 31).

Vygotsky, in contrast with Piaget, regarded language development as stemming primarily from social forces and posited the following developmental sequence: "first social, then egocentric, then inner speech" (p. 35). Vygotsky did not see egocentric speech as an offshoot of autism, destined to wither and die, but rather as a crucial step forward, which in all likelihood "does not simply atrophy but 'goes underground,' i.e., turns into inner speech" (p. 33), and eventually into verbal thought. In effect, Vygotsky saw egocentric speech as occurring when children begin to talk to themselves as they had earlier talked to others.

One reason why journal writing may promote reflection derives from its being a kind of inner speech captured in writing. Of course, the act of writing is bound to transform thought in important ways. The obvious differences between thinking and writing are cited by many scholars—especially the greater time and conscious effort required for writing. Yet it would seem that journal writing is more closely allied with inner speech than are more formal, presentational types of writing. In fact, many writers use the journal as a place to think on paper, to talk to themselves in writing.

A key factor in the ability to write reflectively is the development of an awareness of one's thought processes. According to Vygotsky, an increased awareness of these processes and the ability to verbalize this awareness develop as children learn "scientific concepts" as a result of instruction at school; by scientific concepts Vygotsky meant abstract concepts such as "exploitation," as opposed to everyday concepts such as "brother" (1986, pp. 163-171). Becoming aware of one's mental functioning introduces important new possibilities:

> In perceiving some of our acts in a generalizing fashion, we isolate them from our total mental activity and are thus enabled to focus on this process as such and to enter into a new relation to it. In this way, becoming conscious of our operations and viewing each as a process of a certain *kind*—such as remembering or imagining—leads to their mastery. (1986, pp. 170-171)

In the passages on awareness quoted here, Vygotsky was referring to reflection, not reflective writing. The view of writing he subsequently articulated was based on the idea of writing as primarily a form for presenting ideas rather than for formulating and shaping them. For Vygotsky, writing occurred in a kind of vacuum without the presence of a fellow speaker and listener; it was a monologue rather than a dialogue.

Vygotsky was aware, however, of the importance of writing for raising one's awareness or consciousness:

> Written speech is considerably more conscious, and it is produced more deliberately than oral speech.... Consciousness and volitional control characterize the child's written speech from the very beginning of its development. Signs of writing and methods of their use are acquired consciously. Writing, in its turn, enhances the intellectuality of the child's actions. It brings awareness to speech. (1986, p. 183)

This greater consciousness helps explain the difference between writing and other forms of reflection. Thinking, talking, and writing are obviously all ways of assimilating ideas, but writing, with its capability for being reread and revised, is, for many people, characterized by a higher level of awareness. As one student explained to me in an informal interview, "Of course, I always have interesting thoughts when I read, but unless I write them down in a reading journal, most of them are gone with the wind. The next day I can't recall them at all." The epigraph to the last chapter of *Thought and Language* conveys a similar sense of the evanescence of thought that is not captured in writing:

> The word I forgot
> Which once I wished to say
> And voiceless thought
> Returns to shadows' chamber.
> (Osip Mandelstam, quoted in Vygotsky, 1986, p. 210)

Expressive Language

Like the work of Vygotsky, the theories of James Britton help to elucidate why journal writing is often conducive to reflection. Britton's concept of expressive language, which he adapted from the linguistic theory of Edward Sapir, quite accurately describes the language most often used for journal writing. In Britton's (1982) view expressive language is "language close to the self" (p. 96). He elaborated:

> Expressive language is giving signals about the speaker as well as signals about his topic. And so it is delivered in the assumption that the hearer is interested in the speaker as well as the topic.... It's relaxed and loosely structured because it follows the contours of the speaker's preoccupations.... It's the language of all ordinary face-to-face speech. So it's our means of coming together with other people out of our essential separateness. But it's also the language in which we first-draft most of our important ideas. And ... it's the form of language by which most strongly we influence each other. (1982, pp. 96–97)

Here Britton was referring particularly to expressive speech. He went on to discuss expressive writing, which he felt derives much of its importance from being "primarily written-down speech" (1982, p. 97). Expressive writing is also characterized by its personal nature, its closeness to the self: "In it, we make sure the writer stays in the writing and doesn't disappear" (1982, p. 97). Because expressive writing has its roots in expressive speech, there is also an important affective reason for its ability to free the writer. As Britton put it:

> Expressive forms of speech capitalize on the fact that both speaker and listener are *present*: expressive writing simulates that co-presence, the writer invoking the presence of the reader as he writes, the reader invoking the presence of the writer as he reads.... And whether we write or speak, expressive language is associated with a relationship of mutual confidence, trust, and is therefore a form of discourse that encourages us to *take risks*, to try out ideas we are not sure of, in a way we would not dare to do in, say making a public speech. In other words, expressive language (as a kind of bonus) is a form that favors exploration, discovery, learning. (1982, p. 124)

Expressive writing is the language of exploratory journal writing, whereas "transactional language," the equivalent of the more formal language used in a public speech, is the language most often used in formal essays or reports. Although Britton admitted that "expressive writing is very little encouraged in most schools" (1982, p. 129), he affirmed its crucial importance for education.

In a discussion of early language development, he pointed out the vital link between expressive language and reflection. Once children are able to develop mental representations using language, it then becomes possible for them to go back and modify or refine those representations: " ... we may deliberately go back over experiences in order to make sense of them. That is to say, we work upon the representation to make it more orderly, more coherent" (1982, p. 82). According to Britton, we may do this in the form of an inner dialogue, but this dialogue will be shaped by our past experiences in conversation (1982, p. 115; 1970, pp. 204–205) in much the same way that Vygotsky envisioned inner speech developing out of our experience with social speech.

For this reason, expressive writing lends itself to reflection. Often, according to Britton, reflection is encouraged when writers take on what he referred to as the spectator role:

> As participants we generate expectations from past experience, put them to the test of actuality, and modify our representation of the world (our predictive apparatus, the basis of all our expectations) in the light of what happens. As we go back over the same experience, now in the role of spectator, we may make further and probably more far-reaching adjustments—for, as we have seen, we are likely to refer to a more extensive set of values than we are free to do as participants. (1970, p. 118)

According to Britton, there are times when our experience is so unlike what we had expected that we feel "a *positive need* to take up the role of a spectator and work upon it further—in order, as we say, 'to come to terms with it'" (1970, p. 118). Often on such occasions we also take up a pen.

However, although people seem to have a strong need to achieve a kind of order, to work things out using expressive language, this process, in Britton's view, is not entirely a conscious or orderly one. The value of expressive writing often derives from its spontaneity, its freedom to follow a fleeting intuition, rather than from a strict adherence to conscious goals. Much of what Britton said in his essay "Shaping at the Point of Utterance" relates to the power many people experience in journal writing:

> I want to associate spontaneous shaping, whether in speech or writing, with the moment by moment interpretative process by which we make sense of what is happening around us; to see each as an instance of the pattern-forming propensity of man's mental processes. Thus, when we come to write, what is delivered to the pen is in part already shaped, stamped with the image of our own ways of perceiving. But the intention to *share*, inherent in spontaneous utterance, sets up a demand for further shaping. (1982, p. 141)

Asking students to keep a journal is a natural way for teachers to encourage the human "pattern-forming propensity."

Problem Spaces

Reflection is closely connected to metacognition, loosely defined as thinking about thinking. However, the possible role of journal writing in encouraging metacognition has not received much attention from cognitive researchers. Two researchers who have concentrated on "compositional tasks" such as planning a vacation or writing an essay rather than more easily manipulated and measured logico-mathematical tasks are Bereiter and Scardamalia (1983, 1985; Scardamalia & Bereiter, 1985; Scardamalia, Bereiter, & Steinbach, 1984).

In "Teachability of Reflective Processes in Written Composition" (Scardamalia et al., 1984), the authors are concerned with encouraging the development of reflection, which they view in the manner of Piaget as "a dialectical process by which higher-order knowledge is created through the effort to reconcile lower-order elements of knowledge" (Scardamalia, Bereiter, & Steinbach, 1984, p. 173). The researchers developed an experimental instructional approach to promote reflection among a group of sixth graders who were planning to write compositions. In this approach, teachers and students modeled their planning processes by "thinking aloud" in front of the class. It was the researchers' hope that such planning methods would eventually be internalized.

More interesting to me than the experiment itself was the theory on which it was based. Thinking-aloud studies of expert writers indicate that they do indeed engage in reflection during the writing process (Flower & Hayes, 1980, 1981). School-age writers, on the other hand, seem not to do this (Burtis, Bereiter, Scardamalia, & Tetroe, 1983), relying instead on "primarily linear, nonreflective processes," which Bereiter and Scardamalia describe elsewhere as the "knowledge-telling strategy" (Bereiter & Scardamalia, 1983). Many of the instructional attempts to encourage the development of reflection in inexperienced writers are based, implicitly or explicitly, on the model of reflection as a kind of internal dialogue. Based on the thinking-aloud protocols of expert writers, however, Scardamalia, Bereiter, and Steinbach (1984) believe that a more likely model would be one of problem solving based on Newell's (1980) concept of problem spaces. Like any model, this one tends to oversimplify the complex thinking required for writing; however, it also suggests possibilities that may be important in understanding the power of journal writing.

According to Scardamalia, Bereiter, and Steinbach, the content space is concerned with beliefs. It is here that "one works out opinions, makes moral decisions, generates inferences about matters of fact, formulates causal explanations, and so on" (1984, p. 176). The content space often impinges on daily life and is not just activated when planning a composition. The rhetorical space, on the other hand, relates only to writing: "The knowledge states to be found in this kind of space are *mental representations of actual or intended text*—representations that may be at various levels of abstraction from verbatim representation to representations of main ideas and global intentions" (1984, p. 176).

This model coincides with many previously developed cognitive descriptions of the composing process. For example, Collins and Gentner stated:

> It is important to separate idea production from text production. The processes involved in producing text, whether they operate on the word level, the sentence level, the paragraph level, or the text level, must produce a linear sequence that satisfies certain grammatical rules. In contrast, the result of the process of idea production is a set of ideas with many internal connections, only a few of which may fit the linear model desirable for text. (1980, p. 53)

Scardamalia, Bereiter, and Steinbach proposed that reflection in writing occurs when there is interaction between the two problem spaces, roughly analogous to the turn-taking of speakers in a conversation. The authors believe this view helps to account for the differences in the processes of experts and novices. Whereas experts readily shuttle back and forth from one space to the other, novices succeed in transferring information from the content space to the rhetorical space but are unable to make "the return trip." This results in "a simple think–say process of composition" and restricts revision to surface changes that remain limited to the rhetorical space (1984, p. 178).

This model suggests certain possible reasons for the power and usefulness of journals. Although journal writing is subject to some of the constraints of the rhetorical space, such as linearity, it is much more intimately related to the content space than is more traditional writing, which is geared toward the production of a rhetorically effective text. Thus, while journal writing preserves some of the more obvious advantages of writing over thought or speech, such as the permanence that enables it to be reread and revised, it capitalizes on the freedom from the necessity to produce a polished text, freeing the writer from many of the usual demands of the rhetorical space such as the conventions of a particular genre, elegance of style, or even something seemingly as basic as correct spelling and grammar.

Journal writing may also help students avoid some of the problems that have arisen up in cognitive skills training—specifically the problem of cognitive overload (see, e.g., Perkins, 1985, pp. 353, 357). Journal writers don't have to struggle to keep everything in their minds. By getting their thoughts down on the page quickly without the usual monitors regarding form and correctness (Krashen, 1981), their minds are more free to concentrate on the concerns of the content space.

Theoretically, freeing writers from some of the demands of the rhetorical space enables them to "play" in their writing in ways that may have important metacognitive benefits. Bruner (1985) suggested a possible connection between play and metacognition when he observed that as children play the connection between means and ends is loosened. Based on his studies of children's play, Bruner speculated about the implications of play for the development of metacognition:

> It may be a bit of an exaggeration, but may it not be the case that what we speak of as unprompted metacognition or monitoring, or reflection could be an internalized form of play? After all, the commonsense way of referring to a metacognitive approach to a problem is to say that we are "playing around." (pp. 603–604)

Journal writing, too, may be an important form of play for some writers as they experiment with language and follow their ideas wherever they lead. When students are not worried about pleasing a teacher or getting an acceptable grade and at the same time are freed from their own rigorous demands on themselves by the need to start writing immediately, they often write in unexpected and creative ways.

EDUCATIONAL THEORY

I had completed all of the reading described so far before I began to collect and analyze my students' journals. When I started to look at real data in the form of journal entries, the ideas I had gained from this reading provided useful analytic tools. For example, some students did use their journals in playful ways, reinforcing Bruner's suggestion of a link between play and metacognition. Other students seemed to be talking to themselves in the journals, using a version of Vygotsky's inner speech. In practically every student journal, I found evidence of Britton's expressive language.

One emerging theme, however, was not adequately explained by my reading. As I began to respond to the students' journals, I found that some students used language in a way that made it easier for me to write meaningful responses to their entries. I noted in the field log that journals in which students made connections between their own lives and the class reading seemed to open up a dialogue between us. On the other hand, journals that primarily summarized the book and excluded the student's personal reactions seemed to close off discussion, making it difficult for me to think of an appropriate response. In the field log, I began referring to the difference between "open" and "closed" journals and noted that reading the closed journals felt like being "in a conversation where the other person was not fully participating; there was no sense of open dialogue in these 'closed' journals." My differing reactions to the two types of student journals were apparent from a quick glance at my response letters. The letters to students who were writing in a personal vein were at least twice as long as those to students who wrote what I perceived to be impersonal, objective journal entries.

There was something about responding to the reading in a personal way that I valued. Indeed, I seemed to need the students to include something of themselves in the journals to enable me to write a genuine and meaningful response. As I wrote in the field log: "Perhaps reflection is by necessity a *personal* response—a taking hold of the idea being discussed and saying 'This is how I see it.'" Articulating my thoughts about a possible link between personal response and reflective journal writing during one of the interviews, I seemed to be talking to myself as much as to the student interviewee:

> ... when I say "reflective writing," I'm not just talking about any kind of thinking. I'm talking about a more specific, smaller type of thinking. And I think that one of the really important parts of my definition is getting personally involved in whatever it is you're thinking about. That somehow connecting your own life with what you're reading or what you're writing seems to be a very important part of what I mean when I say "reflective writing." I did a lot of that in the journals I wrote for courses at NYU, and it's one reason I got interested in journal writing, because it seemed different from writing a more formal essay, a more formal paper.

After the interviews were completed, I read an article that helped to clarify these emerging ideas by referring to the concept of connected knowing as described in *Women's Ways of Knowing* (Belenky, Clinchy, Goldberger, & Tarule, 1986). According to the author of this article:

> The voice of connected knowing carries with it an intimacy that presumes a sharing of self and other, a felt relation between knower and known. The voice of connected knowing is attuned to creating continuity between the

so-called private language of self-reflection and the formal designs of public speech. We can recognize this voice by certain stylistic markers—it includes references to the self; it may include the vocabulary of feeling; it recognizes temporal flux and change; it is a voice in which there are echoes of internal dialogue brought out into the open. (Helle, 1991, p. 54)

My initial attempts at coding the students' journals for reflective writing had identified many of these same characteristics—personal comparisons, identification or empathy with characters or ideas in the reading, open expression of emotion, and dialogue with self or reader.

Connected Knowing

A careful reading of *Women's Ways of Knowing* revealed that the authors' concept of connected knowing was helpful in understanding some of the patterns that were emerging in my study. These new insights related not just to the students' journal writing but also to my responses to their writing. Like many of the women interviewed in *Women's Ways of Knowing*, I valued connected knowing as a way of accessing knowledge. Without being consciously aware of it, I had long used this approach to learning—entering into my reading in a personal way by considering how I would have responded to a situation in a novel or by testing out theories in my nonfiction reading by mentally applying them to people or situations in my own life. In the learning logs I kept for my doctoral courses, I was able for the first time to employ connected knowing explicitly in writing about serious academic content. Since this approach had long been a part of my mental makeup, the chance to use it in my writing was empowering. Not surprisingly, I responded positively to students who used a similar connected-knowing approach in the journals they kept for my class. With the concept of connected knowing, I suspected that I had found a frame for analysis that would prove productive, and I began to consider how this concept related to the data in my study.

A key idea in this regard is empathy. Belenky, Clinchy, Goldberger, and Tarule (1986) explained:

Connected knowing builds on the subjectivists' conviction that the most trustworthy knowledge comes from personal experience rather than the pronouncements of authorities.... Connected knowers develop procedures for gaining access to other people's knowledge. At the heart of these procedures is the capacity for empathy. Since knowledge comes from experience, the only way they can hope to understand another person's ideas is to try to share the experience that has led the person to form the idea. (pp. 112–113)

According to the authors, connected knowing differs dramatically from separate knowing, which is "essentially an adversarial form" (Belenky et al., 1986, p. 106) in which knowers present their ideas in the form of arguments:

> Separate knowers speak a public language. They exhibit their knowledge in a series of public performances, and they address their messages not to themselves or to intimate friends but to an audience of relative strangers. Often, the primary purpose of their words is not to express personally meaningful ideas but to manipulate the listener's reactions, and they see the listener not as an ally in conversation but as a potentially hostile judge. (p. 108)

Separate knowing has its roots in the 17th-century epistemological shift that led to the development of modern scientific method and the valuing of objectivity. This concept, inspired by the rationalism of Descartes, holds that "neither bodily response (the sensual or the emotional) nor associational thinking, exploring the various personal or spiritual meanings the object has for us, can tell us anything about the object" (Bordo, 1986, p. 450). Whereas the key to connected knowing is "attachment," the key to separate knowing is "detachment," a concept that has been held up as the ideal not only in scientific research but also in the ways of speaking and writing that traditionally have been validated and valued in the academy.

While pointing out the need for both approaches to learning, Peter Elbow (1973) helped differentiate separate and connected knowing through his discussion of "the doubting game" and "the believing game." Separate knowers prefer to play the doubting game, in which the goal is to find weaknesses in positions that differ from their own. These knowers attempt to extricate the self from the knowing and to arrive at impersonal meanings by excluding feelings and beliefs. For connected knowers, however, it is more natural and more comfortable to play the believing game, which entails "trying on" another person's ideas. Playing the believing game does not mean that the other person's ideas will eventually be accepted, but it does mean "sitting on the same side of the table" as the other person and trying, temporarily, to see things from his or her perspective. Interestingly, the most salient examples of connected knowing in *Women's Ways of Knowing* were found in descriptions of conversations. In talk with a receptive other, the connected knower finds a comfortable and rewarding way to learn.

However, it is separate knowing, not connected knowing, that continues to be held up as the ideal in most U.S. schools and colleges. Some of the women interviewed by Belenky, Clinchy, Goldberger, and Tarule, especially among those attending prestigious universities, had mastered separate knowing and used this approach in writing papers for school assignments. But often the effort to detach the self from the writing led to "absence of interest, anomie, and monotony" (p. 110). One of the women interviewed expressed a nagging dissatisfaction: "I can write a good paper, and someday I may learn to write one that I like, that is not just bullshit, but I still feel that it's somewhat pointless. I do it, and I get my grade, but it hasn't proved anything to me" (p. 108).

Connected knowers usually don't feel distanced in this way from their learning. Belenky, Clinchy, Goldberger, and Tarule asserted that, for women, believing often comes more naturally than doubting, "perhaps because it is founded upon genuine care and because it promises to reveal the kind of truth they value—truth that is personal, particular, and grounded in first-hand experience" (p. 113).

Although connected knowing is rooted in life experience and often begins with attempts to understand other people, it frequently extends to comprehension of ideas: "The mode of knowing is personal, but the object of knowing need not be" (p. 121). A significant way in which learning logs and reading journals differ from more formal academic writing is that writers have an opportunity to engage with ideas in personal ways.

The History of Connected Knowing

While the term "connected knowing" was coined in the early 1980s by feminist researchers (Gilligan, 1982; Lyons, 1983), the concept is not a new one but has a long history in human learning and educational scholarship. In 1958, for example, Michael Polanyi, a scientist turned philosopher, articulated the crucial importance of connected knowing in his complex theory of personal knowledge. Polanyi (1958a) emphasized the participation of the knower in shaping knowledge and discredited the ideal of separate knowing by speaking of the human "passion for understanding" and the "intimate indwelling" with ideas that occur as we construct knowledge.

According to Polanyi, truly objective science is not only undesirable but also impossible: "Contrary to usually accepted opinion, every branch of natural science makes value judgments of some kind" (1958b, pp. 79–80). He went on to state that "no knowledge of nature lacks some measure of indwelling of the observer in his subject matter" (1958b, p. 80). But to Polanyi this participation of the knower in the known did not represent a threat to an otherwise "pure" knowledge:

> The participation of the knower in shaping his knowledge, which had hitherto been tolerated only as a flaw—a shortcoming to be eliminated from perfect knowledge—is now recognized as the true guide and master of our cognitive powers. (1958b, p. 26)

More recently, other scholars have talked and written about the importance of connecting with knowledge in personal ways. One of the most influential is James Britton, whose work was discussed earlier in this chapter. Another educator who speaks and writes about the importance of a personal approach to knowing is John Mayher. According to Mayher (1990), the present "commonsense" educational system, which privileges disembedded thinking, has many deleterious consequences:

> When school knowledge remains disembedded and unconnected to the learner's experience, and, worse, when neither teacher nor student recognizes or tries to deal with the gap between the label and the experience, the only "learning" that is possible is what I have sometimes called verbal short-circuiting, in which the concept comes in the ear or the eye and goes out the pen but never gets sufficiently acted upon in the brain to find a permanent home. (p. 79)

In Mayher's proposed "uncommonsense" approach to schooling, this emphasis would be turned upside down. Crucial to uncommonsense education is the recognition that "there is no knowledge without a knower" and that "human beings are active meaning makers who are continually learning—making personal knowledge—when they can act according to their own purposes" (p. 79). In uncommonsense education the emphasis on the personal is very strong. In fact, it is this aspect that "provides a radical challenge to the commonsense approach because it insists on the importance of the student's personal connections to the material being learned, and of his individual reasons to be learning it" (p. 79). Like Polanyi, Mayher has questioned the commonly accepted distinction between thought and feeling:

> Learning is not something distinct from living but an integral part of all life processes.... These processes engage all aspects of our minds: our feelings and perceptions as well as our constructs and conceptions. There can be, there-

fore, no meaningful separation into cognitive and affective learning, since every idea has a feeling component, and every feeling also involves an idea. Thus the basis of all learning is personal meaning making, which is an active process. (Mayher, 1990, p. 104)

One of the reasons why school writing feels so alien to many people is the stated or unstated injunction not to express feelings or emotions about the topic. Yet if Mayher is correct, this prohibition is based on a false assumption. Our feelings are always intertwined with our thoughts, and we would probably be better thinkers and writers if we were allowed or even encouraged to admit this.

ANALYTIC FRAMEWORKS

As I began to collect and respond to my students' journals, I realized that I responded more positively to entries in which students reacted to their reading in a personal way or wrote introspectively to analyze their own writing processes. Later, when I completed the interviews with the five student participants and began to analyze the transcripts, I discovered the relevance of the concept of connected knowing and decided to use it as a frame through which to analyze the data in my study.

Some readers may question the validity of using a concept developed in a study based only on women as an analytic frame in a study of both male and female journal writers. Several factors support my decision to do so. First, Belenky, Clinchy, Goldberger, and Tarule explicitly stated that separate and connected knowing are not "gender specific" (1986, p. 102). They suggested that more women than men may gravitate toward connected knowing and that more men than women may favor separate knowing, but they were quick to point out that no research has been done to investigate this possibility. Second, connected knowing has been a useful analytic tool in other studies of thinking and writing that, like mine, include data from classroom observation, student writing, and interview transcripts (see, e.g., McCarthy & Fishman, 1991). Third, and most important, initial analysis of the student journals in my sample suggested that the tendency to rely on separate or connected knowing was not directly related to gender. Some of the most striking examples of connected knowing were found in the journals of male students, and many examples of separate knowing occurred in the journals of female students.

Because *Women's Ways of Knowing* was based solely on interviews with women and analysis by female (and feminist) researchers, there has been a tendency to essentialize the findings of this study in a way that I find problematic. Writing about gender differences in language use, Toril Moi (1985) pointed out that empirical studies of speech samples from males and females have demonstrated very few linguistic distinctions between the two groups. The significant differences more often relate to how men's and women's language is interpreted rather than to actual linguistic differences. Moi pointed out the dangers of presenting masculinity and femininity as "stable, unchanging essences, as meaningful presences between which the elusive difference is supposed to be located" (p. 154). Even when the cause of the supposed difference is seen as social rather than biological, the effect of this type of binary thinking is to dangerously oversimplify the complexities of human experience and language use. In my study, the concept of connected knowing provided a useful means of explaining the different ways in which various students used their journals—differences that were not linked to gender in a rigid way.

In order to understand fully the concept of connected knowing, it is necessary to see how it fits into the authors' larger scheme of intellectual development. The authors of *Women's Ways of Knowing* had originally intended to analyze their interview materials using the categories of intellectual development developed by Perry (1970) based on interviews with male undergraduates at Harvard. After an initial analysis of interview transcripts of the 135 women of different ages and socioeconomic and educational backgrounds in their study, however, they concluded that Perry's categories were not adequate for capturing these women's stances toward learning. So, building on Perry's work, Belenky, Clinchy, Goldberger, and Tarule devised a system of five epistemological perspectives, which they felt more adequately described the positions of the women in their study. The authors pointed out that these perspectives are not intended to represent a linear progression or developmental hierarchy and stated that future researchers will have to determine whether these categories have any "stagelike qualities" (p. 15).

The five perspectives are:

1. *Silence.* Knowers operating from the perspective of silence perceive themselves as lacking a mind or voice of their own and hence feel totally dominated by external authority.

2. *Received knowledge.* In this position knowers feel able to "receive" knowledge from external authorities but are incapable of creating their own knowledge.

3. *Subjective knowledge.* Subjective knowers believe that they create their own knowledge, which is personal, private, and subjective. Those who operate from this position trust their intuition and discount the views of external authorities.

4. *Procedural knowledge.* Knowers in this category are concerned with developing reliable procedures to obtain and communicate knowledge. Procedural knowers access knowledge in two distinct ways: separate and connected knowing. The authors suspect that procedural knowers who tend toward connected knowing may have an easier time making the transition to the fifth perspective, constructed knowledge, than those who rely primarily on separate knowing (1986, p. 14).

5. *Constructed knowledge.* Constructed knowers see all knowledge as contextual and view themselves as creators of knowledge. Both subjective (connected knowing) and objective (separate knowing) strategies are seen as useful for constructing knowledge.

Although I was not familiar with the work of Belenky, Clinchy, Goldberger, and Tarule as I was conducting my study, I realized retrospectively that during the course, and even more so during the interviews, I had posed questions that elicited important information about the students' stances toward learning. As I began to analyze this information, I found that the five epistemological perspectives provided a useful way of categorizing the students as learners—and more specifically of describing the role of journal writing in their learning. I soon discovered, however, that these categories should not be viewed as fixed or mutually exclusive. Most learners shuttle back and forth between two or more categories at any given period in their lives, and one's approach as a learner is often influenced by the specific learning task.

As I completed the reading journey described in this chapter, I was convinced that the concept of connected knowing helped to explain my positive reaction to the learning logs I had kept as part of my doctoral studies. The freedom to write about ideas without disengaging my feelings had felt liberating and intellectually powerful. And some of the student journal writers in my study seemed to be experiencing a similar liberation. In the next chapter, readers will learn more about these students as we enter the world of practice—my own writing classroom, where this study of journal writing took place.

3

The Writing Class: Journals in Context

On the first day of the spring 1992 semester, I hurried through corridors crowded with students. My usual first-day nervousness was heightened by the knowledge that these new classes would provide the data for my study of student journal writing. Because the classroom was on a floor undergoing renovation, the elevators and the main stairs had been sealed off to protect the college community from asbestos fibers and other debris from the construction. To get to the classroom, it was necessary to use the fire stairs from the floor below, which remained open for safety reasons. The following excerpt from the teaching journal I kept for a professional development seminar will give a sense of the setting in which this study began:

> When I open the fire door, I enter a surreal environment lined with firebrick and fitted out with fire hoses and extinguishers. On one of the stairs my foot slips on something gritty, and I realize that a sandbag used to prop open the door has burst, scattering sand all over the floor.
>
> As I leave the stairway and walk down the hall to the classroom, the light emanating from work lights dangling on wires in their yellow plastic cages casts an eery glow. "It's going to be a long semester," I think as I pass the door to the adjoining classroom with its yellow and navy poster announcing: "Danger: Radioactive Materials."
>
> My first reaction on entering the classroom is relief. The space is intact. One corner of the ceiling has been damaged by water seeping down from the floor above. The plaster is peeling and crumbling but does not appear to be in danger of falling.
>
> The room is large, about 25 feet square, with high ceilings. There are six very large windows, three on the west side and three on the south side. The windows are covered with tattered shades, but they have a great advantage over the windows in the newer buildings in the college: They open.
>
> The metal desk/chairs are lined up in neat rows facing the blackboard. A few students are already in the room, sitting quietly. I put my briefcase down on the desk at the front of the room and ask the students to help me move the chairs into a circle. Someone has written, "I love Paul!" on the board. But

as usual there's no chalk on the ledge, so I rummage through my briefcase for the box of chalk I always carry. I move to the blackboard and write the course name and section number.

The students who soon filled the room, all classified by the college as "advanced ESL writers," were a diverse group. The 21 students came from 11 different countries and spoke nine different native languages. The length of time these students had lived in the United States ranged from 1 to 9 years. Eight had graduated from U.S. high schools, and six had attended other colleges, three of which were in the United States.

The 23 students in the second class had been born in 11 countries and spoke 12 different first languages. They had lived in the United States from 6 months to 11 years. Nine students in the second class had graduated from U.S. high schools, and six had previously attended another college, only one of which was in the United States.

After a brief introduction to the course, I asked the students to write a short essay explaining their theories about the best way to learn a second language. I recommended that students illustrate their theories by referring to at least one specific experience—either positive or negative—from their own lives.

I looked forward to reading these essays and expected that the students would have many different ideas about the optimal conditions for language learning. During my long teaching career, I have learned that any classroom contains students with widely divergent learning styles. The next section explores some of the theories about teaching I have developed over the years.

STANCE OF THE TEACHER-RESEARCHER

In qualitative research, where the researcher is the primary "instrument" for recording, analyzing, and interpreting data, it is important to acknowledge openly one's basic values and beliefs in an attempt to keep them from interfering with the research. For a teacher-researcher, this means articulating and examining the assumptions underlying classroom practice.

Throughout their reading of this book, readers will undoubtedly continue to gain insight into my classroom practice. But let me start with "the facts." I have spent most of my professional life teaching what is now termed developmental writing but used to be called remedial writing. After completing BA and MA degrees in literature and working for 4 years as an editor,

I accepted a part-time teaching position in 1974, tutoring college students who needed help with writing. A year later, as a result of a budget shortfall, all one-to-one tutoring was eliminated. At that time, I was hired as an adjunct instructor in the same program and began teaching developmental writing workshops. In this first teaching experience, I was working with native speakers of English, who were often struggling to master standard English.

When the program in which I was working was abolished in 1980, I moved to the college in which this study was conducted, where I worked part-time for the next 12 years. Initially, I taught developmental writing workshops for native speakers. However, in 1982 I was asked to teach a comparable writing class for bilingual students, and over the next few years, the emphasis of my teaching and research shifted to working with second-language learners.

Although my career has been devoted to teaching developmental courses, I don't regard my students as remedial writers, and they have justified my faith by producing some extraordinary writing. In fact, excellent writing by students enrolled in ESL courses provides the basis for a textbook I co-authored with Steven Haber, *In Our Own Words: A Guide with Readings for Student Writers* (Mlynarczyk & Haber, 1996).

I continue to enjoy the challenges and rewards of teaching writing to students who are culturally and linguistically diverse. However, my teaching methods have changed considerably since my early years in the classroom. When Gay Brookes observed my classes in 1983 as part of her doctoral research on promising practices in the teaching of writing, she discovered "a highly successful teacher of writing to ESL students" but one whose success was difficult to explain: "In many ways, her teaching seems quite ordinary and even hides from view its promising practices.... Her classroom was more teacher-directed than some of the other successful teachers. She didn't run a modified student-directed workshop as they did" (Brookes, 1987, p. 296). In trying to puzzle out the secret of my success, Brookes speculated that it might lie in my tendency to reflect on my teaching and make adjustments based on these reflections: "It was as if the sessions the observer visited, which began at 2:50 and ended at 4:05 on Tuesdays and Thursdays, were just the tip of the iceberg. Beneath the surface was an ongoing class. It seemed to continue in students' and the teacher's minds, at home and in her office throughout the week and the semester" (Brookes, 1987, p. 293).

Brookes was right, I suspect, in identifying my tendency to reflect on my teaching as being an important part of who I am as a teacher. Yet one of the subjects I have reflected on over the years is something I'm less proud of—the tendency, also noted by Brookes, to run a teacher-directed class. Soon after entering the NYU doctoral program in 1989, I realized that most of my learning occurred not during teacher-led, large-group discussions but in small-group talk with classmates. In the spring of 1990, I taught an entry-level ESL class, which I set up as a student-centered workshop. In this class small groups of students worked independently to produce a class magazine of student writing. On the whole this experiment was extremely successful, but at times I had to struggle with my desire for control, as on this occasion recorded in my teaching journal of March 13, 1990:

> Change is good. It can rejuvenate you and give you new ideas, but too much change can lead to chaos. And I've just about reached my limit for today. I feel that I'm losing control of the class.
>
> We had to move to the fifth floor because our regular classroom was too noisy. And what do I find? This new classroom is just about as noisy as the one we left because of the blower for the heating system. To make matters worse, I have a bad cough and laryngitis. I am beginning to feel that I am swimming against the current. During this class several of the Russian students wandered in and out of the classroom at will, and I began to have that sinking feeling in the pit of my stomach. I started to wonder if perhaps I had let all this comfort and informality go too far.

Fortunately, once I got my voice and my classroom back, I also regained my perspective on the value of student-centered learning, which took a variety of forms that semester: the students met regularly in small groups to discuss *Animal Farm*, the assigned reading; they shared their journals with student partners; they edited and illustrated a class literary magazine. The students not only contributed and edited their writing, but produced beautiful art and design work. The night before turning in the final copy of the magazine for duplication, several students were up all night, polishing the last-minute details. By the end of the semester I felt validated for making this pedagogical change and wrote in my teaching journal:

> With this class I could really feel myself letting go of "teaching" so the students would be free to do more learning. It's true that I often have a difficult time getting the class's attention. But instead of being afraid that I am losing control, I feel immensely pleased that these students are gaining a language in which to communicate with others.

Not only my pedagogical style but also my thoughts about the best way to teach writing have evolved over the years. Like most writing teachers who taught during the 1970s, I was greatly affected by the process approach to writing (Emig, 1971). Around 1980 I began asking students to write multiple drafts of their essays, delaying their concern with grammar and mechanics until the end of the writing process. I came to see that all writers—and second-language writers especially—need to read a lot, and I was pleased when our department instituted the policy of asking students in ESL classes to read "real" books in place of the previously assigned textbooks.

My approach to teaching writing has also been shaped by my past experience as an editor and tutor. In 1983, when Brookes asked what I felt was most important to my students' improvement in writing, I identified three factors: "practice [with writing], attitude, and individual tutoring" (1987, p. 298). Interestingly, these three components are central to journal writing: Journals give students extensive writing practice, the opportunity to express and perhaps to change their attitudes toward writing, and the chance to develop a personal relationship with the teacher. The third factor, my belief in the importance of individualized instruction, has been an important theme throughout my teaching career. Perhaps because of my previous background as an editor working on texts with individual authors and as a tutor meeting with students one-to-one, I have always found this type of personalized teaching particularly valuable for my students and enjoyable for me.

What students should write about—the appropriate content for composition—is an important issue for all writing teachers. In my case, the question of how to integrate personal with academic writing has been central. In an article published in 1991, I stated that my primary concern was

> encouraging students to find their own voices, to discover a reason for wanting to exert the tremendous effort needed to learn to write in a second language. In my experience, this motivation is most likely to develop when students are writing about subjects that are relevant to them personally. After students have become engaged with writing, we should help them *begin* to move beyond the strictly personal by encouraging them to place themselves within some larger issues and to explore these issues in writing. (Mlynarczyk, 1991a, pp. 19–20)

The sequence of essay assignments I developed during the semester in which this study took place was typical of this approach (see Fig. 3.1). Each of these essays was drafted and revised after the students received written feedback on their first drafts from a peer reader as well as from me.

My interest in journal writing originated in the mid-1970s, when a colleague loaned me a copy of Peter Elbow's *Writing Without Teachers* (1973). Elbow's emphasis on the benefits of exploratory freewriting led me to experiment with having students freewrite in class. I was often struck by the power of this writing, which seemed so different from the strained essays produced for more structured assignments. In addition to its greater power and clarity, the freewriting often seemed to be more correct as well. I frequently asked students to freewrite anonymously, hoping to encourage even more freedom, and I found myself saving samples of student freewriting long after I had pitched the practice essays.

Most of this freewriting was written in response to prompts about attitudes toward writing or past writing experiences. For example, I sometimes asked students to write for 10 minutes about a pleasant experience they had once had with writing, or about their earliest memory of writing, or about their attitude toward writing in English as opposed to their native language. In the early 1980s I began to see the potential for having students freewrite about their reactions to the books we were reading. Before that time I had often written detailed "study questions" for the reading and asked students to turn in their answers. But a colleague suggested that the students might

---

Essay 1: Students were asked to write a personal essay describing and analyzing an important experience in their own lives.

Essay 2: After reading five selections related to cross-cultural communication in the textbook *Guidelines* (Spack, 1990), students were asked to write an essay analyzing how the ideas in these readings compared with their own attitudes and experiences. Students were expected to refer to the readings directly by using quotations, summarizing, and/or paraphrasing.

Essay 3: Students were asked to write an in-class essay analyzing an important theme in the assigned class reading, *A Place for Us* by Nicholas Gage (1989), an autobiographical account of a young Greek immigrant's life in the United States. Important themes in the book had been identified during a brainstorming session in the previous class.

Essay 4: This assignment, which occupied about a month of class time, involved a sequence of tasks in which students interviewed an immigrant, transcribed a segment of the interview, reported on the interview to a small group of classmates, and finally wrote and revised an essay analyzing the theme of immigration in the person's life.

FIG. 3.1. Essay assignments.

learn more by answering their own questions, not mine. Eventually, I came to see the validity of this suggestion, and I worked out a simple format for an informal reading journal that I collected and responded to once in a week. In their journals students were asked to do four things: (a) identify five unfamiliar words in the reading, guess the meaning from context, and later look up the dictionary meanings; (b) write a question about the reading that could be used for class discussion; (c) write a brief summary (less than half a page) of the week's reading; and (d) write a reflective journal entry about the week's reading.

This fourth part of the journal was, in my mind, the most important. The instructions on the journal form read:

> Freewrite about your personal reactions to the section of the book you read for this week. What were your thoughts and feelings about what you read? What did you like in the reading? Was there anything you didn't like? In what way did your reading connect with experiences from your own life or with your previous reading?

The reverse side of this form was left blank to encourage more writing, and I urged students to staple additional pages of freewriting to the form. I found that a considerable number of students, often those who rarely spoke during class, wrote long, reflective responses to their reading. Soon I was convinced that this freer approach was much more effective in getting students to connect with their reading (and to improve their writing) than my previous practice of using study questions. I enjoyed reading the students' personalized reactions to the books we were reading. And although I did not correct or grade the journals with letter grades, I did mark them with varying numbers of pluses based on the quantity and quality of the writing. I noticed that students who wrote most prolifically in their reading journals often improved greatly on their timed essay writing as well. Eventually, my interest in learning more about this type of informal writing intensified and led to the research described in this book.

THE WRITING TEST

Although the ostensible goal for the developmental writing classes at this college is to prepare students to cope more effectively with writing tasks in their subsequent college courses, neither students nor teachers can long ignore the pressures of the institutionally imposed final exam, a test that is much discussed and much feared by ESL students.

All the students in the two classes involved in this study had taken this exam at least once before, since a different version of the test is administered to all incoming students as part of the freshman skills assessment program, which also includes tests of reading and math. For the writing test, students are asked to write a short argumentative essay on one of two questions, usually related to controversial issues in contemporary U.S. society. The time limit of 50 minutes is strictly enforced, and students are not allowed to use dictionaries.

This test, intended to determine "minimal competence" in writing, is scored by anonymous readers using a holistic scale, ranging from a high of 6 to a low of 1; in order to demonstrate competence, students must score at least 4. Every test is assessed by two readers. If there is a discrepancy between the two scores, the essay is read by a third reader, whose score determines the outcome. In an attempt to assure consistency of scoring, readers are provided with a set of criteria and trained in "norming" sessions where they score and discuss sample essays. Incoming students who get 4s from both readers are allowed to register for freshman composition and to take regular, credit-bearing college courses. Students with lower scores are placed in developmental writing courses and prevented from taking many other courses. Incoming students who fail the writing exam are placed at the proper level in the developmental course sequence by full-time writing instructors, who reread all failing essays. These courses are designated as being for native speakers of English (two levels of instruction) or bilingual students (three levels).

Although exit from the lower level courses is determined by writing tests developed by teachers in the program, exit from the top level, in which this study was conducted, is determined solely by scores on the writing assessment test. In order to pass the course, a student must receive a 4 from both readers; these exam readers are instructors teaching the same level but not the classroom teacher.

Students in the developmental writing courses are often demoralized by their predicament. If they were placed directly in the course, they may be surprised to find themselves subject to a computerized control during registration that restricts them from taking other courses they need. If they have taken previous courses in the developmental sequence, they may be nearing the crucial 60-credit mark, after which they will not be allowed to register for any other courses if they have not yet passed the writing assessment test. Often those who are most discouraged are the repeaters, students who have previously failed the course and who must continue to register for it until they pass the exit exam. Ironically, many students who are having difficulty passing the writing proficiency exam have high grade-point averages and are having no difficulty in their other courses.

Using an anonymously scored assessment test as the sole exit criterion from the remedial program is demoralizing not only for students but for teachers as well. My own dissatisfaction with the test has grown steadily. When I was interviewed about my teaching in 1986, I was only mildly disturbed by the constraints this test imposed. I explained that I usually devoted the last 5 or 6 weeks of the 14-week semester to test preparation, although I would have preferred to spend this time focusing on writing that was personally meaningful to the students or that would better prepare them for future college writing tasks. But, I concluded philosophically, "That's how it goes" (Cummings, 1988, pp. 64-65).

By the winter of 1992, I was far less sanguine. As I looked back on the previous semester, I wrote in my teaching journal:

> My predominant impression was frustration with the test. I felt that for the last 6 weeks of the semester, my teaching was totally dominated by test preparation that had nothing whatever to do with what I really believe about the best way to teach writing. I remember remarking to a colleague that the more I learn about the theory underlying writing instruction, the more trouble I have in helping students prepare for this exam.

Even though the exam violates what I believe about teaching writing, I feel obligated to help students get through it so they can proceed with their education. But I also hope that through their journals and other course writing, my students will experience writing as a way of developing their thinking and expressing meaningful ideas.

THE JOURNALS

In the third class of the semester, I explained to the students that they would be keeping journals as part of their coursework, and I distributed the handout reproduced on the next page as Fig. 3.2. The purpose of the journals, I told the class, was to "talk about yourself as a reader, talk about yourself as a writer, what your experiences have been, how you're reacting to the book that we're reading, your feelings about the things you write for this class...." In explaining what I had in mind for these journals, I referred to my own journal writing experience to acknowledge that there might be a personal dimension to the reading/writing journals:

I was in a class last spring at NYU where we wrote about our early reading experiences, memories of our mothers reading to us, our fathers reading to us when we were little, memories of storytelling. And, you know, it got very personal. So these journals may end up getting more personal than we think at this point, and that's okay. But I'm not really seeing this as just a personal diary but focused more on you as a reader and writer.

Because I hoped that extensive journal writing would help the students develop fluency in English, I emphasized that I wanted them to write a lot—at least five times a week, for a total of at least five pages a week.

I'd like you to follow these guidelines for your reading/writing journal. Although I will occasionally suggest topics for the journal, most of the time you will decide what you would like to write about.

1. *Content:* Basically, this journal is a place for you to write about yourself as a reader and a writer. Of course, readers and writers are also people. So if there are personal things you would like to discuss in your journal, that's fine too.

2. *Length:* Writing regularly is important, so I would recommend that you write in your journal about 5 times a week, even if it's only for 10 or 15 minutes. Each week you will be expected to write at least 5 pages (10 pages if you double space).

3. *In-class writing:* During each class meeting we will spend about 10 minutes freewriting. Be sure to add these writings to your journal.

4. *Writing about reading:* Every Friday you should come to class with a journal entry about your reaction to the chapters in A *Place for Us* assigned for that week. You can get some ideas for writing about reading from the Introduction of *Guidelines* (Spack, 1990, pp. 1–11). We will also discuss how to write about reading in class

5. *Form for journal:* Be sure to date every entry at the top of the page. Write on white notebook paper and put all entries in a plastic ring binder. Please write in pen and only use one side of the paper. Your journal will be much easier to read if you double space (I'll explain).

6. *Response to the journal:* I will collect your journal every 2 or 3 weeks and write a letter of response to you. Sometimes you will also be asked to let a classmate read your journal. It's fine to write about private things in your journal, but be sure to mark them in some way so that you can remove them before you let someone else (either me or a classmate) read your journal.

FIG. 3.2.   Guidelines for reading/writing journals.

I stated that "Writing about reading is an important part of the journal" and gave a fairly detailed explanation of what I had in mind. I said that every Friday, students should come to class with journal entries about the chapters assigned for that week and recommended that they read the introduction to the assigned textbook, which recommended keeping a "reading/writing journal" and provided examples of actual entries written by ESL students (Spack, 1990, pp. 1–11). I pointed out that it was acceptable to summarize the reading but made it clear that this wasn't the primary purpose of the journals: "What I'm more interested in is your own reactions.... A lot of times, it's another story from your own life that relates to the stories in the book."

Another topic that I emphasized as I introduced the journals was the students' right to privacy:

> It's very important for you to understand who's gonna read this journal as you're writing it. Because some things are very private and personal, and if you knew somebody else was going to read it, you either wouldn't write it at all or you would write about it in a very different way than if it was your own personal diary and only you were going to read it.

I reminded the students that they should look through their journals before turning them in to me and remove any entries they wanted to keep private.

At this point I introduced the idea of freewriting (Elbow, 1973) as a useful technique for journal writing. When I asked how many students had used this technique before, more than half the students raised their hands. I asked one student to explain what freewriting meant and then expanded on her comments:

> It's very different from trying to produce this beautiful essay to get an A from your teacher because freewriting is not graded. It's to get the thoughts out of your head and onto the paper. Grammar is not important. Spelling is not important. Don't worry about it. Don't stop to look up words in the dictionary. Just write freely.

But what happens, I asked the class, if your mind is completely blank? "You're out of luck," said Rita, a student from Israel who often spoke in class. We all laughed. Then I said, "No, you're not," and explained how I handled the times when I was tired or distracted and the words didn't want to come:

> What works for me is to write the same sentence over and over again, like, "I can't think of anything to say. I can't think of anything to say. I can't think of anything to say." It takes about three of those, and I get so bored with

writing that same sentence, that some idea will come into my mind, sometimes a pretty good idea.... So if that happens to you today or at home when
you're writing, don't sit there for a long time without writing. Keep going like
that, and then some new idea will come to your mind.

I ended this discussion by asking the students to write their first journal
entry—a focused freewrite about "your attitude toward writing, particularly
your attitude toward writing in English, which might be different from your
feelings about writing in your native language." I explained that it was
important for students to be aware of their attitudes toward writing, "not to
have a real positive attitude, but to be honest about your feelings, whatever
they are." Then I read four short descriptions written in previous semesters
to give the students a sense of what a journal entry was like. I explained that
I always write in my freewriting journal while the students are writing in
theirs and that I don't like it if anybody talks to me or to other students
during this time: "So let's write now. Freewriting as we talked about it. Your
attitude.... Something that came into your mind as you heard me read.
Write about your own attitude toward writing in English."

Introducing the Research Dimension

Several weeks into the course I explained to both classes that I planned to
use their journal writing as the basis for a research study. I made it clear that
I was not changing the way I taught in order to conduct the study but simply
analyzing, in a more systematic way, the journals that had long been an
important component of my approach to teaching writing. I explained that
student involvement in this research was completely voluntary and that
there was no penalty for opting not to participate. If a student did not want
to be involved in the research, he or she would simply not sign and return
the permission letter that I distributed. Students who chose not to participate were still expected to submit their journals, but their journal writing
was not used in my analysis. Students who did choose to participate were
assured of complete anonymity and were told that they would be referred
to by pseudonyms in the written report of the study.

In explaining the nature of the research, I emphasized the students' roles
as collaborators: "Once you get involved in this kind of research, we're all
participants together, and it's a kind of sharing of the research really." Most
students did decide to participate—19 of the 21 students enrolled in the
first class and 18 of 23 in the second class.

Receiving the Journals

"To teach," said Nel Noddings, "involves a giving of self and a receiving of other" (1984, p. 113), and I was often reminded of these words as I began to read the students' journals. About 2 weeks after the semester began, I collected the journals from the first class. All but 3 of the 21 class members turned in journals, in which they wrote primarily about their reactions to *A Place for Us*—summarizing, explaining connections between the book and their own lives, analyzing Gage's writing style, expressing likes and dislikes about the book.

A few students, however, used their journals as personal diaries without commenting directly on the reading. In the field log I noted that some students had "almost a compulsion to work on the most important personal problems." For example, one student in the first class, an older man from Colombia, wrote:

> Today at 3:05 p.m. sitting in my room, I begine to write about my live. I don't know why I want to do this, it have never occured to me to write about that. I stop and think why. Some thing came to my mine and I belive that the reason why I want to write about it, is because of the book, A Place for Us.

A few days later this same student announced in his journal, "Today I would like to write about me," and ended his entry with a postscript: "P.S. Please excuse me for not writing about the book this time. I need to put in paper what I was felling and the journal was the only thing that came in my mind." Although this student was not strictly adhering to the journal guidelines, I was not disturbed and noted in the field log, "I think the students will know the best way to use these journals. I can't know what's best for each of them."

Another student who chose to write about herself rather than the assigned reading was Rita, the woman from Israel mentioned earlier, who wrote 11 pages in which she examined her attitude toward writing. In reviewing the audiotape of my explanation of the journal guidelines, I noticed that I had suggested that students could continue the entry about attitudes toward writing at home if they wished. Rita, as it turned out, was the only student who followed this suggestion. I judged her journal to be highly reflective in the way she seemed to step back and examine herself as a writer:

> I'm very confident in my speach or my verbal capacity. I feel no matter where I'll be or when I'll do it I will always have my strength in a verbal ways. My confidence, my power and my strength are all in this part of my character.

Factors that might have played a part in Rita's reflective approach to journal writing included her age—at 40 she was the oldest student in the class. She was also the mother of two children and had gone through difficult life experiences such as a recent divorce, which might have encouraged her to become more analytical. Another older student, a man who had been born in Bangladesh and later lived in Germany as a member of the U.S. Army, also seemed to be among the more reflective students. And his journal illustrated Britton's thesis (1970, p. 118) that disturbance or pain often leads to reflection and in many cases to reflective writing. This student wrote:

> Writing about the day to day life, and the complexity of our vicious world gives me the knowledge to fight in tough times. We learn from mistakes. If I document an experience in black and white, later on it gives me some background knowledge of the same problem and how to react on it. Our world is not a bed of roses. So we have to learn from our mistakes.

A week later, when I collected the journals in the other section, I was pleased by the high level of participation (every student except one turned in some writing) but surprised by the content. More students in this class used the journal solely for personal expression and failed to comment on *A Place for Us*. In this class, as in the other one, I noted that many students used their journals to write analytically about themes in their reading or in their own lives. For a class of 23 students the number of stories dealing with personal trauma seemed very high. One of the primary uses of journals is as a kind of therapy, a way of getting unpleasant feelings out in the open so the writer can process them, thus freeing the mind for more productive activities (see, e.g., Baldwin, 1977; Britton, 1970; Rowe, 1978). In this class many students were using the journals in this way.

Not all the journals, however, focused on painful or upsetting experiences. Several students spoke of positive experiences with journal writing in the past and seemed to welcome the chance to keep a journal for this class. For example, a young woman who had come to the United States from Hong Kong only 6 months earlier wrote:

> Writing is familiar with me cos every time when I'm feeling the need of writing, I rush to get a pen and paper at once. I like my diary very much, it recorded my happiness, my sadness, failure and success. When I opened it, all the good and bad memories are being recalled on my mind just like a film playing in a theatre.

This student, like most of her classmates, tended to be quiet and reserved in the classroom. After reading the students' first journal entries, I felt that I had learned more about them than I had through several weeks of classroom interactions. By enhancing my understanding of the students in my classes, journals provide a valuable database for the decisions I am constantly required to make as a teacher—decisions ranging from what books to assign to how to respond to a particular student's writing.

Responding to the Journals

I planned to collect the journals every 2 weeks and write a personal letter of response to each student. The decision to respond in letters rather than by writing comments directly on the journals was motivated by my desire to have a computer record of all my responses. I also liked the idea of responding in a sustained text rather than a series of fragmentary comments. Although writing these individualized letters was time consuming, it was also rewarding because it gave me a chance to communicate with the students about their individual concerns. (See Appendixes B through E for samples of these individual response letters.)

After responding to the first set of journals, I wrote in the field log:

> Basically, I enjoyed reading these journals and did not find it an onerous chore. What I'm trying to do is to ask questions for further thought, something that is not easy for me. And also I'm trying to send the message that it's good for the students to use these journals as they see fit.

Most important, in responding to the journals I tried to develop an atmosphere of trust and support. Martha Cummings (1988), who studied a series of writing conferences I held with four students, noted this tendency, which she referred to as face-work, "work to protect or restore the positive self-image the student wishes to present" (p. 155). She said that what distinguished my conferences from the hundreds of others she had analyzed was "the amount of work [I did] to make these students feel important and special, to let them know how much [I] value[d] their contributions" (p. 155).

Midway through the course nearly all of the students were turning in their journals, and many were writing prolifically and reflectively on a variety of topics. At this point I started writing some of my responses in the margins of the journals rather than in separate letters. I explained the reasons for this change in the field log:

It's 8 p.m. on a Sunday and I'm buried under these journals but still finding them interesting. One thing that started to happen this time was that I started to write comments directly on the journals.... I just wanted more of a speech-like dialogue, just little comments like "I agree," "interesting." The first time I felt compelled to do this was with Roberto's journal. But now as I'm getting to know all of the students better, I'm feeling the need to do more of this.

I was also beginning to suffer from "researcher overload." On several occasions I found it impossible to write a separate response letter to every student. Instead, I responded in a letter to the whole class, in which I quoted passages from some of the journals, an idea I had gotten from Spack and Sadow (1983). (See Appendix A for samples of my response letters to the whole class.)

In another one of these class letters, I urged the students to reread their journals when they got them back. In class, I explained the reason for this advice:

... you spend a lot of time writing something. You give it to the teacher. The teacher spends a lot of time reading it and writes some comments.... I think probably most people do look at the teacher's comments. But they don't take the time to reread *their* stuff. So, I know, from unfortunate personal experience, that I tend to do the same thing because I'm so busy, as you all are. But I feel like you've put all this effort into the journals. You really should read them more than once, more than when you're writing them.

I suspected that some students read my responses but neglected to take another look at what they had written. Reasoning that reflection involves looking back on what has been said and thought and revising it in light of new information, I thought it was important for the students to reread and reconsider earlier journal entries. By getting students to reread their journals, I hoped that some of the less reflective writers might begin to see these ideas differently and perhaps re-examine them in later journals or at least in their own minds.

Using Journals to Prepare for the Final Exam

By the last month of the semester neither the students nor I could any longer ignore the impending final examination. During this period the students wrote one in-class "agree-or-disagree" essay each week, which I scored using the official grading scale. I asked students who did not receive a passing score to improve their papers by rewriting. My rationale was that once students had the experience of writing a passing essay, they would more likely be able to repeat it under test conditions.

At this point in the semester, virtually all the class work became focused on passing the all-important final exam. I asked the students to brainstorm about possible questions on the final, and each class decided on two current topics to use for exam preparation. On their own, the students found newspaper or magazine articles on these topics and wrote informal summaries and reactions that they discussed in small groups in class.

I also encouraged the students to use their journals to explore issues related to the final exam. I wanted to see if they could demystify this test by writing about how it is graded, their own strengths and weaknesses as writers, how their emotions might affect their performance on the test, and so on. In the last class before spring vacation, I responded to the students' journals in a letter suggesting some questions they might want to discuss in their next journals: "What are your feelings about taking this test? How do you think the test is graded? What kind of paper is most likely to pass this test? How do you feel about the assigned topics? What is most difficult for you personally about this test?"

Most of the students did respond to these questions, and I continued to use my open letters of response to share some of the insights that were emerging in the journals. For example, in a letter to the second class I included the following excerpts from student journals:

On the time pressure of the final exam: Many people wrote about this. Here is one comment: "My major problem in final essay is timing. Timing kills my thoughts, because one thought that is in my head: 'How much time I still have?' Your final essay has to be short and sharp like a gun shot."

On the type of writing required: "I wonder why the questions in the exams are all argumentative. Why there is not other kinds of questions like descriptive essay or story writing? It should have a larger variety of choice. As I hate writing argumentative essay very much, I am quite worried about the exam. It is a fact that many people can write good descriptive essay or story but not argumentative essay. Like me."

On the need to change the system: "I think that they have to change that system. I guess that almost all the people that are taking this course feel the same way as I. If I don't pass this course, I will not be able to take some courses that I want to take for next semester."

I ended my response letter by reminding the students that I wanted them to use the journals to develop a strategy for doing well on the final exam: "What are some specific things you can do to improve your chances of passing the exam? Write out a plan for yourself that will help you to do your best on this test."

END-OF-SEMESTER QUESTIONNAIRE

As the term neared its conclusion, I was relieved that the avalanche of data was about to cease but gratified that my interest in the journal writing of second-language learners had yielded such rich materials. In order to gain additional insights into how the students felt about the course and particularly about the journals, I wrote a three-page questionnaire and distributed it during the last week of classes. The questionnaire was supposed to be anonymous, but more than half of the students chose to sign their names. Fifteen out of 21 in the first class and 13 out of 23 in the second class returned the questionnaires. The responses are summarized in Table 3.1, which reveals certain patterns. The answers to Questions 1 and 2 indicate that the students in the first class had a stronger sense of their own improvement both in writing and in attitude toward writing than did the students in the second class. This is somewhat ironic as the passing rate in the second class was substantially higher than that in the first class—83% compared to 71%. Yet the negativity expressed by students in the second class was in keeping with my impression, mentioned many times in the field log, that the students in the second class seemed more negative and more passive than the students in the first class. Although a majority of the respondents in the second class felt that their writing had not improved, they did feel their attitude toward writing had improved. Of the 13 respondents, 11 indicated that they left the class feeling positive about writing. Three of these students mentioned the journals as a significant factor in their changing attitudes. In the first class all 15 respondents said that their attitude toward writing had either improved during the semester or remained positive.

A majority of the respondents from the first class had not kept a journal before, whereas a majority in the second class had. The previous journal-writing experience of the students in the second class supports my impression, mentioned in the field log early in the semester, that the students in this class were unusually proficient writers for this level of instruction. Ironically, their prior writing experience may also help to explain their more

TABLE 3.1
Responses to Questionnaire

1. Has your writing improved this semester?

	Yes	No
First class:	15	0
Second class:	6	7

2. Has your attitude toward writing improved?

	Yes	No	No, but positive to begin with
First class:	13	0	2
Second class:	8	2	3

3. Have you ever kept a journal before?

	No	In first language	In second language	In both languages
First class:	9	3	2	1
Second class:	4	4	3	2

4. Was the journal helpful for you?

	Yes	No	Not sure
First class:	14	0	1
Second class:	11	2	0

5. How much time did you spend on the journal each week?

	It varied	Not much	1-3 hours	3-7 hours	13-14 hours
First class:	1	2	2	2	2
Second class:	1	2	5	5	0

6. Which type of teacher response did you prefer?

	Individual letter	Group letter	Didn't care
First class:	11	1	2
Second class:	13	0	0

7. Do you plan to continue your journal?

	Yes	No	Undecided
First class:	7	1	7
Second class:	7	2	4

negative attitudes; many of these students may have been dismayed to find themselves in a developmental writing class.

A large majority of respondents in both classes said they found the journal helpful. In answering the question about writing improvement, five students in the first class said that they felt their improvement was attributable to the journals. As I analyzed the students' anecdotal comments about how the journals led to improvement, certain categories emerged. Most of these categories recurred in the case studies are discussed at greater length in later chapters.

The most commonly mentioned benefit of journal writing was increased fluency—including writing speed, improved vocabulary and grammar, and ability to think in English. Many students felt their increased fluency resulted from the freedom of this type of writing. One student wrote, "My freewriting has become much more smooth when my mind is relaxed. My thoughts well up while my pen flows. Several times, I was even surprised at myself that I could write so much and a few sentences with complex grammar, I wrote without hesitance." Another benefit that several students mentioned was increased self-assurance about writing in English and a newly found sense of control. One student explained, "It gives you confidence in the second language and helps you control your fears about the test." Quite a few students mentioned that the journals helped them to develop and organize ideas. For example, one student wrote, "There are things that I wrote in my journal for this class that I've been planning on jotting down for as long as I could recall."

Students reported a wide variety of strategies for deciding what to write about in the journals. One student explained, "It is freewriting. I wrote first sentence and then I continued writing almost without any stops." Another said, "I didn't dicide. It came by itself." A total of five students mentioned that they usually took their journal topics from their reading in A *Place for Us*. One of these students said she always started her journal entries with a quotation that generated a strong reaction and went on from there. Many students said that the ideas in their journals related directly to experiences in their own lives. Approximately half of the respondents said they planned to continue writing in their journals even after the course ended.

UNANSWERED QUESTIONS

One of the strongest endorsements of the value of journal writing came not in response to the questionnaire, but as part of a student's journal.

About 3 weeks before the end of the term, a young woman from Hong Kong wrote:

> The writing of the journal is really a breakthrough in my life. I seldom write as much as this journal assignment. Sometimes, I just don't believe it! It's a good practice for me to express myself on the papers. Although I am poor in spoken English, through the writing of the journals I can express my feelings no matter it is positive or negative. Also this is one of the best way to lesson the pressure deep inside me. Of course, if I have a good reader, I feel much better because I can share and open myself with her.
>
> Today everyone is kind of busy in one's daily life. Each of us has problems of his own, but, it is rather difficult to find your friend when one is in depression. Therefore, writing is necessary in life.

As I ponder this affirmation of the value of journal writing in a bilingual student's life, a little voice keeps nagging at the edges of my consciousness: "Sure, for students like this one, keeping the journal was a truly rewarding experience. Not only did it help her to improve her English, but it also helped in her personal life, substituting for the friend she was too shy or too busy to find in her life outside the classroom. But what about the other students—the ones who didn't sign the permission forms to be a part of the study, the ones who wrote in their journals only erratically or not at all? What was their experience of being asked to keep a reading/writing journal?" I had to admit that these were valid questions although difficult ones to address. I decided to examine the data more closely to see if I could discern any patterns among the students who failed to turn in their journals regularly.

In each class, I had collected the journals six times. I felt satisfied with the response rate of students who had turned them in five or six times. After all, most of these students were taking heavy course loads, and some had families, worked many hours a week, or both. I could easily understand how a student could slip up once or twice. But I was more concerned about the students who had turned in the journals three times or less. Among this group, some students had extenuating circumstances such as illness in the family that prevented their full participation in the journal writing. Still, seven students out of the 44 enrolled had attended fairly regularly but had turned in three or fewer journals. These less than enthusiastic journal writers represented nearly 16% of the total enrollment.

I've been teaching long enough to know that no teaching method will be enthusiastically embraced by all students. And the differences found in any classroom—variations in personality and learning style—are compounded when the students come from different countries and speak different native languages. My feeling at the end of the semester was that, all things considered, the reading/writing journals had been extremely helpful for most of the students.

Based on my knowledge of the writing abilities of the students enrolled in my classes, I was pleased by their performance on the final exam. Both classes exceeded the department average on the final exam. In the first class, 71% of the students passed, 15 out of 21. In the second class, 83% passed, 19 out of 23. These rates compared favorably with the overall passing rate for all students enrolled in the course that semester—69%. I was also pleased with the quantity and quality of journal writing and felt that most students had benefitted significantly from keeping a journal. But still I wondered why some students had not participated fully.

Among the group who failed to submit the journal only one time, the omission tended to come at the end of the semester, either the last or next-to-last submission. At this point in the semester many students were beginning to feel the pressure of the final exam and were also working hard to complete the required work in their other courses.

But I continued to wonder about the seven students who turned in three journals or fewer. Why didn't they become fully engaged with journal writing? I will never be able to answer this question definitively. But through the ethnographic interviews that took place after the semester ended, I received many new and sometimes unexpected insights into the students' experiences with and attitudes about journal writing. The next four chapters present detailed portraits of five of these students.

4

Roberto: Validation
Through Connected Knowing

> I've been writing for three year in english. I know for a fact now that you can
> use writing as your best friend. Writing how you feel can make you realize
> many things. You can develop a lot of knowledge and open mind thinking.
> No one will listen to you as a notebook can. No one will listen [to] your
> thoughts about politics, problems, love, faith as a good diary can. A piece of
> paper never lets you down.

The writer of these words is Roberto, an 18-year-old student from Colombia,
who at age 13 immigrated to the United States with his family. Roberto
attended and later graduated from a public high school. He lives with his
parents and younger sister and has an older sister who attended college
briefly before getting married. Roberto and his sister represent the first
generation in their family to attend college. Upon entering college, Roberto
was placed in only one developmental course—the writing class he took
with me during his second semester.

The passage quoted above is part of a longer entry written in class on the
day I asked the students to begin their journals by freewriting about their
attitude toward writing in English. As I look back on Roberto's journal for
the semester, I'm not surprised that he was able to explain at the outset why
he perceived the journal as personally meaningful. For Roberto, having the
chance to freely express his thoughts and feelings in a journal was a
validating experience. And, for the most part, this validation occurred as
he connected his school learning with his life outside school—his experiences as a "proud Colombian," a struggling immigrant, a language learner,
and a young man attempting to come to terms with his personal relationships. Every page of Roberto's journal contained reflection on subjects that
were relevant to the course and meaningful to him personally.

Soon after I began reading and responding to the journals, I realized that
many of Roberto's entries epitomized what I hoped students would gain from

keeping a journal. His journal writing was enthusiastic, prolific, and personally engaged. Roberto appeared to connect easily with A *Place for Us,* in
which Nicholas Gage (1989) described his experiences as an immigrant,
who at age 9 came to live with his father in America after his mother had
been killed by Communist guerrillas in his native Greece. For the first 6½
weeks of the semester, Roberto devoted all of his at-home journal entries to
this book.

When I began to analyze the student journals using the concept of
connected knowing, I realized, with some surprise, that several of the
students who employed this way of knowing most powerfully in their
journals were male. Although Belenky, Clinchy, Goldberger, and Tarule
(1986) had stated that connected knowing was not limited to females, they
suspected that more women than men might favor this approach to learning.
Yet among the students I interviewed, it was two young men who relied most
often on connected knowing in their journals. My subsequent analysis of
their journals has made me skeptical of essentialist approaches to anything
as complex as learning. Cultural background, native language, previous
educational experience, social class, and personality may be just as powerful
as gender in influencing a person's preferred approach to learning. Therefore, throughout this book, I focus on connected knowing not as a female
quality, or a male quality but as a human quality from which all students can
benefit.

CONNECTED KNOWING
IN ROBERTO'S JOURNAL

Examples of connected knowing occurred on virtually every one of the 65
pages of Roberto's journal. In fact, his inclination toward this approach to
learning may have been a reason why he enjoyed the journal and why he
had no trouble generating ideas to write about. In analyzing Roberto's
journal, I identified six stylistic or content markers of connected knowing:
references to the self, open expression of emotion, recognition of temporal
flux and change, hints of internal dialogue brought out into the open,
empathy and identification as ways of gaining access to other people's
knowledge, and knowledge seen as deriving from personal experience.
These markers were developed from descriptions of connected knowing in
Women's Ways of Knowing (Belenky et al., 1986, pp. 112–124) and from
Helle's commentary on that work (1991, p. 54). To demonstrate the

prominence of connected knowing in Roberto's journal, I discuss each of the six markers in turn.

References to the Self

As is characteristic with connected knowers, Roberto often referred to himself in the journal as he compared characters or events in A *Place for Us* with people and experiences in his own life. For example, his first journal entry about the book began:

> I felt very familiar with the book A *Place for Us*. There wasn't a single thing the little guy lived that I didn't, or, at least, similarly. The first thing that shocked was the sacrifice that his mom Eleni did for him. Although my parents didn't have to give their lives for me, they left a culture where they were always welcomed to a place where nobody would know if you die. My dad gave up his lifetime savings to buy all the plain tickets, he gave up having his own business and here he can't get a job. All that my parents have in their mind is our future and they really push me into not giving up my dreams. (For the complete text of this entry see the first item in Appendix B.)

In subsequent weeks, Roberto continued to use the journal to connect his reading with his own life and experiences outside of school. For example, in the following entry Roberto explained how Nick's experiences in hanging out with the tough boys in the neighborhood compared with memories from his own childhood:

> Chapter nine brought me old memories of my early years. How nice it was to be with boys of the same condition and talking in the same manner. Being wild. This was an unforgettable part of life. Playing the innocent but being the bad boys in the street. Trying hard to be the gangsters of the moment. Risking your bones just so a girl can pay attention to you. I think we all get to a point where you feel ready to be self sufficient or, put in another way, *uncontrolable*. This is where the old conflict starts. Your old folks trying to keep you out of trouble don't get nothing but hostile looks. You feel like the street corrupted boys are your family and your own family is the opresor. This was how my father and I started. While the gang was playing soccer in the street, hanging out, I would be helping him or in the house watching them from the window.... You don't realize they are the bad guys until something puts a stop. For Nick, it was that beating that he got in his old neighborhood. For me it was my family (my father's side).

It was clear from my interviews with Roberto that reflecting in writing came naturally to him. He had ready access to many memories from the past and often revised past interpretations in the light of present experience. In our first interview Roberto explained how this process worked when he was writing about A *Place for Us*: "It was mostly about memory, right? ... I had to go back, I was back in my city. I was doing the same things then."

The way Roberto used his journal to go back into his past experience, reinterpreting it in the new light of his reading, relates directly to Britton's explanation of the way in which readers take up the spectator role to create new knowledge through connected knowing:

> Looked back on, the experiences others have related merge into the experiences we have had ourselves: as a basis for making generalizations, judgements, evaluations, decisions, we call upon both. We become experienced people, in other words, as a result of the fusion of other people's experiences with our own. (1970, p. 116)

Throughout the course, Roberto's journal continued to exemplify the type of fusion that Britton had in mind.

Open Expression of Emotion

The acknowledgment of emotion has been identified as another hallmark of connected knowing. This feature was present in Roberto's journal from page one. When he thought about how Nicholas must have felt after his mother, Eleni, was killed by the Communists in Greece, he related this to his feelings for his own mother: "I can't think of losing her, let me die before I have to see [my parents] leave, I couldn't handle it. I know my mom would give everything for me just as Eleni did."

As the weeks passed, Roberto became even more comfortable with journal writing, and the openness and emotionality of his entries increased. This sense of freedom was reflected in the way he freely switched from one topic to another, asked questions, and held extended dialogues with characters in the book. At times there was a stream-of-consciousness quality to Roberto's journal writing, for example, in the entry in which he philosophized about the meaning of the birth of a baby in A *Place for Us*: "Everytime a baby is born the feeling for life becomes stronger. It's the essence of hope for many and a proof that miracles do exist." Later on the same page he broke in, as if he had just become aware of what he was writing: "God knows an hour ago I wanted to have none [no children]. Now ... hum?!?? I must be going crazy."

If we accept Mayher's notion that thought and feeling cannot be separated (1990, p. 104), then one of the advantages of journals from an educational point of view is the possibility of expressing emotion in connection with learning. The heightened emotions that are often expressed in journals may, in fact, lead to more lasting learning.

Recognition of Temporal Flux and Change

According to Belenky, Clinchy, Goldberger, and Tarule (1986), connected knowers are usually sensitive to the possibility of flux and change over time. There are numerous signs of this recognition in Roberto's journal, both in his predictions of what will happen later in the book and in comments he makes about his own life—for example, when he writes about his desire to improve his economic situation or recognizes that his attitude toward his father may change as he gets older. Roberto's recognition of temporal flux and change was particularly evident in his last journal entry, where he wrote about the significance of opening his first bank account:

> I look at all the years before I get some degree. It disappoints me. Will I make it? What could make me change my life and force me to do something unexpected? It's scary. Will I still have my mother tomorrow? What if I'm forced to quit school? I better stick to the present and enjoy it. I've found out through grown ups that life is full of up and downs. One day you have it all. The next you may be wondering what will you eat tomorrow.

In this entry Roberto actively questions himself about the future, indicating his knowledge that things change over time. The questions also signify the presence of reflection, as each question could provide the basis of another reflective journal entry with Roberto's ideas continuing to expand.

Internal Dialogue

Writing in the connected mode has a feeling of dialogue about it—either a dialogue between writer and reader or an internal dialogue within the writer. This dialogic quality was often present in Roberto's journal. On several occasions, for example, he addressed me, the reader: "I hope I'm not boring you my dearest teacher but this book just touch me where it hurts: poverty and adjusting to the new culture." But even when he did not address me directly, I felt privileged to "listen in" on his ongoing internal conversation.

Several times, Roberto's dialogue took a form not used by any other student. He addressed his writing directly to the characters in the book, characters in an imagined scenario, the American public, or even, in one case, to Jesus. The most extended of these invented conversations was with Nicholas Gage's father, Christos. Roberto acknowledged the freedom he felt in the journal as he introduced this dialogue:

> Now lets move to something completely different and since this is called free writing I'll take it as so. I'm going to speak to Mr. Gage about some cultural things that he must forget in America if you don't want to harm your daughters instead of protecting them.

Interestingly, Roberto shifted into the dialogue form in the middle of this passage, as the pronoun switched from "he" to "you." He continued his advice as follows:

> First of all Mr Gage, you are no one to choose your daughters' man. You didn't bring daughters into the world to sell them or to fix them up with your ideal man. You must allow them to date and if they feel ready for marriage be ready to support them. This is america, buying wives is a nonsense of Greece's free market. Your daughters need to know what is out there in this world full of evil. They must go through a process of learning by experience. Why do you want them married anyway? So they can bring kids into the world and become shortminded and stupid like you? Let them enjoy the youth and be prepare for the real world. Let them get married for love, not for slavery.... Forget about your pride and just think what's best. Shut up!

This excerpt provides one example of Roberto's asking questions in his journal—something he often did, which again reveals the dialogic nature of his writing. Some of these questions, as with the previous examples, were rhetorical. Others were real, open-ended questions. For example, in writing about the Greek attitude toward women, as revealed in *A Place for Us*, he asked, "Why do some cultures relate women to house and kids?" And in contrast to the rhetorical questions that, in effect, answered themselves, this question provoked a long and thoughtful discussion about stereotyping based on gender roles. By asking and answering his own questions, Roberto sustained a dialogue within the pages of his journal.

Empathy and Identification

Empathy and identification with other people and their ideas are extremely important ways of acquiring knowledge in the connected mode, and these features were evident from the beginning in Roberto's journal. In fact, I commented on this in my first letter of response to him:

> You do a great job of explaining how you identified with the boy Nick in sentences like: "I know exactly how the boy felt. Knowing that you had felt more pain than any of them could imagine makes you not fit in, not until you find someone with similar experiences."

Later, Roberto continued to empathize with the characters and their problems, for example, by seeing glimpses of his father in Nick's father, Christos, and comparing his own habit of finding escape by driving to Nick's way of escaping by going to the movies. At times, Roberto's identification was so strong that he almost seemed to be living vicariously through his reading. For instance, in describing his frustration in school after he moved to the United States at the age of 13, he revealed how he resented people who considered him "dumb or retarded" simply because he couldn't speak English. He set out to prove his intelligence by getting the highest grades in the class on math tests and he seemed to relive those experiences as he read about Nick Gage's schooling in the new country:

> It felt good when I earned my respect, now, I can't wait to finish this book and read that Nicholas earned his, I want to live that feeling again through Nicholas. I want to read where the teachers who looked down on him had to praise him, they really looked stupid I believe, just like mine.

In our final interview I asked Roberto about his tendency to identify in a personal way with his reading. In describing the process, he explained that the author "was describing the feeling first. I recognized the feeling and then I recalled." Roberto illustrated this idea by referring to incidents in the early part of the book:

> ... cause he [Nicholas Gage] really saw and described a lot of things that I really saw and described within me, too, when I saw them. He was talking how he was too mature for American kids, how he felt uncomfortable cause he was dressed poorly, and they have, like, nice [clothes], and they were rich and everything. And I was picturing *myself*. I wasn't picturing what was written in the book. I was picturing what I saw.

More than any of the other students I interviewed, Roberto identified with the struggles of the young Nicholas Gage. A question that naturally arises is whether the connected-knowing approach that Roberto used in his journal was merely a factor of his strong personal identification with a book that he perceived to mirror much of his own life experience. Roberto did state during an interview that *A Place for Us* was "a special book" for him. However, he continued to write from a strong position of connected knowing after finishing the book. He explained that he always found something to identify with in his reading:

> I always *identify* something, like when I was reading [Unamuno], he was talking about a guy who was a volcano of passion, remember? And I also thought of that guy as my father or me, like we are like that. And I wasn't picturing that guy. I was picturing me. So that's what happen. But then some other things, when they're describing places, if you want to understand it, you have to picture yourself there. And, you know, some things are not related to you. Then you picture things they are describing. But when something really hits you, and you recognize the feeling, that's when you don't picture what they are writing; you picture what you saw.

Besides providing an articulate explanation of the processes of connected knowing, Roberto's comments also elucidate the insights of reader response theorists who concentrate on the active role of the reader in constructing meaning from a text (see, e.g., Rosenblatt, 1968, 1978). For Roberto, empathizing while reading was crucial for understanding. In our first interview he expressed surprise that all readers do not identify in this way: "I felt like I was there, like I was in the ship with them [the Gage children]. I don't know the way it happened. It does not happen to everyone who reads?"

Acknowledging that empathy and identification have a valid role to play in education may seem alien or even wrongheaded to those who believe that education should train students to be objective and to distance themselves from their feelings. However, I agree with Robert Coles, who believes that a student's empathic response to reading should be cherished as an impor-tant learning experience:

> That side of ourselves [the emotional side] is not set apart from our intellect. In order to respond, one remembers, one notices, then one makes connec-tions—engaging the thinking mind as well as what is called one's emotional side. How to encompass in our minds the complexity of some lived moments in a life? How to embody in language the mix of heightened awareness and

felt experience which reading a story can end up offering the reader? Not that a novel cannot, also, be an occasion for abstraction, for polemical argument. But it can, as well, insinuate itself into a remembering, daydreaming, wondering life; can prompt laughter or tears; can inspire moments of amused reflection with respect to one's nature, accomplishments, flaws. (1989, p. 128)

Roberto's journal reveals him to be the kind of engaged reader that Coles described. By entering into his reading in an active way, he makes it his own.

Knowledge Derived From Personal Experience

According to the authors of *Women's Ways of Knowing* (1986), connected knowing grows out of the belief, often held by subjectivists, that the most reliable knowledge results from personal experience. There are several places in Roberto's journal where he stated this belief explicitly, for example, when he wrote about "the importance of a hiding place" to temporarily escape from personal problems. For Nick Gage, this place was a movie theater, and Roberto felt that "what he really did there was study himself and what he wanted." Roberto identified strongly with Nick's need for temporary escape:

> It's great to feel empty after a trip to your hiding place and I can now feel all the thoughts that went through Nicholas head while he was sitting in the movies. You reach many peaks: The hero, the miserable, the smart, the unreasonable, the forgotten, the most popular. This is where you mold yourself according to yourself....

Ultimately, in Roberto's view, a person's development is in his own hands: " ... you mold yourself according to yourself." In two entries written in class (one of which was excerpted as the epigraph for this chapter), Roberto expressed the belief that even in formal educational settings, learners must generate knowledge for themselves.

HOW ROBERTO USED THE JOURNAL

In analyzing the students' uses of the journals, I asked whether the student wrote primarily to fulfill an assignment or for other reasons as well. There were many possibilities: using the journal to communicate in a more personal way with the teacher, to prepare for the final exam, to develop the

TABLE 4.1
How Roberto Used the Journal

A Place for Us	In-class entries	His own topics	Final exam	Responses to my questions
44 pp	8 pp	11 pp	2 pp	0 pp
68 %	12 %	17 %	3 %	0 %

craft of writing, to generate new knowledge, and on and on. I realized, of course, that these different uses were not mutually exclusive. In Roberto's case, merely calculating the number of pages spent on different types of writing was quite revealing. Table 4.1 indicates that Roberto used the journal primarily to write about his reactions to A Place for Us (68%). Because of his strong inclination toward connected knowing, these entries based on the assigned reading often related directly to himself and his own life. In contrast with many other students, Roberto did not use the journal to set up a two-way communication with me, hence the 0 in the category designated "responses to my questions." He ignored the requests contained in my response letters to write about his past experiences with reading and writing, focusing instead on self-generated topics. When he finished reading A Place for Us, he had no trouble generating new topics for writing (17%), which ranged from his thoughts about what he was learning in his classics course to his decision to open a savings account.

Although the numbers in the table reflect Roberto's priorities for journal writing, the interviews and the journal text itself reveal a subtler view of the purposes of journal writing for this young man. The most important of these purposes are working on personal problems, validating the self, expressing deeply felt ideas, and venting about the exam.

Working on Personal Problems

An extremely important purpose of the journal for Roberto was to work on problems he was facing in his life. While writing about A Place for Us, he managed to sort out many of his own feelings about being an immigrant, struggling with a new language, and facing poverty and discrimination. One of the most important issues that Roberto confronted in the journal, a topic he also chose for his personal essay, was his problematic relationship with his father—a charismatic hero in his early life in Colombia but also an alcoholic who in the past had sometimes physically abused his wife and children.

In the final interview I asked Roberto to select three entries from his journal that had been especially meaningful to him, entries he wouldn't want to lose. He chose three selections from the early part of his journal, all of them passages in which he wrote about himself or his family members in connection with *A Place for Us*. In explaining why he chose these particular entries, Roberto said that he looked for parts that he remembered "perfectly," passages where he was "really opening up" and "searching there for truth." These entries, he explained, "didn't take a lot of making up." Instead, "they just were there, coming out by themselves.... I didn't really force myself to write this."

He selected his first entry about *A Place for Us*, which I commented on earlier in this chapter; an entry in which he compared his family's situation to that of the Gage family and concluded that things could always be worse; and an entry in which he talked about conflict between fathers and sons. This third entry appears below:

> Chapter five introduced us to a new kind of problem faced by many of us and now face by Nichola: Growing with some love but with a strong resentment to your father. Going to bed at nights with a lot of words in your mouth held only by fear is not my idea of a night. Watching the darkness, your body shaking of unger [anger] hoping that some day you'll be stablished and secure so you can face your father and ask for many explanations is not the way a child should grow. Even when you are able to face your father, no matter how much you said, it's never enough. That resentment keeps coming no matter how much you understand your father now. I guess that when I get to be in his shoes that will change completely. I know life would have been much more easier if I had had my father on my side and not seen him as my opresor. Maybe I'm saying the wrong things, maybe he was teaching me some lessons. I guess I'm to young to say the final word about my father, I'm only eighteen and am just starting to know what's out there. I do thank him for all the sacrifice he's made and for not leaving us when a lot of times that was his easiest choice.

In the interview Roberto said that when, in his reading, he came to the part where Gage described his anger toward his father, he immediately recognized the feeling. He explained, "You can't say anything cause he's your father, cause you have to keep that within you, and, I mean, it grows and grows." At this point Roberto paused for 37 seconds before continuing:

> Of course, after I wrote this, everything *changed*. I mean, right after this I remember I was also thinking about why he was really doing that. He wasn't that bad man that I used to think of. So right after I wrote that, I mean, it

never happened again. I mean, I just kind of *forgave* my father after I wrote this. I kind of say, "Hey, why am I making my life miserable when this has been so long, and he was really doing it for my own good?" So I'm *glad* I wrote this. Because I think of him now as someone who has earned my respect a lot. He's worth loving.

After the last sentence, there was another long pause, this one lasting 30 seconds. And then Roberto looked at me, indicating he had finished commenting on the passage about his father.

That Roberto was aware of the significance of the journal entries he wrote about his relationship with his father was supported by the amount of time he had spent talking about this subject in the previous interview. When I asked whether the topics he wrote about in his journal were things he had thought about before, he said "sure" but explained that the act of writing these things down caused a big change: "I took it in a way like, okay, I write this now so I don't have to think about it anymore." After I explained how a colleague of mine used her journal to vent her anger and frustrations so that she could then go on to work on her writing with a clear mind, Roberto brought up the subject of his anger toward his father and explained that writing about this in his journal had helped him to see his father more clearly: "It's sort of getting the bad image out so you can study the other image."

Roberto's experience supports the idea, often mentioned in the research on journal writing, that making thoughts tangible, getting them from the mind onto a piece of paper helps to objectify them so that they can be dealt with more rationally. For Roberto, revisiting his old anger from a new perspective as a college student enabled him to analyze his childhood problems from a more mature point of view. Intriguingly, there is a shift in perspective about halfway through the entry just quoted, when Roberto starts to imagine the situation from his father's point of view ("I guess that when I get to be in his shoes that will change completely").

Some might argue that Roberto's increased understanding of his relationship with his father was irrelevant to the course I was teaching, that instead of writing about personal problems, Roberto should have been perfecting his grammar or working on essay structure. In fact, the possibility that school journals may encourage students to open up about personal problems has led to their censure by some parents and organizations. Phyllis Schlafly (1984), for example, edited a book entitled *Child Abuse in the Classroom*, condemning the use of personal journals in schools. (See Gannett, 1992, for a detailed discussion of recent attacks against journal writing in educational settings.)

In my mind, however, education should not and, in reality, cannot be separated from the rest of life. Gannett expressed my view as well when she wrote:

> Although it is still common to think of the healing function of writing as unrelated to intellectual growth, it should be obvious ... that writing to heal is a form of intellectual empowerment which allows for the development of a self that is sufficiently integrated to be capable of knowing. (1992, pp. 145–146)

Besides leading to emotional healing, Roberto's use of the journal to come to terms with his relationship with his father is an example of the kind of active meaning making that most powerfully drives language use and language learning.

Validating the Self

Although Roberto perceived the journal's value to be the opportunity it gave him to reflect on his relationships with his family, another strong purpose of his journal was self-validation. This should come as no surprise since, as Cummings has argued, students who are placed in a writing course because of failing a writing exam have experienced a serious blow to their self-esteem and are in need of positive "face-work" to repair their damaged pride (1988, pp. 154–166).

Roberto, who had been rewarded for his good writing in high school, was shocked to be placed in a developmental English course in college. Near the end of our final interview he reminded me that he had once said he "came really afraid to this class" because of unexpectedly failing the placement test. But, on the other hand, he "came really confident" because of positive experiences with writing in high school. He told me that he kept reminding himself, "I can learn this.... I can pick it up. I'm not far cause I used to be a good writer in high school."

In a sense, the journal offered him a chance to prove, from the beginning of the semester, that he was indeed a good writer. Both the content of his journal, with many entries devoted to his triumphs over adversity, and the obvious attention he put into producing good writing gave him a chance to validate himself as a human being and as a writer. During an interview Roberto told me that when I introduced the journal assignment, he resolved, "Hey, let me do something good with this."

This was not the first time that Roberto felt he had to prove his worth in a school situation. As mentioned earlier, one of the reasons he identified so strongly with Nicholas Gage was that both of them had been regarded as inferior by school authorities because they could not speak English. In his journal Roberto explained how he proved his intelligence by excelling in math. But later, as he said in an interview, he also validated himself through his writing.

When he first moved to the United States, he was placed in his high school's lowest level ESL class, where he worked hard, especially on his writing: "It was the thing that I enjoyed the most, so I did all my writing homework." After 2½ years in the ESL program, he was moved into mainstream courses. During his last semester of high school, he was placed in the most advanced English class. Feeling self-conscious about his accent (he was the only nonnative speaker), he never spoke in class, but he impressed the teacher with his writing, "She thought I did the *best*, that lady.... She used to tell me, like, 'I don't believe it. You know, you don't speak in class, and you come out with this writing.'"

Roberto returned to the theme of validation through writing in our final interview when I asked him to read aloud the journal entry about his attitude toward writing. In reading the segment about his teacher's astonishment at the difference between his writing and his speaking, he commented: "Oh, this is true. Yeah, I remember well. Makes me feel good."

In both of my interviews with Roberto, he brought up his high school English teacher's reaction to his writing. For example, in the first interview we had been talking about his high school English class, and he broke into my talk—one of the few times that he interrupted me—to say: "But she loved, she *loved the way I wrote*. She loved it."

Like Roberto's high school teacher, I was impressed with his writing. Because I found his journal so engaging, I wrote long letters of response— one typed page or more (see the samples of these letters in Appendix B). In the first of these letters I said that I found his journal "very moving to read" and that I liked the way he "relate[d] the book to his own life and predict[ed] what [would] happen next." Early in our first interview I said that I had some questions about his journals because they had been "so interesting to read." Breaking into my stream of talk, he asked, "You liked them?" In the interviews Roberto revealed that he cared a great deal about impressing the teacher with his writing. So when I asked whether he thought about the reader when he was writing, his answer was unexpected: "Well, I don't really think about the reader. I really think about what I want to say."

By looking closely at Roberto's journal and the interview transcripts, I have come to understand how his obvious pride in his teacher's positive reactions fits together with his statement that he doesn't think about the reader. In his writing, Roberto wanted to satisfy both himself and the teacher. He tried to please the teacher by making his writing as "good" as possible—by choosing engaging topics and crafting his language. But he didn't let the teacher's interests determine the content of what he wrote. Instead, he kept his mind focused on what he wanted to say. The figures in Table 4.1 support Roberto's assertion that he did not allow the reader to influence the content of his journal entries. In contrast with many of the other students, he never used the journal to ask me questions or even to answer the questions I asked him in my letters of response. (For samples of these questions, see the last two paragraphs of my first letter of response to Roberto included as Entry 3 in Appendix B). Like many other talented writers with whom I have worked, Roberto was really writing for himself, though he hoped the teacher/reader would like it too.

Expressing Deeply Felt Ideas

Another important purpose the journal served for Roberto was providing a socially acceptable outlet for his imagination and lively intelligence. During the interviews, Roberto painted a picture of himself as a loner who usually hid his true feelings from the world. He recalled that as a child growing up on the streets of Bogota he had been outgoing and something of a hero among his peers, "one that everyone listens to and makes everyone laugh." But when he moved to the United States and entered the alien culture of a large, urban public high school, things changed drastically.

In the first interview I asked Roberto if the reflection he did while reading *A Place for Us* was a new experience or whether he had done this type of thinking before. He felt that he had been a reflective reader for some time and mentioned the insights he had gained into his own life by reading *Siddhartha* just before graduating from high school. When I asked whether these thoughts were stimulated just by the book or partly by class discussions, he explained that his high school "was not like college where you can really raise your hand and say, 'But I feel this way.'" He suspected that, like himself, some of the other students in his advanced English class might have had strong reactions to the books they were reading, but "if they say something, they will be looked as uncool or stupid or something," so "you just kept it to yourself." As the only nonnative speaker in this advanced English class, Roberto felt especially vulnerable and explained, "I found myself being very quiet in that class, not talking to anyone, while they would just be cursing everywhere, like doing their thing." Instead, he channeled his energy into the papers he wrote for the course and was gratified by his teacher's positive reaction: " … that's the only way you could express yourself in that class."

When I asked whether he ever talked about the ideas he expressed in his writing with anyone else, either friends or family members, he said there was only one friend with whom he could discuss serious issues, a Peruvian immigrant who had moved to the United States about the same time he had: "I can discuss anything with him, and he won't be stupid, and he won't be uncool. I can discuss anything from abortion to what happened to a friend of ours." But except for this one close friend, he explained, "I don't open myself to anyone."

In the same interview Roberto described his identification with a character he had encountered while reading a work by Unamuno for his high school English course:

> [Unamuno] wrote about some guy that he was very hard, very cold. But he called him a volcano of passion, right. When he exploded, he would cry. The next minute he will be again a rock, cold as a rock and cool, and cold and everything. But he was a volcano of passion. And I *loved* it. Then I went back and said, "Hey, in a way this is me." And, I mean, some people, most of the people don't think, how should I say it? They don't think I can think…. But I think, I think for myself and I don't open myself to anyone. And I may seem just a cold person, or someone who is irresponsible, and many people get that feeling from me…. But [pause] the people who really know me, they know how I am, and I really, I mean, I really related myself to that guy, that guy in the book.

This exchange is particularly significant in revealing Roberto's perception of himself. He had used the "volcano of passion" metaphor in describing his father in his personal essay, where he wrote, "I discovered that night something about my father: The hard, stone hearted man was a volcano of deep feelings." He referred to this concept once again in the final interview, when he reminded me that he identified both himself and his father with Unamuno's "volcano of passion."

This metaphor also relates to the ways in which Roberto used his journal. With the exception of his one close friend, Roberto did not talk about his deepest thoughts with other people. They might not have understood, might have thought he was "uncool" or laughed at his ideas—or at his accent. But in the journal he felt free to open himself and explore the ideas that he could not share with others.

Even in the college writing course I taught, where the atmosphere was more conducive to the discussion of ideas than in his high school English class, he felt constrained. Early in the term I noted in the field log that Roberto seemed to "radiate" energy and enthusiasm to others in the class. But he actually said very little. About a month before the end of the semester I noted: "Although Roberto smiles a lot, he seems shy to me. He never talks in the large group and has not signed up for a conference with me."

In commenting on his experiences in my class, Roberto said that in the small-group work, students just stayed on the surface of things, not really expressing their true feelings: "Nobody dares. Nobody dares. I didn't want to dare to be the first one" to talk about serious issues. Another problem was the short amounts of time allotted for group tasks. Roberto explained, "When we were in groups, like, 'Okay, next, next, next. Oh, we're done. Okay. Good.'" I tried to confirm my sense of Roberto's attitude toward social interactions: "You don't want to be just out there. You don't want everybody to take one look at you and know everything about you." He agreed, saying, "No. I don't go into that." And then he moved the conversation in a very interesting direction, saying, "I was very open in this journal." I agreed, "You were, you were," and asked if he could explain why he felt free to be so open in the journal when he felt inhibited in class discussions.

He replied, "You said that, you know, it was basically between you, and you know what I mean. You don't want anybody else to know it. But I *liked* that. I felt comfortable writing that." When I asked if my responses influenced what he wrote the next time, he said: "No. I just [pause], I just wrote. I knew you were the outside reader, not a psychologist or someone who's getting to know this person."

Thus, the journal served an important purpose for Roberto by providing a socially acceptable outlet for his imagination and a place to examine some of his own most deeply felt ideas. During the interviews he said he would not have kept a journal if it hadn't been assigned for class. Because he didn't feel comfortable talking about serious ideas with most of his peers, the thoughts that found their way into his journal would have gone unexplored. As he wrote in one of his journal entries: "For some reason I feel much better writing this thoughts than telling them. Telling doesn't help. Writing really makes me realize what [I] am thinking and the value of it."

Venting About the Exam

In comparison with some of the other students who used the journals to describe their fears about the final exam, to develop practical strategies for doing well on it, and to write additional practice essays, Roberto's writing about the test was minimal. About 2 weeks before the end of the semester he wrote a two-page typed entry in which he focused on the feelings of shame and anger he had experienced as a result of failing the placement test:

> When I got the results I felt insulted and blamed the people who graded them. If you had asked me then how do I think they grade the exam I would have answered that they look at your nationality and if you are Colombian they'll fail you no matter what.

He went on to write about how this experience brought back unpleasant memories from high school:

> I hope to do well in this test. I want to feel comfortable at school and feel free and equal to everybody. For some reason I don't feel well being stuck in [this class]. It was enough in High School when I had to be in the ESL program for almost three years. It was degrading enough and it affected my relationship with other students to the point where I was miserable. People used not to be friendly with new immigrants and look down on them.

Shortly after Roberto wrote this entry, I began to fear that he might fail the test again. I judged that his first in-class practice essay would receive a failing score of 3 because of repeated problems with comma splices and a few subject–verb agreement errors. In an attempt to help Roberto with these mechanical problems, I hastily scheduled a conference, the first and only time we met privately during the semester. By the time Roberto arrived in my office, he had, without my suggesting it, rewritten the practice essay, which I now judged as a 5 because of its strong writing style and interesting ideas.

When the day of the final exam arrived, I noticed Roberto sitting near the back of the room, looking nervous as did most of the other students. Of the two possible topics, he chose to write about whether or not schools should offer supplementary programs such as sex education and free breakfasts for needy children. His exam essay consisted of four cautiously constructed paragraphs and contained five minor errors in spelling or usage—though not a single comma splice or agreement mistake. Two of the questions on the back cover of the exam ("Where were you born?" and "What language did you speak first?") were left blank.

Both anonymous assessors rated Roberto's essay a 4, a judgment with which I concurred. Compared with the lively essays and journal entries Roberto had written during the course, his exam essay was, in my opinion, pedestrian and uninteresting. However, it served its purpose. In the eyes of the institution, Roberto had demonstrated "minimum competence" in writing and could now participate fully in the academic life of the college.

THINKING AND WRITING PROCESSES

One of the primary purposes of the interviews was to gain insight into the students' thought processes, writing processes, and language learning. In Roberto's case these interviews yielded surprising information about his reaction to freewriting and the role of translation in his journal.

Freewriting

As I read Roberto's journal during the semester, I had been struck by the stream-of-consciousness quality of his writing. Thus, I was surprised when I learned during the interviews that he carefully planned his entries before he began to write. He explained that as he did the reading, he made notes of topics he might like to write about in the journal. For every chapter he generated about 10 possible topics and then picked the four he liked the most. Later when he sat down to write, he would try to visualize the entire entry in his mind before beginning to write.

Because Peter Elbow's (1973) version of freewriting had proved to be useful in my own writing, I was surprised to hear that this technique, as I had presented it to the class, didn't work for Roberto:

> I can't like just put my pen and write whatever. No. I can't do that. You know, I've tried it, and I end up like changing my whole topic, and changing to other things. I mean, when I realize, I say, "Oh, man, do you know what you wanted to say?"

Fortunately, Roberto felt free to ignore my instructions, using the writing process that felt right to him.

Roberto's need to conceptualize the whole piece before starting to write supports the conclusion of Tarvin and Al-Arishi (1991) that reflection requires a period of passivity prior to beginning an activity such as writing or discussion. Roberto's experience suggests that some popular strategies such as freewriting and brainstorming may actually discourage reflection by requiring instant responses. In any case, Roberto and several other students had major problems with my advice to "just keep writing."

Roberto said he needed about 5 minutes for quiet reflection before beginning a journal entry; after that initial planning period he did seem to experience a sense of freedom. When I asked if he ever got stuck once he had started writing, he replied, "Not really.... You know, other than the 5 minutes that I spend getting the idea. You know, once I put the pen." "It just comes out," I finished his sentence.

For Roberto the freedom he experienced once he had started writing seemed to represent a major difference between journal writing and essay writing:

> To write an essay, you have to think about the body, you know, you have to think about an order; you need an order for everything. And that takes a long time to figure out in mine. So in a journal you just put a picture of what you're gonna say and write. But for an essay, you know, you have to put a lot of pictures like, "This should go in this paragraph; oh no, this should be in this paragraph. I'd better put it in the second paragraph." And think of that. It takes time.

Roberto's comments support the idea described in chapter 2 that the power of journal writing to promote reflection may result from its freedom from some of the demands of "the rhetorical space." When writers don't have to think so much about organizing their ideas and expressing them in a rhetorically effective way, they are more free to explore the content of their writing. Roberto explained quite clearly the benefits of this freedom to pay more attention to "the content space," the domain of developing ideas. For Roberto, the journal led to a comfortable experience with writing. As he put it, "So by writing *a lot*, you got the experience to get used to the English language.... I mean just to practice is the word. To get comfortable with the language."

In the journal Roberto enjoyed the opportunity to choose his own topics and the freedom from the necessity to organize carefully and write convincingly, common requirements of essay writing:

> ... in a journal you have a great domain of things to pick up from. And you can even talk about the different aspects of things. You don't have to stick to a particular question. So journals are more freely written. You're not limited to some rules or anything.... And with an essay you are just limited to what they want. You can't just change topics on an essay like you would, you know, in a journal.... You have to stick to a point and prove a point. And here [in a journal] you don't have to prove nothing if you don't want to. I mean, you just make sure it's understandable.

The last part of this statement reveals that in the journal Roberto didn't feel totally freed from the demands of the rhetorical space. His writing still had to be understandable to a reader. He stated elsewhere that in the journal his goal was to produce good writing, and he was quite concerned about matters of style and correctness. In the final interview Roberto elaborated on his approach to journal writing: "When you really have a nice idea, ... you have to put it in a way that it's gonna look nice on paper." He explained how this process worked for him, "This is where the mind comes and plays around. Like, you cross out. 'No, this don't sound good. No this don't sound good.' And you spend a lot of time trying to highlight your ideas."

From talking with Roberto, I learned that his journal, which I had assumed to be a spontaneous outpouring of thoughts and emotions, was really a much more carefully crafted attempt to "highlight" his ideas. Nevertheless, Roberto said that, when compared with essays, the journal gave him increased freedom to experiment with ideas and follow his thoughts wherever they might lead.

Translation

Because of the increased freedom of journal writing as well as its closer link with spoken language, I suspected that writing extensively and regularly in journals might help ESL students make a breakthrough to thinking in English. In fact, the case study of Lan in chapter 7 suggests that this did happen for her. But I was surprised to learn from Roberto that almost all of his journal entries had been translated from Spanish. In the first interview I asked him to describe his "experience" with journal writing: "What kind of experience is it? Well, I usually will think in Spanish. I haven't been using the language [English] so much, so I think in Spanish. And everything I write is already in Spanish." Roberto's ESL teachers in high school had told him that he should try to think in English, but he hadn't been able to manage this because he socialized almost entirely with Spanish-speaking friends, sat next to Spanish speakers in classes, and did most of his reading in Spanish.

Roberto's pride in being Colombian and his concern with achieving elegance of style may have been other factors in his reluctance to think in English. He felt uncomfortable and constrained when thinking in English. Moreover, he was proud of his Spanish heritage and didn't want to lose it. In another conversation he described how he refused to let his 10-year-old sister speak English in front of their parents, "who don't speak a *word* of English." It was extremely important to him that she not try to hide things from her parents by speaking in English *and* that she not lose her fluency in her native language.

There were times, however, when ideas for writing came to Roberto in English instead of Spanish. He explained that for some topics such as abortion, he did think in English because he had first heard or read about these topics in English: "… when you hear something you like, and you keep it as it is, right.… It might sound nice in sentences that you hear. You keep that in the way they are. You don't translate them. You can't translate them." Other times he encountered Spanish expressions that "could look good if they came on paper. So you think of those nice phrases … and you figure how to translate them and you put them down."

Roberto's sensitivity to language and his desire to write and speak with flair were signs of his strength as a writer. Like other excellent bilingual writers, Roberto took the best from both languages, carefully tailoring his thoughts, and the language in which he chose to express them, according to the situation.

Awareness of Thought Processes

It is possible that by capturing thoughts on paper in a journal, writers may become increasingly aware of their thought processes. Thus, it stands to reason that journal writing might lead to heightened metacognition. Roberto felt that keeping a journal did help him to become more aware of his thinking. As he explained, "it makes you decide where you really are standing." In elaborating on how the journals affected his thinking, it is significant that he mentioned some of the distinguishing characteristics of connected knowing. He said that when you are asked to write in a journal about your reading, you begin to think, "'Hey, this really affects me.' … Then you start looking back, like, 'Hey, this happened to me. This happened to some of my family.'"

Like other highly reflective writers with whom I have worked, Roberto spoke of his tendency to "talk to himself." As I was transcribing my interviews with him, I often had to add quotation marks as he addressed comments to himself. When I asked about this during our final interview, he immediately understood what I meant and recounted some of these silent conversations with himself:

> I'm like, "Okay, Roberto. What should you do now?" Or I tell myself like, "Don't tell her. Don't say this." You know, I warn myself of things too, like, "Be careful here. You might get tired of what you're doing there."

After this comment, Roberto looked at me in surprise and said, "You mean not everyone does it?" To be truthful, I don't know the answer to this question. I suspect that all people do "talk to themselves" to some degree, that this is the "inner speech" that Vygotsky hypothesized (1986, pp. 15–35). I also suspect that the students who write most reflectively in their journals are those in whom the capacity for inner speech has become highly developed through habitual reflection. For them, the journal provides a natural extension of their thought processes as they think through and write down some of these inner reflections.

For some people, inner speech may even at times serve as a substitute for social speech. Roberto felt his tendency for talking to himself had developed because of feeling left out at home. He described his situation as a schoolboy in Colombia:

> In school I was always talking whatever came to my mouth, and laughing. I was really the happiest boy when I was in school.... But when I came home, and I was through, you know, I was always thinking and thinking. No one really stopped and listened to me.

Perhaps Roberto's habit of creating dialogues in his mind, the types of dialogues that were frequent features of his journal, began during this time in his life.

ROBERTO'S STANCE AS A LEARNER

One of the advantages of interviewing the students at the end of the semester, after I had already come to know them through their journals, essays, and classroom interactions, was that I was able to gain a deeper understanding of their overall approach to learning than is normally available to teachers. This added insight, gained primarily through the interviews, helped me to assess why each of the students used the journal in such different ways.

There are numerous indications in Roberto's journal and in the interviews that he usually operated from the fifth epistemological perspective described by Belenky, Clinchy, Goldberger, and Tarule (1986), that of constructed knowledge. In moving from procedural knowledge to constructed knowledge, the processes of self-reflection and self-analysis are crucially important:

> It is in the process of sorting out the pieces of the self and of searching for a
> unique and authentic voice that women [and men] come to the basic insights
> of constructivist thought: All knowledge is constructed, and the knower is
> an intimate part of the known. (Belenky et al., 1986, p. 137)

Undoubtedly, Roberto's inclination to reflect on his own experience and his
school learning using connected knowing had been an important factor in
helping him achieve this sophisticated epistemological perspective at an
early age.

Moreover, Roberto's intellectual and emotional development continued
throughout the semester he spent in my course and afterward, as he began
to take mainstream academic courses. The progress in Roberto's thinking
and his increased sense of integration with other students became obvious
during the interviews when he described a philosophy course he was taking
during the summer session.

Constructing Knowledge

At the beginning of my course Roberto described his view of knowledge in
an in-class journal entry responding to a short essay entitled "What True
Education Should Do." In this essay, Sydney Harris, the syndicated colum-
nist, contrasted the transmission model of education, in which knowledge
is handed down by authorities, with the Socratic model, in which knowledge
is developed through a dialogue between teacher and student. Harris'
sympathies lie with Socrates, as he explained in his concluding paragraph:

> Pupils are more like oysters than sausages. The job of teaching is not to stuff
> them and then seal them up, but to help them open and reveal the riches
> within. There are pearls in each of us, if only we knew how to cultivate them
> with ardor and persistence. (1990, p. 10)

Roberto concurred with Harris' position (his entire response appears as
Entry 2 in Appendix B). This journal entry has strong overtones of subjective knowing, the third epistemological position, where knowers rely heavily
on intuition and believe that all knowledge is self-generated: "You never
stop getting knowledge from yourself," "You are never to old to explore all
the knowledge within you." Yet there are also indications of the value of
procedural knowledge. Teachers can be useful in getting you started with
the examples to play with; later Roberto mentions that to develop one's
mental capacity fully, a good teacher is necessary. Finally, in this entry there

is a sense that knowledge is constructed. By studying with good teachers, by playing with problems, by listening to the knowledge within, each learner can construct knowledge for himself or herself.

In my final interview with Roberto, I asked him to read this entry aloud and verbalize any thoughts he had as he was reading. After reading the sentence that stated, "We all have the same capabilities. It's just that one uses more of it than others," he elaborated:

> Yeah, some people are lazy. I've discovered that. Some people prefer not to spend their time thinking, prefer not to *waste* their time thinking, when it's really good. And it's good for people. There's nothing wrong with thinking or they don't believe it's cool or, I don't know what they think about it. But just limit themselves to class materials. And you really have to explore your thinking.

In explaining a position he had taken early in the semester, Roberto took an even stronger position. Not only is it possible for learners to construct knowledge for themselves based on what they have learned in school, it is their obligation to do so. For Roberto, constructed knowledge was what education was all about.

Thinking of constructed knowing as an obligation makes it sound like an onerous chore. For Roberto, however, this was definitely not the case. In fact, through his journal and interviews, he revealed himself as experiencing the kind of "passionate knowing" that is characteristic of the most highly developed form of connected knowing, which occurs when learners "use the self as an instrument of understanding" (Belenky et al., 1986, p. 141). For Roberto the construction of knowledge often occurred as he "played" with ideas, a habit of mind exemplified in a journal entry he wrote about concepts he was encountering in a classics course he was taking the same semester as the ESL writing course. The entry began with Roberto speculating about "the pagen Gods and how this stories became part of the Greek culture wich later influenced our world greatly." Soon he was writing in the connected mode:

> I wonder what I'd be like being under the existence of this gods, all they do is fool around with mortals. It'd be wonderfull to make a sacrifice to Cupid or Aphrodite so she could make the girl of my dreams fall in love with me. How nice it'd be to ride Helius' chariot and see everything from far away. What if Athena made my clothes and, with Hephaestus, they built a place for me in Manhattan even greater than the white house. I wonder how Nectar and Ambrosia tastes, I bet nothing on earth, even my favorite shrimps, tastes

like that. How different my house would be if Hestia (God of hearth) lived there, I bet my parents would let me go everywhere I want at night.

In this entry, as well as in many others, Roberto was engaging in powerful thinking and writing, that resulted in part from the increased freedom of journal writing—the freedom to play with ideas, to set out on paper thoughts that arose in connection with concepts he was encountering in another course. Although the classics professor had not assigned a journal, Roberto explored ideas from this course in the journal he was keeping for my course, a practice I supported. By playing with ideas in this way, Roberto was also furthering his thinking in ways that support Bruner's (1985) speculation about a possible link between play and metacognition.

Studying Philosophy with Plato et al.

At the time of Roberto's final interview, he was completing an introduction to philosophy course he had elected to take in the summer session a course he had enjoyed immensely. The topic of what and how Roberto was learning in this course recurred throughout the interview, and this discussion helped to explain the ways in which he integrated separate and connected knowing to construct knowledge. About halfway through this interview I said to Roberto, "And I'm wondering whether sometimes schools and teachers encourage students *not* to be reflective. Do you think that there are ever teachers who just say, 'I don't care what *you* think. Just tell me what happened.'"

He thought for a while and then said, "But there are subjects that your opinion doesn't matter. Like philosophy. In that philosophy class, we have a lot of things to say, and a lot of things to really oppose .... But the class is not *about* that. They [the professors] don't care [about] your opinion. They just want to know what *they* [the philosophers he was reading] wrote."

According to Roberto, some of the students in the class were getting personally involved with the ideas they were studying: "A lot of people just raised their hand and said, 'How can this be true?'" The professor tried "to be as nice as possible," but she seemed to be more concerned with "covering" the curriculum. As Roberto explained it, "So, you know, when you touch about things about existence, God, a lot of people tend to get excited. And she might try to deal with it, but when it gets to a point, she goes, 'Okay. We're just studying this, and you have to know this.'"

I asked Roberto how he had approached the first philosophy paper, for which he had received an A. He said that he had been careful to keep his own opinions out of the paper: "I gave her what she was asking for." When I asked whether he had gotten personally involved with the ideas for this paper, he answered, "Not really. I didn't cause, since the beginning she warned us, 'This class is not about your opinion.'"

Secure in his own perspective of constructed knowledge, Roberto was not upset by his professor's stance:

> I took the class as something interesting to *know*, how these people used to think and how they came out with explanations for things that we still ask ourselves. But I have my beliefs. You know, I believe in God. I believe a lot of things. And it would be really hard to get me out of those things. So I just took the class to get knowledge of what some people believed, about what some people followed, and so that's how I took that.

Although the professor had not asked the students to keep a journal about their reactions to what they were reading, I asked Roberto to envision a different scenario:

> Can you imagine if this teacher had said, " … there'll be two sides to this class. The part that you're gonna be graded on will be your understanding of the books and the ideas in the books. And in that part of it, your opinion will not matter. You know, I just want to see if you understand the ideas." And she might say, "We'll have two papers and a final exam, and those will be graded, and that will determine your grade. But there's also going to be another part of this course, which is required but you're not graded on it. And that is to keep a journal as you do this reading, where you can express your own opinions if you want to. Just do some informal"/

At this point, Roberto broke into my talk excitedly, "Oh, that'd be great!" "Would it?" I asked. He replied, "I mean, you'd come out with the best journal. Cause there are things that really hit you. Like what do you think exists? There are a lot of things you can write about that…. I would have come out with pages and pages." But because journal writing was not required and the students were expected to keep their personal reactions out of the papers they wrote for the course, the questions that Roberto would have pursued in a journal went unexplored.

Later in the interview, while we were discussing his journal entry on what education should be, particularly his comment that "you never stop getting knowledge from yourself," I said that perhaps this belief helped to explain why journal writing had been so rewarding for him. I speculated, "Because if you believe that nobody can really give you knowledge, that you have to develop it from within, then if you limit yourself to just [pause], well, if a teacher or course says, 'I don't care about your opinions,' then you're sort of limiting that part of you." Roberto responded, "I mean, there is not much time to spend [referring to his philosophy course, where the professor felt the need to cover a lot of material].... So what I did is, I did my best in studying those theories. I did my best on *knowing* them, and then on my own I can think."

But I wonder, looking back on this interview, when Roberto will find the time to think the thoughts he would have put into a journal for this course. And how much will be lost if these fleeting reflections are never captured in writing? Of course, it's impossible to answer these questions. But as the interview continued, I got a hint of what Roberto might have written if journal writing had been an integral part of the philosophy course. When I mentioned that he seemed to feel a lot of sympathy with Plato and to make connections with his ideas, he expressed his thoughts about the philosophers he was reading in a kind of spoken journal entry:

> It was great; I mean this class was great. We started with Plato. We all sympathized with Plato. Then we moved to Descartes, and we were surprised by his thoughts. He denied matter. It's like, "How do I know that I'm not dreaming right now?" ... And we all, we didn't actually sympathize with him. We just said, "He could be right, but I don't like it." And then we moved to Hume, and we were surprised also. Like this is true. But how can he not have God? Cause most of us believed in God. And most of us were thinking the same thing. I know I was. It was like, "He's right." He gave an excellent study on the naturalistic view of morality. He gave a nice *study*, I mean a nice research.... And I said, "Yeah! He's right!" I mean, that's what you do, that's exactly what you do, but how can he not have God around? And then at the end with Immanuel Kant, we all sympathized, "Yeah, he's the mind of reason that discovers that there is always a universal truth about morals that we have to follow." ... So I guess they all have a good point. You just sympathize with all of them.

In this extract from the final interview, Roberto vividly demonstrated his stance as a learner. By combining his own style of connected knowing with the separate knowing approach advocated by his philosophy professor, Roberto was actively constructing knowledge. He had also begun to think of himself as a contributing member of a learning community. In striking contrast with the feelings of alienation he experienced in his high school English class, he now saw himself as one learner among many. As he spoke of the other students in the philosophy class, "they" had become "we" and getting excited about ideas was no longer regarded as "uncool."

5

Cliff: Unspoken Words
From the Deepest Part of the Mind

When I think about writing, the first thing that comes in my mind are words
full of expressions and meaningful thoughts. Writing has been very helpful to
me special[ly] since it has power over me, that lets out the unspoken words
and thoughts from the deepest part of my mind. This might sound unusual
but it's true. I don't often talk about death in my family or me being a diabetic.
But in writing I usually write about these subjects.

With these words describing his attitude toward writing in English, Cliff
began the journal he would keep for the rest of the semester. He had been
born in Ethiopia and was a native speaker of Amharic, but had moved to
the United States at the age of 14 after completing the ninth grade in his
native country. He came to the United States to live with his older sister at
the urging of his father, who wanted his son to master English and complete
his education here. At the time of this study, Cliff was 21 years old and in
his third semester of college. He had not yet decided on a major field of
study but was considering engineering.

THE PAST IS PROLOGUE

Before coming to the United States, Cliff had studied English for many years
in Ethiopia, beginning in the first grade, when he learned the English
alphabet. He began reading in English in the third grade, starting with
"popular things" and year by year developing his English. By the time he
entered the ninth grade, all of his classes, except for Amharic, were taught
in English. As Cliff explained, "Whether you want it or not, you have to
speak English." Doing well in English is essential to moving on to higher
education. Students in Cliff's school were tested in the sixth and eighth
grades to determine whether they could continue with their schooling. The

most difficult subject for Cliff was Amharic, "the only course that I didn't do well."

School Attitudes Toward Reading and Writing

Although the examinations given in the sixth and eighth grades tested subject mastery rather than writing ability, students in the Ethiopian schools were required to write, and this was a problem for Cliff. The teachers assigned topics for writing, and the students were expected to read their writing aloud in front of the class. Cliff felt that the teachers singled him out as a poor writer. As he put it during an interview:

> I hated writing—especially in my language because the teachers didn't like my writing so much. They compared me to the other students. And every time when I write something, they said, "Why don't you do this way? Why don't you do that?" And so I get offended, and I said, "Forget about it." And now I cannot remember what I wrote because, you know, I was rejecting it so often. Always they tell me, "This is not good. This is not good."

The negative evaluation of Cliff's writing ability affected not only his attitude toward writing but also his assessment of his chances for success in life: "I thought that I wasn't writing well, and I couldn't make it in the future. I lost hope right there." (See Entry 6 in Appendix C, entitled "My Past History as a Writer.")

Family Literacy

Cliff's feelings of inadequacy as a writer affected him at home as well as at school. Literacy was highly valued in his family, which consisted of his mother, father, two brothers, and two sisters. Both parents were fluent in English though they spoke Amharic at home, and reading was an important activity within the family. When Cliff was growing up, both of his parents spent a lot of time reading the Bible as well as other books. And Cliff's sisters and brothers used to read also. In an interview Cliff stated, "I'm telling you, all the time they read books." Sometimes his sisters would read aloud to Cliff. However, he went on to explain, "But I don't read books. I had a bad memory of reading books. I said, 'Forget it. Reading books is bad.'"

In Cliff's family writing was encouraged as well as reading: "All of my sisters kept a diary. Like they write every day what they did. I'd say, 'What's the use of keeping anything written down?' I'd say, 'Why don't they keep it in their heads?' But they write it down." Cliff stated in a journal entry that he sometimes sneaked into his sisters' room and read their diaries. Explaining his interest in their writing, he wrote:

> I personally found it exciting seeing how words can give a powerful meaning and reveal our deepest emotions. Most significantly, they wrote about things they don't usually say out loud, which helped them to communicate with their inner thoughts and express it in words. Unfortunately, I didn't see it work for me.

In an interview Cliff explained how his family's and his school's prescriptions about reading and writing affected him:

> I hated reading books. I hated writing things down. I liked only math class and physics, this kind of thing, geography. But, you know, everybody's telling me how to do this, specially my father. "You're supposed to read," you know. "Read me this book." And this kind of got into the way that I hated doing it. But I never tried to force myself to write or, you know, keep anything like a diary.

Both at home and at school, Cliff felt stigmatized because of his lack of interest in or facility with reading and writing.

High School in the United States

When Cliff arrived in the United States at age 14, he enrolled in ninth grade in a public high school, where he was placed in an ESL program. Most of the students in his class were native speakers of Spanish although there was one Ethiopian student, who spoke Amharic. At first Cliff looked to this student for help, but he soon realized that he wasn't likely to get much assistance from the other Ethiopian student:

> He showed some resentment—I don't know why. He doesn't want to even be with me. When I ask him something because I don't know what's going on, he said, you know, "Go ahead and ask your teacher." And I said, "Forget it. I won't bother you no more."

Cliff believed this student's hostility was probably related to political differences because the other student came from the northern part of Ethiopia. As Cliff explained, "They feel, I don't know, different." Undoubtedly, both of these students brought to their U.S. classroom feelings related to the civil war in their home country. In commenting on the war, Cliff said, "So many people died. So many people. And they are still dying. They're fighting, fighting, fighting. The whole reason is because we are this and they are that." Spurned by the Ethiopian student, Cliff began to reach out to the Spanish speakers in his class and felt that they helped him much more "even though we don't speak the same language."

Cliff did well in this ninth grade ESL class, and the next year when he enrolled in a different high school for tenth grade, he was placed in a regular English class. One of the first reading assignments was a Shakespeare play, which Cliff found extremely difficult: "It takes me the whole night to find the meaning. It was tough. It was tough." This class was also difficult because the other students mocked his speech. As he explained in an interview, "At that time when I speak, they pick up the accent, and they say, 'Oh, he speaks like that!' They laugh. So I did bad. So I didn't speak at that time."

After 3 or 4 weeks in this class, Cliff's teacher began to wonder why he never spoke during class. In an interview, Cliff described a classroom encounter with this teacher:

> The teacher asked me to answer questions. She looked in the list and said, "What's your name?" I said, "Cliff." "Yeah, answer the question. You never raise your hand. What's wrong with you?" I said, "I don't know the answer." And she said, "How come you don't know? You didn't read the book?" "I read the book." "Okay, talk to me after class."

Cliff explained to his teacher that he had done the reading but didn't understand it and didn't feel his English proficiency was strong enough to enable him to keep up with the work of the class. The teacher checked his file and confirmed that his placement, based on his previous record, was correct. However, Cliff asked to be transferred to an ESL class, and in this class with other nonnative speakers of English he had no trouble keeping up with the work. He also felt more comfortable and free to participate in class discussions: "Nobody could speak better than I could."

Like many ESL students, Cliff was required to study a third language to fulfill his school's second-language requirement:

> I had to take other languages besides my own and English in high school because they said, "You need a extra language." [Spoken loudly] *They didn't consider my language as a language. I don't know why.* They put me in Spanish class. I don't know why they put me in Spanish. And I start learning Spanish, which I found very easy to spell than English. Whatever you see, you write it.

Although Cliff was upset that the school authorities didn't accept Amharic as an "official" second language, his proficiency in Spanish has proved useful to him in various part-time jobs.

By the time Cliff graduated from high school 3 years later, he felt that his English had improved tremendously and that he had learned "how to write in American style of English." In our interviews he spoke enthusiastically of his overall high school experience in the United States: "High school was *good*." He expressed concern, however, that he was losing some of his proficiency in his native language. He felt that his writing ability was stronger in English than in Amharic and that his active vocabulary in Amharic was decreasing.

College Experiences with Reading and Writing

Upon entering college, Cliff was placed in a section of the intermediate ESL writing course taught by a woman I'll call Martha, an experienced adjunct instructor who was completing her doctoral studies. Cliff's experience in Martha's course was critical in transforming his view of himself as a reader and writer of English. During the interviews he talked extensively about this course and also wrote about it in his journal. In our first interview Cliff explained that he came into Martha's class hoping for the best:

> When I came in the class, I said, "Maybe this is a nice teacher." I always say that. I say, "Maybe this is a good teacher or it's not a good teacher." And I was sitting up front—I always sit in the front. She said, "We gonna do this. And I want you to have this, this, this, this. And, you have to bring this in the next class." I said, "Maybe, oh boy," I said, "this is not a good teacher." But after a while, you know, I saw the way she teached, and I understood it also. It's much more than the other classes, and I got a lot of things out of it.

Martha had also been a positive influence for Lan, who is profiled in chapter 7. Both of these students told me during interviews that Martha conveyed a strong message to her students that writing was important in their lives and that, through hard work, they could succeed in learning to write effectively. Martha demonstrated her care and concern by holding her students to strict standards. Cliff explained Martha's role in his development as a writer in a journal entry written for my class:

> In American high school … I didn't achieve, or let's say, I hadn't obtain new and important skills. Since my arrival, I was in the ESL class, English as

Second Language class. Basically, it involved having to describe what I learned and what I seen in the form of essay, Introduction, Body, and Conclusion.

When I enter college, my attitude toward writing changed. I started in [the intermediate level] class. At first, I didn't like the professor. She seemed strict and uncommunicable. I said to myself, "Here you go again," expecting rejection, like in the past. But to my surprise, she was open and encouraging towards writing. Her ability to make direct communication enable me to write more until I achieved basic skills in writing, Punctuation, Dependent and Independent clauses, Etc.... I still thank her for the change she helped me obtain towards writing. If it hadn't been for her, I would be still the old me who hates writing.

Not only did Cliff feel grateful to Martha for her role in his changing concept of himself as a writer, but I too benefited from her work. Cliff entered my course with a positive attitude; he saw writing as an important means of communication and was eager to continue the development he had begun the previous semester. As he explained at the end of the journal entry just quoted, "Now I am in this class learning and enjoying the world of writing which I took for granted in the past." Although journal writing hadn't been stressed as much in Martha's class as in mine, Cliff had written some journals for that course, usually personal entries consisting of two to three pages.

HOW CLIFF USED THE JOURNAL

In many ways, Cliff's experience with journal writing in my course was similar to Roberto's. Both students began the course with positive attitudes toward writing. They had developed confidence in themselves as writers and believed that keeping a journal could help them work out their thoughts and express meaningful ideas. Both students were highly reflective writers and used their journals to write about subjects that were personally important. For Roberto, this reflective writing centered on his relationship with his father; for Cliff, on his life as a diabetic.

However, the two students' approaches to journal writing differed in significant ways as well. While Roberto's journal had been characterized throughout by its conversational quality and shifting topics, Cliff's journal read like a series of essays. He usually titled his entries and often typed them, sometimes including earlier drafts that had been edited and corrected. At the end of his first journal submission, he wrote on a separate page a title for a piece he planned to write later, "The Biggest Turning Point." This entry

TABLE 5.1
How Cliff Used the Journal

A Place for Us	In-class entries	His own topics	Final exam	Responses to my questions
6 pp.	14 pp.	25 pp.	21 pp.	10 pp.
8 %	18 %	33 %	28 %	13 %

was included in his next journal. Table 5.1 summarizes the amount of space Cliff devoted to different types of writing.

Cliff wrote only six pages about *A Place for Us*. His priority, as shown in Table 5.1, was to explore his own topics, which he did in four entries totaling 25 pages; three of these pieces were related to his life as a diabetic. Although Cliff was definitely willing and able to generate topics for himself, he also devoted a considerable portion of his journal—10 pages, or 13%—to writing detailed answers to the questions I posed in my written responses. Cliff was expansive in responding to my questions about his past experiences as a reader and writer. He devoted seven entries to answering my specific questions about the final exam, which appeared on a class handout distributed before spring vacation. In addition, he wrote four practice exam essays that are included in the 21 pages of writing about the final exam. The most significant uses Cliff found for his journal were working on personal problems, reflecting on writing and reading processes, communicating with readers, and preparing for the final exam.

Working on Personal Problems

Cliff's conception of the function of writing in his life did not waver from the beginning of the semester until the end. On the first in-class freewrite, which serves as the epigraph for this chapter, Cliff stated his belief that writing "has power over me" and that it "lets out the unspoken words and thoughts from the deepest part of my mind." His answers on the end-of-semester questionnaire were consistent with this view of writing. In response to the question "How did you feel about writing a journal for this class?" he wrote: "I like writing a journal since it allows me to express my feelings."

In using writing to express his feelings, Cliff chose the two topics he had mentioned in the early freewrite: death in his family and his own struggle with diabetes. For his personal essay, in which the assignment was to describe a memorable experience from the past, Cliff wrote a moving essay about his younger sister who had died 2 years earlier at the age of 7 as a result of congenital heart disease. He had loved his sister very much, and this essay was the first time he had written about her death. He explained during an interview that by describing the experience in writing, he was able to express himself more completely: "When I speak, you know, I usually leave out things." When asked on the end-of-semester questionnaire to indicate the paper with which he was most pleased, Cliff selected this essay about his sister "because it say[s] what I had in my mind for long time."

Cliff usually chose to write about personal topics in his journal, which included three gripping entries about his life as a diabetic: "The Biggest Turning Point," a lengthy narrative describing his diagnosis as a diabetic 5 years earlier; "The Other World!" a creatively written description of what it feels like to experience an insulin reaction (Entry 4 in Appendix C); and "The First Incident," a frightening first-person account of an insulin reaction he had experienced 2 years earlier.

During the interviews with Cliff, I was reluctant to probe the painful areas of his sister's death and his diabetes. This was one of several times in which my role as supportive teacher conflicted with my role as ethnographic interviewer. I didn't want to risk the discomfort that might result for both of us if I asked Cliff to talk about these emotionally charged subjects. I have no doubt, however, that writing about them reinforced Cliff's recently acquired belief in the value of writing. During an interview he explained what he gained from writing about deep, personal subjects:

> When you speak, you limit yourself from saying certain things. And then when you write, you feel secure enough to put it, and you could avoid showing somebody else. So you could feel free to express what you have in your mind fully. But when you are talking, you are communicating with somebody, so you try to avoid saying this and that. But then when you do write it down, it comes out of your mind, you know. Maybe you don't have to worry about it no more. You said it already, you know.

In the second interview Cliff reaffirmed the therapeutic value of writing about problems:

> For example, if you have something in your mind, usually for a long time that thing always bothers you. It will keep on bothering you even if you do something else. When sometimes in your life that thing connects to what happened before, that thing will become a new thing, and you feel bad inside

cause you haven't said it. But if you write it down, somehow [it] all comes out. You don't have a problem because you've said it already.

Cliff's description of the catharsis he experienced when he used the journal to write about disturbing thoughts from the past is strikingly similar to Roberto's observation: "I write this now so I don't have to think about it anymore." Both students would undoubtedly agree with Britton, who (in a passage cited earlier) explained the value of reflecting on previous experiences in the spectator role: "As we go back over the same experience, now in the role of spectator, we may make further and probably more far-reaching adjustments—for, as we have seen, we are likely to refer to a more extensive set of values than we are free to do as participants" (1970, p. 118). Cliff's and Roberto's comments on the resolution that sometimes occurs as a result of writing about personal problems support the validity of Britton's statement. There is something about concretizing the problems in writing and, as Britton suggests, bringing new perspectives to bear on them that often leads to a sense of release.

In the following excerpt from the final interview I asked Cliff to describe the importance of writing in his life:

> **Cliff:** I think it's very important. Now I see what I could do with it.
> **Rebecca:** What can you do with it?
> **Cliff:** I mean, like I told you, I could express myself very deeply, you know. Write down thoughts. [pause]

However, because Cliff had not always been an enthusiastic writer, he could empathize with other students who did not welcome the chance for self-expression that the journal offered but did the writing simply to complete an assignment: "Some people feel that they have to write it because you ask them to. Even if they write it in clear way, they don't get much out of it. But if you want to write it, you know, you have so much ideas, you could write it down."

Through his own experience Cliff had discovered something that I have learned from many years in the classroom: Students will become truly engaged writers only if they view writing as personally satisfying and not just something they do to fulfill a course requirement or get a grade. Cliff's changed conception of the role of writing in his life provides eloquent testimony to his evolution from a reluctant writer to one who views writing as a source of inner satisfaction and a constructive way of dealing with personal problems.

Reflection on Writing and Reading Processes

From the beginning of the semester it was obvious to me that Cliff took himself seriously as a writer and hoped that this course would give him the chance to develop new and more effective writing techniques. When I asked the students to describe their feelings about being in the class, Cliff wrote one of the most positive responses:

> ... I feel [this course] is a bridge that connects the future me to the presant one. I am learning new ideas which can be helpful, and improve my writing ability. For example, knowing how to write as a famous author with words of sound and picture that are interesting for the reader. I am also very sure that by the end of the semester, I will acquire all the skills expected of me. I feel great knowing that I am in this educational class which has already placed me and my fellow students in the right track, becoming excepted writers.
>
> I really enjoy having to talk and exchange information about our essay with one another. Because this shows me where my mistakes are and I am not understood by the reader. Clearly, if I improve this skills with the help of this class, one day I will become the greatest writer ever lived.
>
> All these dreams can come true with the support of this class only. No one else!!!!

Like Roberto, Cliff often used the journal for self-validation, in this case verging on grandiosity as he proclaimed that he would become "the greatest writer [who] ever lived." Despite the exuberance of this statement, I interpret it not primarily as self-congratulation, but rather as an attempt to ingratiate himself with his new teacher. After all, according to Cliff, he would achieve his lofty goal "with the support of this class only. No one else!!!!" I have more to say later in the chapter about Cliff's strategies for dealing with teachers. But for now I would like to consider his active attempts to become a more accomplished writer, as I believe that his concern with writing techniques reflected a genuine interest.

About a month into the course, when I asked the students to freewrite about their reactions to a personal essay written by another student in the class, Cliff was one of the few students who focused on writing techniques that helped this writer achieve her effect. He mentioned a specific detail that he felt was especially effective and went on to say, "I also liked the sounds that are in this writing. Such as 'Mm—, and La La, and Ha! Ha!'"

In my first letter of response to Cliff's journal, I praised his view of himself as a writer: "It is clear that writing is important in your life. I really loved the way you expressed your ideas about writing.... In your next journal, could you write a little bit about certain pieces of writing that were especially meaningful to you?"

In contrast with Roberto, who ignored the questions I asked in my response letters, Cliff answered each of my questions at length. And it was through these journal entries that I learned much of the information about Cliff's past experiences as a reader and writer, summarized at the beginning of the chapter. As he entered my course, Cliff saw himself as part of the larger literacy community, one who was qualified to make judgments of other writers, whether fellow students or professionals. In keeping with his expressed goal of becoming a great writer, Cliff later speculated in his journal:

> In high school, in a class discussion, when the teacher asked the question [about what makes a writer great], most students said, their ability to make a story interesting, mysterious, relate the story to most people's life style or problem and uniqueness. I agreed with these points since that is what I expect from THE BEST WRITER OF OUR TIMES.

As a result of Cliff's transformative experience in Martha's class, he was trying on new identities—what I would describe as "literacy identities." In his journal and during the interviews, he eagerly embraced various roles such as the critic of published writing and the thoughtful responder to student writing. Cliff regarded himself as an important part of the community of writers and readers, one who could not only reflect on his own writing and reading processes but actively critique the work of others.

Cliff was an ideal research participant because of his psychological insight and awareness of his own inner processes. For example, in an entry entitled "My past as a reader," Cliff recounted the negative experience of his early reading ("I was dragged by my father and teachers into reading books which I hated so much"). He particularly hated his seventh-grade geography book:

> The [English words] were new and I had to stop and define the words that I found important in every line. After a while, I started simply reading, reading the book instead of stopping for difficult word. This helped me read fast but with little understanding. Basically, I can call it, eyes movement for left to right.... The pressure from father and teacher forced me to read the book with a complete mental block. And prevented me from reading any other books since I thought every book is like my geograph[y] book.

Cliff's dislike of reading persisted throughout his high school years in the United States. He read only small parts of the assigned reading, just enough to answer the teachers' questions. But when he entered college and took the intermediate writing course with Martha, his view of reading changed: "Couple of words from my professor opened the mental block that was caused by my geography book. She said, 'Read books that you like outside the class requirement.' Since then, I read 10–15 books with my own will and interest that I felt comfortable and relaxed with, without any pressure." He concluded this entry by awarding his own ratings to 10 of these books on a scale from 1 to 5.

Cliff's description of his development as a reader has much to teach us. As a boy, Cliff saw reading as a task that was imposed on him by his teachers and a demanding father, all of whom strictly prescribed what books to read and how to read them. In high school as well, Cliff regarded reading as something to do for school, not for himself. It was only after entering college that Cliff realized he could take charge of his reading. As a result of his experience in Martha's course, he became an avid reader who chose books for enjoyment and actively judged them according to his own criteria. The change in Cliff's approach to reading paralleled his changed approaches to writing. And by his own report, both writing and reading had acquired a new meaning in his life.

Communicating With Readers

Cliff's journal entries and the comments he made during the interviews made it clear that he placed an extremely high value on the need for writers to communicate effectively with their readers. In an early journal entry he wrote, "If readers are asked about what makes a writer one of the best, most probably they would say, their ability to communicate with the reader clearly." He returned to this theme in his next in-class journal entry, in which I asked the students to describe their feelings about sharing their writing with classmates in small groups. In his response, Cliff emphasized the need for group work to ensure clear communication with readers:

> If it had not been for the group work, each of us can not see were [where] and what gives a reader problems when they read our work. The reason for it is we, as a writer, have some knowledge of what we are writing about but the read[er] does not. That is when we see what information is still in our mind that suppose to be in our written work. This eventually helps us see and focus on the subject we, as a writer, tend to forget.

During the interviews Cliff returned again and again to his major concern: communicating effectively with readers. For example, when I asked him whether he consciously used techniques of fiction writing in the personal narratives he had written for his journal, he said that he had not deliberately employed specific techniques. Instead, he concentrated on the reader, thinking: "Let me write it this way so they [the readers] could see what I was feeling at that time, or what I was trying to explain." Rephrasing what I heard Cliff saying, I echoed: "So your goal was really to communicate with a reader." "Yes. Very clearly," he replied.

On the final exam as well, Cliff's feeling of competence as a writer was related to his belief that he could communicate with his readers. When I asked during an interview what kind of essay he tried to write on the test, he explained, "One thing I knew was that I could write effectively. I knew I could do that, make it effective and show the reader that my point is right. That's basically what I was trying to do." In the next section we see what strategies Cliff used to achieve this goal.

Preparing for the Final Exam

About a month before the end of the semester, I urged the students to use the journals to discuss their feelings about the final examination. In an entry entitled "My Feelings towards taking the test," Cliff openly discussed his fears:

> Taking any kind of test is frightening. But specially, seeing what will happen to me if I didn't pass the test, it will make me more scared and adds a lot of anxiouty in taking it. I think that I have enough skills to pass the test. But considering the time lime[t], it will make the test hard. I don't like timed test since it makes me lost my consentration and think about the time left to finish the test.... I like to give all of my essay a lot of thoughts before I write them down. But, I guess, I couldn't do that on the final test.

About a week later he again examined his feelings about the test in an entry entitled "What it means to me weather I pass or fail the test":

> I think and I am sure that no one wants to repeat the cours again. From my point of view, after working for whole semester, writing and writing so many essaies, I wouldn't feel that I stepped forward or achieved any thing in the past semester if I fail the final exam. And the most thing that I hate in life is doing the same thing over again. So, if I fail the test, I will be fill up with anger and hate towards the class. It will take a long time before I can convince myself to open up and learn from my mistakes. I know this is very self destructive and unreasonable. But that is how my body reacts to my failur on

the final test. Angry—because I put a lot of effort for passing the class and hatred—because I going to spend another semester in which I could have achieved in this semester. I hope I wouldn't have to go through it.

I was impressed by Cliff's understanding of the emotional aftermath of failing the exam. I had seen this reaction of anger and frustration many times in working with repeaters. During the interviews, I learned that Cliff was writing from experience because he had had to repeat the developmental reading class.

A few weeks before the end of the semester when I started to score the students' practice essays on the 1-to-6 scale, I began to fear that Cliff might fail the exam because of grammar and spelling problems in his in-class writing. When Cliff received a failing score of 3 on one of his practice essays, he immediately signed up for a conference with me, and we met exactly one week before the final exam. In this conference, which I audiotaped and transcribed, I focused mostly on "the little things," spelling, articles, and verb endings. At one point I apologized for being such a perfectionist, but Cliff responded, "That's good. I want to make sure that everything is right." I especially emphasized the need for him to work out a way to improve his spelling of common English words and used as an example the word *parents*, which he had misspelled in his practice essay.

Clearly worried about the possibility of failure, Cliff used the week before the exam to develop strategies that would improve his chances. I described his attitude in the field log: "Cliff was very active and positive. When he left my office, I felt that somehow he was going to figure out a way to pass the final." I learned during the interviews that my perception of Cliff's approach was correct. He went home and read through his practice exam essays, making a list of all the words he had spelled incorrectly and memorizing them. In a subsequent interview he explained the strategy he adopted: "In the exam, since you told me that they would look at the spelling, I decided, 'Maybe I'd rather not use that word. Let me use the one I know.' You know, that kind of thing, and I studied a lot of words before I took the exam."

Cliff told me that on the exam he avoided certain words: "Even though I know them before, but I said, 'Maybe that's not right. Why take a risk?'" He admitted that this did inhibit him as a writer: "I didn't feel as good because I feel if you use a good word, makes it smooth. But if you use, you know, regular words, most often used by everybody, it makes it look cheap."

Despite Cliff's dissatisfaction with using a more limited vocabulary, his play-it-safe approach paid off. He passed the final exam with a solid five-paragraph essay that received scores of 4, 4. In this essay, which I judged to be the most correct in-class writing sample Cliff had produced all semester, he also managed to retain his clear thinking and eloquent expression of ideas. Ironically, *parents* was a key word in this essay and appeared, correctly spelled, six times.

THINKING AND WRITING PROCESSES

Cliff, like Roberto, possessed a high degree of metacognitive awareness and so was usually able and willing to provide detailed descriptions of his mental processes. While working on this case study, I have often marveled at Cliff's sophisticated insights into his own thinking and wondered what factors in his mental makeup and life experiences accounted for this awareness. If teachers could solve such puzzles, we might be able to help other, less reflective students to develop some of the qualities that Cliff possessed in abundance. Although I can't fully explain the reasons for Cliff's high degree of self-awareness, the sections that follow provide some intriguing insights into the way his mind worked.

Freewriting

One of the major benefits Cliff felt he had gotten from freewriting was a great increase in fluency and in the ability to write on a wide variety of subjects. As he said during the first interview, "Even if you are in a problem as to what to write, when you start writing, you know, you got used to it, so it comes automatic." In the second interview Cliff reaffirmed that extensive journal writing had given him a chance to experiment with words and to reach "high-level standard English." He felt that his writing fluency improved dramatically as a result of all the practice he got in the journal: "When I start to write something, even though it's not a good word, but I know how to make it up, you know, how to write it, and make a connection to the whole story. Simply before I couldn't do that."

But for many of his journal entries, Cliff didn't use the process of nonstop freewriting I had recommended to the class. He explained in an interview: "Some of the things I have to think about what I'm gonna write. You know, specially the personal things have to come into my memory. It takes me a while because I might do it now, or stop and do something else and come back to it and write again."

Fortunately, Cliff felt free to ignore my original instructions for journal writing and took the time he needed to think before writing. He also used the journal as an opportunity to perfect his word processing skills, typing, revising, and spell-checking most of his out-of-class entries. Not counting the time for thinking, he spent 4 to 6 hours a week on his journal. And like Roberto, Cliff was concerned with quality as well as quantity. As he put it in an interview, "I want to write it nicely."

Thus, "freewriting" may be the wrong term to describe the process that Cliff used for his journal. When he spoke of how the journal helped to improve his fluency and comfort in English, Cliff was acknowledging that he had benefited from the extensive writing practice he got by spending 4 to 6 hours a week writing in his journal. But his efforts to edit, correct, and "write it nicely" kept him from engaging in the nonstop exploratory writing that Elbow advocated in *Writing Without Teachers* (1973). For Cliff, the free exploration of ideas occurred in his mind before he put pen to paper.

Reflection as Internal Dialogue

One of the most intriguing characteristics of Cliff's journal was the way his writing often reflected an ongoing internal dialogue. Several examples occurred in the 10-page entry entitled "The Biggest Turning Point," in which Cliff wrote about the diagnosis of his diabetes 5 years earlier. He described the scene as he waited with his mother in the hospital lobby, portraying his fear and confusion in terms of a mental dialogue:

> The feeling that I had that day was like a blind man walking through a unfamiliar room and pretends he knows the way. I ask this question so many times, "How is Cliff tomorrow compared to today?" There were no answers in bewildered mind of mine.

After the doctor confirmed the diagnosis and explained the necessary diet and medication, he sent Cliff and his mother home to face a new way of life. Again, Cliff described his powerful, new emotions as a conversation between different aspects of himself:

> … After we said thank you and good-buy to the doctor and headed for home, this new person inside of me started to scare me. He said, "How you going to keep me alife? What if you forget to eat and you faint? You will kill us both you know that." When I got home, I went to the kitchen, like usual, and grabed a bread. At that minute, the stranger's voice said, "Hay, what are you doing? You didn't take you medicen. You no longer the old and free Cliff. You are under my control. Now go get your needle and medicen and take it."

The use of different voices to suggest inner reflection was a motif that Cliff repeatedly used in his journal. In "The First Incident," written a month later, he used the metaphor of being taken over by another person to describe his first experience of an insulin reaction. The reaction had occurred at work, and his boss told him later, "You were like somebody that was filled up with super powers and commanded by the devil himself." As Cliff explained at the end of the entry, "Before this first incident, there lived a part of me that I haven't seen or existed. As the ambulance took me to the hospital, I felt as I heard the syrian [siren], that I was dangerous to other people as much as I was to myself." (For additional examples of inner dialogue in Cliff's journal, see Entry 7 entitled "Why Now!" in Appendix C.)

Not only did Cliff often engage in a mental dialogue in his journal, but he also "talked to himself" during the interviews. When I asked him about this in the second interview, he immediately knew what I meant and replied: "As far as I remember, I usually talk to myself." He went on to explain that he had developed this habit during his childhood in Ethiopia, where he was stigmatized because of being overweight. This surprised me because now Cliff was tall and slim. But as a child, he said, he had been "very fat." He went on to describe the significance of obesity in a country where many people don't have enough to eat:

> If you are fat in my country, it means you are from a rich family. They say things to you there. "Oh, what did you eat today? You ate one chicken." You know, this kind of thing. That isolates you from the students. Everybody makes fun of you, even the teachers. I remember the gym teacher said, "Cliff, you start running early, before I send all these students, so you could get there at the same time." That kind of thing. So I didn't bother talking to nobody. I said, "Ah." Even when I got into ninth grade. So that's how it started.

When I asked Cliff to say more about how his habit of talking to himself developed, he explained, "If I say something, nobody understand what I'm saying. Anybody that I talk to. I'm the only one who understands it." Now that Cliff was living in the United States with one of his sisters, he still talked to himself, sometimes even voicing his thoughts aloud, "because to keep them inside is hard." As he saw it, the purpose of these mental dialogues was "arranging things in order."

I asked Cliff whether journal writing was "another way of talking to yourself." "Exactly," he answered. "You could say what you have in your mind. You know, you just quote it the way it comes."

I believe that this inner dialogue, a striking feature of both Cliff's and Roberto's journals, is an important part of the reflective process, conducted in the inner speech that Vygotsky (1986) saw as the basis for all verbal thought. It is likely that students who habitually engage in this type of dialogic thinking will write reflectively if asked to keep a journal. In a significant sense the journal becomes an extension—or an externaliza-tion—of their accustomed thought process. The challenge for teachers is to find ways of encouraging students who do not habitually engage in an internal dialogue to use their journals in reflective ways. I consider this problem at length in chapter 6.

Another intriguing parallel between Cliff and Roberto is that both of them said their habit of talking to themselves developed during childhood as the result of a failure of communication in their families. Cliff mentioned that as a child he was not able to communicate freely in his family. As he put it: "We don't sit around with our parents and talk." Roberto had expressed a similar idea when he said that during his childhood he had been happy and outgoing in school but "when I came home…, I was always thinking and thinking. No one really stopped and listened to me."

These comments suggest that for some people the tendency to engage in a reflective inner dialogue may develop as a substitute for social speech. However, it's important to point out that, as college students, neither Cliff nor Roberto were reclusive or socially maladjusted. Both were well-liked by their classmates and comfortable in discussions with teachers and peers.

The Role of Comparison

Another salient feature of Cliff's journal was his tendency to make compari-sons between what he was reading and his own life, which often took the form of connected knowing. In entries about A Place for Us, he usually approached the book in terms of his own life experience. In one entry, for example, he compared Greek marriage customs with Ethiopian practices. In another he compared a beating that the young Nick Gage had received from a classmate with a similar incident from his own childhood. In an entry inspired by a reading passage in the textbook about the meaning of friendship, he again responded in a personal vein by comparing the Ethiopian concept of friendship to the one he encountered after moving to the United States.

For Cliff, bringing his own experiences to bear on what he was reading was an important step in the reflective process. During the interviews I asked

Cliff about his "tendency to relate one thing to another thing." He knew exactly what I had in mind and replied:

> Basically, I relate things. To everything I relate things. This is the same as that one. It's even people. I don't pick them by their name. You know, this person is like this one. And, you know, what I feel about that person, okay, this person is like that. And sometimes I say the wrong people's name because the feelings that I have toward that person is the same. You understand?

I did understand and was impressed by Cliff's facility in explaining how his mind worked. He went on to say that sometimes at work he called people by the wrong names "because the feelings that I have toward that person is the same. That's how I put it in my head. That's how I register in my head."

Cliff's ability to categorize people and ideas "in his head" through a process of comparison was an important one from a cognitive point of view. He told me that he had developed this tendency after moving to the United States at the age of 14. In making these mental comparisons Cliff was engaging in a type of concept formation that Vygotsky (1986) described:

> ... a concept can become subject to conscious and deliberate control only when it is a part of a system. If consciousness means generalization, generalization, in turn, means the formation of a superordinate concept (*Oberbegriff-übergeordneter Begriff*) that includes the given concept as a particular case. (pp. 171–172)

By making these mental comparisons, by relating one thing to another and grouping them into categories in his head, Cliff was engaging in a type of conceptual thinking that is highly valued by the U.S. educational system. It is interesting that Cliff engaged in the process of categorization and concept formation not only as part of his school learning but as part of his personal life as well.

CLIFF'S STANCE AS A LEARNER

Cliff's preferred learning style is not easily classified by the *Women's Ways of Knowing* typology of epistemological perspectives (Belenky et al., 1986). Like Roberto, Cliff often employed connected knowing in his journal. For example, in his journal entries about *A Place for Us*, he made comparisons with his own life, and his journal contained many of the markers of connected knowing: references to the self, open expression of emotion, recognition of temporal flux, internal dialogues, empathy and identification as ways of understanding the experiences and ideas of others, and a strong sense that knowledge often derives from personal experience. It is obvious from his journal and interviews that he was in the habit of reflecting deeply about the meaning of his experiences. It is also clear that at times he constructed knowledge for himself. For example, when he devised his own rating scale for the books he read, he was claiming the right to decide what makes a book good and to award an appropriate rating. Despite the fact that Cliff often used connected knowing and at times constructed knowledge, he also consistently expressed a strong belief in teachers as important sources of knowledge.

The Role of Teachers

One way for me to gain insight into different students' epistemological perspectives was through their written responses to Sydney Harris' (1990) essay "What True Education Should Do." Cliff expressed skepticism about Harris' thesis that the teacher's job is not to "stuff" students with information but to "help them open and reveal the riches within" (p. 10):

> Education can and should be different from place to place. In the story that we read, Socrates taught students by making them conciously aware of their talent and talking about it. I think this is a good way or methed that can be used to educate people in general, but not to all students. That is because in my opinion it is time taking and hard to get quick results.

Ironically, in differing from Harris on this point, Cliff is, in effect, constructing knowledge—in this case, his own pedagogical philosophy.

Cliff's behavior as a student and statements he made during the interviews confirmed his belief in the importance of forming a close bond with his teachers. Early in the semester I noted in the field log that Cliff always chose a chair close to my desk and participated eagerly in class discussions. During an interview he explained why he did this: "When I sit in the back, I feel that I don't communicate with the teacher. And I feel kind of left out. So I don't want to do that. I said [spoken loudly], 'I want to be in the class.'" For Cliff it was essential to take part in class discussions: "If you don't talk in class, the teacher doesn't know what you really need." As a result of his educational experiences in the United States, Cliff had developed the belief that most teachers were advocates who could give students what they "really need." He told me that he especially liked the teachers of his ESL classes in high school, a feeling that was reinforced by his positive experience in Martha's college ESL writing course.

As a child in Ethiopia, however, his relationship with teachers had been problematic. As he explained during the second interview: "In my country, it's different. You are scared of the teacher because they have a right to, I mean, you cannot say nothing. If I don't pass the test, for example, if I need only one point to pass, I used to get beaten by the teacher." According to Cliff, everyone in Ethiopia accepted this system, but looking back on it now, he no longer condoned the idea of corporal punishment: "That kind of learning is not learning, I don't think. Even though I get beaten up by the teacher, I don't know what my mistakes were. All I remember is if I fail the test, she's gonna beat me up."

This led Cliff to another educational issue about which he felt strongly—his dislike of being forced to do things by teachers. Commenting on the physical punishment that was a feature of his education in Ethiopia, he said: "Sometimes, you know, probably it encouraged me to study a little bit more. But when I think about it, I'm forced to do this, and my mind doesn't want that. If I'm forced to do something, I cannot do it."

Cliff also acknowledged that he did better in courses in which he felt close to the teacher. He illustrated this statement by telling about an experience he had recently had in a math course. Although he usually got As in math, he had gotten a B in this course. And he felt the reason for the lower grade was his inability to relate to the teacher:

Somehow I don't feel, how should I put it? These are strong words. I don't feel as important in the class. You know, the way she teaches. You know, "If you want it, learn. Otherwise, you know, forget it." Maybe she's not that way, but that's what I feel. So when I feel that way, I say "forget it." I don't bother studying it. [pause] But that's bad. I know that's bad.

When Cliff said that it was important for him to feel "close" to a teacher and to feel that he was "important" in the class, he did not mean that he wanted unconditional support and acceptance. In fact, what had pleased him so much about Martha's teaching style was that she was "nice *and* strict," forcing students to correct every grammar error 10 times. What he wanted from teachers was interest in his work, which in his view included constructive criticism.

Although Cliff relied on teachers as important sources of help in his learning, he was not a received knower according to the definition provided by Belenky, Clinchy, Goldberger, and Tarule (1986), who stated that learners operating from this perspective "have little confidence in their own ability to speak" and "still their own voices to hear the voices of others" (p. 37). Cliff knew what he wanted from teachers and took active steps to get it. His confidence in dealing with teachers was often apparent during the interviews as he interrupted to ask questions and to request clarification. Conversation analysts have pointed out that for students to take the lead in this way during interactions with teachers is not the norm. Generally, the teacher's role is "attention-getting" while the student's role is "attention-giving". Often in such exchanges, the attention-giver—in this case, the student—assumes "a certain socially imposed invisibility" (Derber, 1979, p. 40). But analysis of the transcript of the conference I held with Cliff shortly before the final exam showed that he did not fade into the background in this way. Instead, he frequently interrupted the flow of talk, asking me for clarification or additional information. During the final interview I asked Cliff if he agreed with my view that he was assertive in talking with teachers. He seemed embarrassed by this question, laughing and fumbling for words: "I don't know how to put it. Uh. Well, I, I think so. I don't know. I think so." Sensing his embarrassment, I tried to reframe the question:

> Let me put it another way cause it certainly wasn't assertive in any negative way. But it was like, a lot of students act very passive when they're with their teachers, and they just wait for the teacher to tell them completely, you know, lead the conversation. And you seem to be a little different in that you will break into that conversation and sort of ask for what you want. You know, you have some ideas of what you need to know from the teacher, and so you'll ask her.

Cliff agreed with this assessment: "Cause otherwise she gets kind of, you know, go around and around again. You don't reach what you want to say, and you don't communicate specifically." As we see in the next section, this goal of "communicating specifically" with teachers was extremely important to Cliff.

Concern With Communication

In the early stages of analysis, I made many comparisons between Cliff and Roberto. Both students were highly reflective writers whose journals had engaged me from the beginning of the semester. Both usually wrote their journal entries in the first person and often relied on connected knowing. Both were independent thinkers capable of constructing knowledge.

But in one respect they were diametrically opposed. That was in the way they chose to respond (or not respond) to the questions I asked in my letters commenting on their journals. The tables on how the students used their journals reveal this difference in concrete terms (see Table 4.1 and Table 5.1). Whereas Roberto had produced no writing in response to my questions, Cliff had responded to similar questions with 10 pages of journal entries, 13% of his entire journal. During the interviews both Roberto and Cliff were able to articulate their very different reactions to the questions I asked in my letters of response. Although Roberto made it clear that he wanted me to like his journal, he did not answer the questions I asked. As he explained his process for composing journal entries, "I don't really think about the reader. I really think about what I want to say." Based on my two interviews with Roberto, I was convinced of the essential truth of this statement. In his journal, Roberto's first priority was to explore his own topics, not those suggested by his teacher.

Cliff's response was totally different. As we have already seen, he was attuned to the needs of all readers and saw writing as a highly communicative process. And the reader he was most eager to reach was his teacher. During the first interview I mentioned to Cliff that some students never answered the questions I asked in my response letters, but that he "did respond very much to my questions and my responses." The conversation continued:

> **Rebecca:** I was reading your journal this morning. You answered that thing about your past history as a reader, and then you had a couple of other entries. And then you started talking about what makes a really good writer, what kind of books you really like. And you explained how you rate the books. And it was almost like you anticipated a question. Were you starting to ask your own questions then?
>
> **Cliff:** Yeah, kind of, you know. I said, "What is it I have to add to this kind of writing?" I start thinking what I have to write about. Basically, what writing is about. So that's the first thing that came in my mind. It made me talk about what I believed, you know.

It is clear from this exchange that Cliff was trying hard to respond to my interests. In talking about the journal he had kept for Martha's course, he explained his choice of topics, "I wrote personal things that comes in my mind." But in my course he gradually steered his writing away from the personal and toward topics related to reading and writing processes. When I asked him what he remembered about my response letters, he replied:

> Well, you wrote in the journals that I have to, you know, tell you what you wanted to know, so I said, "Maybe I have to write the next one on this idea." So basically that's what I followed up. Then I said, "Maybe let me do this. And let me relate something to that and write something different but such a way that is related to the question that you asked."

Cliff took my requests for information very seriously (for samples of these requests, see Entries 2 and 5 in Appendix C). And I found it significant that while Roberto felt free to ignore similar requests, Cliff interpreted them as a mandate: "I have to tell you what you wanted to know." Clearly, Cliff felt a strong obligation to answer all of my questions.

My own reaction to this realization is one of ambivalence. I'm glad that the journal enabled Cliff to explore and analyze his own experiences and processes as a reader and writer. And I believe that the greater metacognitive awareness he developed as a result of writing these journal entries will be valuable to him in the future. I hope, however, that his responsiveness to my interests didn't cause him to neglect topics that might have been even more meaningful or useful for him.

Ironically, the motivating force behind my questions had been my strong sense of engagement as a reader. As I had explained to Cliff in an interview, "I didn't ask questions as much to some students, but there were other students, and you were one of them, where I always had a lot of questions after I read the journal. It was somehow like a conversation, and it invited me to keep the conversation going." In Cliff's mind, however, these questions were interpreted not as conversational responses but as directives for future writing, reminding me once again of the power differential in all interactions between students and teachers.

Cliff's strong concern with my responses to his writing was revealed at the end of the final interview when I asked him to look through his journal and pick out the entries that had been most meaningful to him personally. Much to my surprise, he focused instead on the brief comments I had written directly in his journal: "It's interesting, the little comments that you write. When I read it again, after I read your comments, I say, 'Oh yeah. Maybe it is interesting.' You know, feedback."

As Cliff continued to peruse his journal, he focused not on his own writing but on my comments. When I asked whether he always reread his journal when I handed it back, he said, "Yes. Specially the comments because I want to know which words I write are very effective. I'm talking to the reader. I want to know the next time when I write. Maybe I'll use those words, make it better next time." Earlier, in talking about his reaction to Martha's comments on his writing, Cliff had acknowledged his need for support and approval from his writing teachers: "She would look at [the journal] and give you a comment, which is very helpful, like you did. I read 'em. I said, 'Oh, good.' Basically, I don't know why I do that, but I judge myself as to what other people tell me."

Cliff's strong need for response and reinforcement from his readers, especially his teachers, was also evident when I asked whether he thought he would continue to keep a journal now that the course had ended. He said:

> I might do it, but just for myself. And I rarely do it for myself. I don't think I'll do it if it is for myself. If I'm doing it for somebody else, I probably will do it. I want a response, personally. I need somebody else to read it and tell me what they think. Otherwise, I say, "Why am I writing it? I know those things in my head. It's in my head. Why am I writing it?"

I didn't point out that earlier in this same interview Cliff had mentioned the therapeutic value of getting disturbing thoughts out of the mind by writing. I did mention, however, that journal writing might be useful to him in the future: "Sometimes writing about personal problems is very, very helpful, just to get it out. If at some point you feel like it might help to do that, you can do it. It doesn't mean you have to do it every day of your life or anything. But you know that it's there whenever you might decide to do it."

Although Cliff and Roberto had different perceptions of the teacher's role as the audience for their journals, they seemed to share a sense that the journal was a safe place where they could openly discuss personal issues. At the end of the final interview, Cliff spoke about rereading his journal and finding it very "revealing." When I asked him if there were any journal entries that he had decided not to turn in because they were too private, he said there were not: "I have no problems showing you." Later he said, "I trust all my teachers. I don't have a problem with that." When I asked him how he would have felt about having a classmate read his journal, he quickly answered, "I wouldn't mind with the students also." Then he laughed and said, "Outside my family is okay with me."

It is important for teachers to realize, however, that not all students share Cliff's comfort and trust in writing about emotionally charged topics in journals that teachers and perhaps classmates will read. The next chapter examines the experiences of such a student.

6

Maribel: Tension Between Private and Public Worlds

I believe that writing is a way of expressing your feelings and communicating with people. Writing is very important. We need writing almost for everything, but sometimes I don't like to write. It's difficult for me to express my ideas on a piece of paper. Sometimes I think that it is because my language, because when I recived letters from my friends, I love to answer them as soon as posible. I answer them in Spanish. Sometimes I like to write, but I try to disregard essays, it is to difficult to put things in order, I mean to express them. Specially in essays that you always have to give examples, and maybe you give them, but you are not sure if they are right or wrong. When I'm writing I'm always afraid to write something wrong, or write something that doesn't relate with the topic.

This was the first journal entry written by Maribel, a young woman who had emigrated from the Dominican Republic 4 years earlier at the age of 14. The members of Maribel's large family—she is the next-to-youngest of 13 children—came to the United States over a period of several years; Maribel was in the last group to arrive. Neither of her parents speak any English.

Knowing no English herself, she enrolled in a public high school. When she was not able to recite the alphabet in English during her admissions test, she was assigned to the lowest level of ESL and demoted from the tenth grade to the ninth. As she explained in one of her essays, "I couldn't believe it and I couldn't defend myself because I didn't know English."

At the beginning of her studies in the United States, Maribel was overwhelmed by her problems with the language. But she took an active and primarily social approach to language learning. She asked an older sister who had been here longer to help her, and she joined the Latin American Club at her high school, where she received extra help with English from other Spanish speakers. By her senior year in high school, she was succeeding in her studies and had also been elected president of the Latin American Club.

When Maribel entered college in the fall of 1991, she was placed in the lower level reading course and the upper level writing course for native speakers, which is equivalent to the course for bilingual students that I was teaching. The decision to place Maribel in a course with native speakers was not unusual, especially considering that she had been in the country for 4 years and had graduated from a U.S. high school. Using the placement essay as evidence, readers try to gauge whether the student has primarily *language problems*, usually errors suggesting interference from the first language, or *writing problems* such as lack of familiarity with the requirements of written discourse or problems with essay organization. Obviously, these placement decisions are not always clear-cut, and errors sometimes occur.

Maribel had not been in the writing course for native speakers long before she realized that a mistake had been made in her case. She found the course very difficult, and although she wanted to do well in it, she sometimes failed to do an assignment simply because she couldn't understand what the teacher intended. By the time Maribel's teacher realized that she had been placed incorrectly, it was too late in the semester to move her to an ESL section. But they both agreed that if she failed the final—and they both seemed to assume that she would—she should register for the writing course for bilingual students the next time around.

When, a semester later, Maribel was assigned to my ESL writing course, she felt much more comfortable being in a class with other second-language students. She had no trouble understanding my assignments and felt that she was making progress with her writing. But I was not so optimistic. Based on her first in-class essay, I feared that she would not make enough progress in one semester to pass the final exam. And when the students began turning in their journals, I was struck by the absence of reflection in Maribel's journal. Her out-of-class entries were all centered on A *Place for Us* and consisted almost entirely of summaries of events in the book. The following extract, taken from the beginning of Maribel's journal (Entry 1 in Appendix D), is typical of her approach:

> They [the Gage children] left their home country Greece because the communist guerrillas occupying it had began gathering children to send them to an indoctrination camps behind the iron curtain. They left their mother and their sister Glykeria fifteen, was missing behind the iron curtain, where they had been imprisoned, tortured and finally executed by the escape. The four travelers set sail to america on March 3, 1949. They passage on the Marine Carp. Their absentee father's American citizenship waited for them in American, whom believed that he's family should stay in Greece because America life is to dangerous specially for teenagers girls.

Her journal continued in this vein for another six pages before she finally mentioned her personal reaction in a brief and undeveloped concluding paragraph consisting of one sentence: "In my opinion I enjoy reading the story A *Place for Us* because all of us immigrant face the same struggle to form a better future."

My letter of response to this first journal submission sent mixed messages. I praised Maribel for her "very complete summary of the chapters in A *Place for Us*," implying that I approved of the extensive summaries she was writing. But I also tried to encourage her to connect with the book in a more personal way: "In the last paragraph you mention that all immigrants face the same experiences. In your next journal, you might want to write about how this book compares with your own experiences." In fact, in subsequent journals, Maribel chose to stick with the approach she had used in her first journal, in which she summarized her reading and appended a very brief personal reaction. As the weeks went by, her journal entries did not become more reflective.

Although at the time I didn't understand how to encourage Maribel to write more reflectively, writing this book has caused me to look more critically at my own responses and see their patterns and weaknesses. It has also caused me to imagine how I could do things differently. I return to this subject at the end of the chapter, where I discuss Maribel's stance as a learner, and in chapter 8, where I discuss my role as a responder. But first I analyze Maribel's uses of the journal and discuss what the journal and interviews revealed about her thinking and writing processes.

HOW MARIBEL USED THE JOURNAL

Soon after I began collecting the student journals, I selected several students and looked closely at whether they appeared to be using their journals to meet some of their personal or academic needs. Maribel was one of these students, and my initial perception was that she was not using the journal for her own purposes. She did not write about topics she had chosen, as most of the other students did at times, and in writing about her reading, she did not find a way to explore personal connections with the material. The numbers in Table 6.1 confirm this observation.

Every one of the 48 pages Maribel wrote in her journal was, in one way or another, a response to a teacher assignment or suggestion. The two largest categories were my assignments—to write about A *Place for Us*, as well as the topics I assigned for in-class freewriting. She also responded to my

TABLE 6.1
How Maribel Used the Journal

A Place for Us	Hunger of Memory	In-class entries	Her own topics	Final exam	Responses to my questions
17 pp.	8 pp.	17 pp.	0 pp.	4 pp.	2 pp.
35.5%	17%	35.5%	0 %	8 %	4 %

request to write about the final exam, although not enthusiastically, as is shown later. Toward the end of the semester, Maribel asked if she could include in her journal some of the entries from a journal about Richard Rodriguez' *Hunger of Memory* (1982) that she had been asked to keep for her reading course. Although I noted in the field log that I was "not too pleased that this time she wrote no journal entries specifically for our class," I was happy to read her entries on *Hunger of Memory*. This book, which I had used in a previous ESL writing course, raises important issues related to language and identity for bilingual students, especially for speakers of Spanish. In responding to Maribel's journal entries on this book, I asked how she felt about these issues. At the end of the semester she used the journal to answer some of these questions, and though her responses comprised only two pages, or 4% of her journal, during the interviews she selected these entries as being the most meaningful ones she wrote.

My initial reaction to the discovery that Maribel did not find ways to personalize her journal was one of surprise. She had spent her teen years in the United States and had graduated from a U.S. high school. Thus, I assumed—rather naively, I now realize—that she would have been strongly influenced by the American values of freedom and individuality. Yet, as the interviews revealed, these features had not been emphasized in her high school's approach to reading and writing.

Maribel's apparent failure to use her journal to meet some of her own needs as a learner is in keeping with the findings of other studies of "remedial" college writers. For example, Sharon Pianko's (1979) study of the role of reflection in the writing of remedial and nonremedial freshman writers at Rutgers University revealed significant differences in the compos-ing processes of the two groups. Pianko felt that one reason for these differences was that the nonremedial writers had experienced writing as a meaningful activity in their own lives and had observed its importance in their families and communities. Pianko speculated that the nonremedial writers were "more capable than remedial students of viewing writing as serving their own purposes" (p. 277). The remedial writers, in contrast, had seen writing only in school settings where it was done to meet a teacher's requirement. Pianko pointed out that such students "rarely, if ever, did self-initiated writing" and commented, "It is not surprising that these writers could not see writing as playing a specific role in their lives" (p. 277).

Although initially it appeared to me that Maribel was not using the journal for her own purposes, I can see now that she did use the journal in ways that were important for her—summarizing her reading in order to understand it more fully and attempting to please the teacher by fulfilling an assignment. It took some time for me to recognize this because Maribel's purposes were so different from my own goals for the student journals—primarily my hope that the students would use their journals to engage in written reflection about the reading and writing they were doing for the course.

Summarizing

Maribel had never kept a journal before she entered my class. But interestingly, in the semester in which this study was conducted, she was asked to keep two. In addition to the journal for my course, she also kept a journal for her upper level developmental reading course. The reading teacher distributed a handout to the class asking that the journals begin with a summary of the reading assignment and end with a personal reaction. Maribel told me during an interview that she wasn't sure what her teacher meant by "reaction," but she had a lot of experience from high school in writing summaries and felt strongly about them: "Oh, for me, I think like a summary is, you know, the most important things about what you read.... You don't have to write everything." Instead, a summary should be "what you got in mind, you know, when you close the book. I think that's the summary of the book."

Maribel's approach to journal writing was influenced not only by her reading teacher's instructions but also by the book reports required in her high school. According to Maribel, the major purpose of these reports, which were presented in both written and oral forms, was for the students to prove they had read the books by giving a detailed summary. In our first interview I asked Maribel, "Did your high school teachers want to know how you related the book to your own life, what you thought about it?" She replied, "No. You don't have to, like, to relate it to your own life. They only want a summary of the book." Sometimes Maribel would give a perfunctory glimpse of her own reactions at the end of one of these book reports, "And when I was, you know, at the end, my reaction. I just saying, 'I like the book.' Or 'This part surprised me.' ... So, something like that, but especially, you know, we talk about the summary of the book." This same pattern of long summary and brief personal reaction described quite accurately the approach Maribel adopted for the journals she wrote for the developmental reading and writing courses she took in college. Summarizing can be a useful and rigorous mental exercise, as Mike Rose (1989), among others, has pointed out, and Maribel herself indicated that the summaries she wrote in her journal augmented her understanding of the books she was reading, although they were not the high-level syntheses Rose had in mind when he extolled the value of summarizing in order to "manage information, make crisp connections, or rebut arguments" (1989, p. 138). Nevertheless, in my view Maribel was limited by her high school's prescription of the acceptable way to write about reading. It was not until the end of the course that she began to see that there were other possibilities.

Preparing for the Final Exam

When, toward the end of the semester, I encouraged the students to use the journals to explore their thoughts and feelings about the final exam, Maribel complied with my request. She was especially sensitive about this exam because she had failed it the previous semester and confessed in her journal entry that she found this subject unsettling. But being a dutiful student, she forced herself to try to answer the questions I had posed about the test:

> How are the final exams graded? I'm not sure how they are graded. But I believe that they are graded by professor that you might know, but you don't know what teacher graded you exam. You pass this exam with 4, 4. I really don't know how long each teacher spend on each paper. The teachers graded this exam looking for grammar mistake, how well you organized you essay, and if you had answered the question.
>
> I preffer not to continue taking [talking?] about this exam because I get score [scared?]. I fail onces, and I don't want to fail again. I'm trying hard and I "hope" that I could pass this exam this time.

In responding to this entry, I wrote at the bottom of the page:

> I understand your feelings, but I'm hoping that through writing about the exam in your journal, you will figure out some useful strategies to help you to pass it. In your next journal, please write about what you can do to improve your chances of passing this exam. Thanks. R.M.

I collected the journals only one more time after this, and Maribel did not write about her strategies for passing the exam. But facing her fears about the test in the journal and in our class discussions marked the beginning of the active preparations that enabled her to pass it. I asked her about this during our first interview: "I did a lot of things there at the end to make ... you aware of how they grade the test and what they look for in a passing essay. And you wrote in your journal that you didn't want to think about it very much. Do you remember that?" She said she did, and both of us laughed. I continued, "That made you uncomfortable, but ... how did you feel about that? About knowing how the whole process worked and how the grading worked?" She said that this awareness, which had not been stressed in her previous writing course, had helped her to develop a clear sense of who her readers would be and what they would be looking for:

> You know, it's good, like, you know, like what they look for, you know, for a passing grade. So when you're writing the essay, you think about that. Like, "Oh, you know, they looking for the grammar, you know, the grammar. And how you organize...." And when you're writing, you think about that because everything that I wrote, I went, "Oh, maybe they like this, you know, because they are looking for it."

When I asked Maribel what specific strategies she had used to prepare for the test, I learned that she had been active and thorough. What she felt helped her the most was rewriting her own in-class practice essays until they were at passing level. Grammatical errors were a serious problem in Maribel's writing, and she developed an approach that enabled her to learn from her mistakes. If she was not sure why something she had written was incorrect, she would ask her tutor at the Writing Center:

> I asked her, you know, why this is not correct and ... why I couldn't use, like, this verb, or why should I use present or past with this, you know. So that's help you a lot because when you write a sentence, and then you remind the mistakes that you made, you don't make it again.

The tutor, an upper division student who had received special training as a writing conferencer, worked patiently with Maribel, helping her to correct her grammatical mistakes without relying on exercises in grammar textbooks. If Maribel didn't have any of her own writing to work on, the two of them would work on the grammar in other student essays.

Another strategy that Maribel found helpful was borrowing and reading student essays from a folder I circulated containing passing essays written in previous semesters. Maribel found that reading other students' essays not only helped her with grammar, but also expanded her view of the possibilities that writing offered, "When you read another essay, you know, from another student, you learn how they organize and how they think about words. You learn a lot from reading other students' essays."

I asked Maribel if she could describe her feelings on the day of the final exam. She said that she went into this exam feeling much more confident than she had the previous semester. Right before I distributed the exam topics, I returned the practice essays the students had written in the last class. I told Maribel that I thought this was her best in-class essay so far and that I would have given it a passing score. According to Maribel, this comment "gave [her] hope."

She went on to write an exam essay that was, in my judgment, her best in-class paper of the semester and fulfilled the university's standards of "minimum competence" in writing. She passed her reading exam as well. Thus, Maribel, like Roberto and Cliff, left the "vestibule" of developmental education, having demonstrated her competence to read and write at the college level.

Although Maribel never did much journal writing that I judged to be reflective, by the end of the semester she had made progress as a writer and a student. The class discussions about what readers expect, as well as the opportunity to rewrite and improve her essays, gave her a more tangible sense of the criteria for passing the final exam. Although most of Maribel's thoughts on these subjects never found their way into her journal, by her own testimony the writing she did there served as a catalyst for the active efforts that enabled her to control her fears and begin her active preparations for passing the final exam.

Responding to the Teacher's Prompts

Compared with the other case study participants, Maribel devoted a larger proportion of her journal to responding to the prompts I gave for in-class freewriting—35.5 % of the total. And when compared with her out-of-class entries, which consisted mainly of summaries of her reading, these in-class entries contained more evidence of reflection. The reason for this may be obvious. The prompts I gave for in-class journal writing required the students to express an opinion; summary was not an option because there was nothing to summarize. For instance, when I asked the students to write about their feelings on working in small groups, Maribel made the interesting observation that although in some ways group work is more relaxing than large-class discussions, it can also put more pressure on individual students because there is a greater need to make a meaningful contribution. As she expressed it:

> I believe that work in groups is helpful because you can share ideas and you can ask any question that you are confuse on it. Also you learn how to express yourself in a group with different culture. I think is helpful but sometimes you don't know how to express your ideas and you feel bad if everybody in the group are giving opinions except you.

Maribel's reflective response to this question encouraged my own further reflection on the subject of group work.

I was also impressed by Maribel's response to my request to write about "what history means to you." She responded:

> We can define history in many ways. History is an events that took place in the pass. Also history started since writing began. We can said that people make history. For instance everything that we do everyday, that's history. I believe that without people there is no history. History is the study of the pass. Everyone has her or his own history. The future is shape by the history. I believe that this is history.

Quite a good definition, I think, and it demonstrates that Maribel was capable of writing reflectively when the prompt called for reflection.

Many times while working on this chapter, I recalled Vygotsky's observation, written in the 1930s in the Soviet Union, that the ability to form true concepts does not develop until adolescence, and even then it must be nourished by the proper climate:

> If the milieu presents no [meaningful tasks requiring the formation of abstract concepts] to the adolescent, makes no new demands on him, and does not stimulate his intellect by providing a sequence of new goals, his thinking fails to reach the highest stages, or reaches them with great delay. (1986, p. 108)

During the interviews it became clear that Maribel's high school had not required or encouraged her to formulate concepts of the kind Vygotsky was referring to. So it was not surprising that when she was asked to keep a reading/writing journal, she did not immediately use it in a reflective way. When I assigned topics that, in effect, required reflection, however, she was capable of responding reflectively. I now realize that Maribel had strong opinions on many of the subjects encountered in her reading. But something was holding her back from expressing these opinions in her journal.

THINKING AND WRITING PROCESSES

In the journal Maribel often relied on certain thinking and language learning processes that had served her well in high school. However, journal writing also offered new opportunities for intellectual growth, and during the interviews I learned more about what Maribel felt she had gotten from the journal.

Freewriting

Although it did not seem to me that Maribel was writing very freely in her journal, it is important to remember that freewriting was a new experience for her, and she felt it had been extremely helpful in allowing her to relax and express her ideas more spontaneously. She emphasized this at the end of our second interview when I asked if there was anything else she would like to tell me that might help students taking the course in the future. She thought for a few seconds and then said that she found freewriting especially helpful because it was like "warming up." Then, when faced with the extreme demands of the final exam, it was easier to think of what to say.

The interviews provided many surprises, and this was one of them. Maribel, a student whom I thought had benefitted little from journal writing, felt the journal had helped her in important ways. One difference she saw between the journal and her previous writing was that she had more control over the topics. Her writing in high school consisted mostly of the book reports discussed earlier, which had to conform to a prescribed format. As Maribel put it, "The teachers give you, like, you know, certain questions."

With journals, on the other hand, there was no set format, and Maribel enjoyed the freedom of being able to choose what to write about. "In the journals you can write, you know, like in this week you write something about, like, the unity of the family, and then the next week you write something about, you know, another topic."

As Maribel and I continued this conversation, I tried to find out whether the journal caused Maribel to think more deeply or whether she only used the journal to record thoughts that she had had while reading. She believed that writing about her reading made a difference:

In writing this, you know, … you got the chance to think about it. And like when you write something, like you write the first paragraph, and then from that first paragraph you keep writing, and you have to, yeah, development.

Maribel went on to explain that reading, in contrast with writing, is "fast and, like, you don't take too much time thinking because, like, it's saying, you know, 'I have to keep reading this.'"

Maribel's distinction between reading and writing as modes of thought meshes with the hypotheses of some of the most distinguished linguists. For example, Vygotsky's associate, Alexander Luria, theorized:

Written speech is an important device in thought processes. Written speech becomes a useful means for clarifying thinking because it involves conscious operations with linguistic categories. These can be carried out at a far slower rate of processing than is possible in oral speech, and one can go over the product several times. It is therefore obvious why we often utilize written speech not only to convey prepared information, but also to process and clarify our thinking. The idea that it is often best to put things down in writing in order to make oneself clear is completely sound. This is precisely why written speech is of enormous significance for processing thought. It represents work performed on the mode and form of an utterance. (1982, p. 166)

For Maribel, the realization that writing could be used not just to present already formulated information for a teacher's evaluation but also to clarify her own thinking represented an important discovery.

Concern With the Concrete

A strong pattern in Maribel's journal and interviews was her tendency to focus on concrete details rather than more abstract overarching ideas. For example, in the entry from her journal about A Place for Us (Entry 1 in Appendix D), she mentioned the exact date of the family's embarkation for America, the name of the ship they were traveling on, and the age of the sister who was left behind.

In the interviews, too, Maribel exhibited pride in her mastery of the concrete. The book she remembered most favorably from her high school reading was entitled The White House. And it was the concrete details of this book that had impressed her:

I like it because it was very nice. Because I didn't know, you know, too much about it. Like, the White House has, like, 150 rooms. You know, I was surprised. Oh, my God! Too much room! For what? You know in one part, the president ... where he does his speech. And like where he goes, you know, to relax and everything. And that when the president go out of the house, that the ... flag, right, has to be on the top. And when he is in the house, it's not on the top. They, like, they take it off, right.

In both interviews, I noticed Maribel's assurance when discussing concrete facts or practical details. This may even help to explain her tendency to summarize in the journal. Capturing the concrete details of her reading by writing summaries seemed to fulfill an important function for her, and in a sense, it was her grasp of such details that helped her to pass the final exam. Once she was aware of "how they make a 4," she developed a strategy that enabled her to reach that mark. But she was less comfortable with the more abstract ideas so highly valued in postsecondary education. During the interviews, when I asked questions requiring inferences, she often had to think for long stretches and had a great deal of difficulty putting her thoughts into words.

Up to this point in her education, Maribel does not seem to have been unduly hampered by her concern with the concrete at the expense of the abstract. However, as she moves into higher level college courses, she will need to develop ways of handling thinking and writing tasks that are increasingly abstract.

Social Approaches to Language Learning

One of the strongest patterns in Maribel's approach to learning a second language was her tendency to use strategies that are social in nature. Oxford (1993) pointed out that social and affective strategies are often overlooked by teachers as well as students because they are not usually discussed in the research on language learning. But, according to Oxford, social strategies such as asking questions and talking with native speakers can be just as important for language learning as cognitive strategies such as reasoning or analyzing, or metacognitive strategies such as evaluating one's own progress or monitoring errors.

Maribel, with her warm smile and outgoing personality, knew that language learning was a social activity. In our first interview, we discussed Richard Rodriguez, the author of *Hunger of Memory*, who effectively cut himself off from his Mexican roots in order to perfect his English. Our conversation led to a discussion of how Rodriguez and Maribel seemed to be on opposite ends of the learning-style spectrum:

Rebecca: He was using English almost as an *escape* from his family, where you describe him off in his room or almost—I picture him in a closet with the door closed.... It was interesting ... what you said about yourself when you came here is just the opposite. But it was another way of dealing with the problems. Whereas he cut himself off from Spanish, and didn't want his mother to try to speak English, and didn't include his family in any of the English learning that he was doing, when you were learning English, if you had any problems, you either went to the Latin American Club to get help/

Maribel: /Yeah, or to my sister, you know/

Rebecca: /Or to your sister/

Maribel: /I was getting, like, more close with someone.

Rebecca: Right. So you don't *have* to cut yourself off to learn another language.

The subject of how Maribel's outgoing personality helped her learn English came up again toward the end of our last interview. I asked whether she considered herself an active person, a thoughtful person, or some combination of the two. She replied, "I think, you know, that I'm an active person." When I asked her how she felt this influenced her approach to language learning, she elaborated:

I think that, you know, an active person is not like as shy, you know.... That person is not afraid to ask a question or to go to someone, you know, if you could help me in doing this. And that's *help* you because if you have a question, and you are shy to ask, you gonna be like, "Oh, I don't know this. I'm, you know, shy to ask." So I think you learn from asking.

As Maribel pronounced this last sentence, her voice was much louder than it had been at other times in the interviews. In an observer comment in my field log, I noted the significance of Maribel's assurance on this point, "She seems absolutely certain that you learn from other people, you learn from asking."

Right after this discussion of the social element in language learning, Maribel told me about her volleyball coach in high school, a Puerto Rican woman, who had been an important role model for her. The coach insisted that her players speak English because not everyone on the team understood Spanish. And even when the girls were in a group of all Spanish-speaking students, she reminded them to speak English since the only way to master the language was by practicing it.

Maribel's active, social approach to improving her writing may help to explain why she succeeded in passing the final exam when several other students I judged to be more skilled and more reflective writers failed. As she moves into the college mainstream, however, Maribel will need to learn how to use language as a means for interacting with ideas as well as with other people. In order to conceptualize how this kind of intellectual growth could be facilitated, it is important to understand more about Maribel's approach to learning.

MARIBEL'S STANCE AS A LEARNER

Before commenting on any student's approach to learning, it is important to point out that each of us operates from a variety of epistemological perspectives, depending on the situation and our own place in it. From what I learned about Maribel during the interviews, I was convinced that she had developed active learning strategies that served her well in social situations. But within the classroom Maribel was more constrained. She also seemed inhibited during the interviews, which were in a sense an extension of the classroom as I had been Maribel's teacher. During the interviews none of the other students had as much difficulty as Maribel in expressing herself. Her speech was full of disclaimers ("I don't know," "I guess") and fillers ("you know," "like") as well as pauses and hesitations.

The lack of reflection in Maribel's journal writing and her tendency to focus on concrete details rather than abstract ideas was reminiscent of some of the women in *Women's Ways of Knowing* who were categorized as operating from the position of silence:

> Because [the silent] women have relatively underdeveloped representational thought, the ways of knowing available to them are limited to the present (not the past or the future); to the actual (not the imaginary and the metaphorical); to the concrete (not the deduced or the induced); to the specific (not the generalized or the contextualized); and to behaviors actually enacted (not values and motives entertained). (Belenky et al., 1986, pp. 26–27)

Although this passage accurately describes the approach Maribel often used in her journal, she more often assumed the perspective of received knowledge.

Received Knowledge

Women operating from this perspective—like the men described in the equivalent position in Perry's (1970) study—tend to see most things in concrete and dualistic terms: right and wrong, good and bad, black and white. For received knowers, there are not many gray areas. Maribel demonstrated her adherence to this position in her first journal entry, included as the epigraph for this chapter. Here she admitted that she had trouble writing essays because she could never be sure whether her examples would be "right or wrong," and she was "afraid to write something wrong."

Received knowers, as the label implies, accept teachers and textbook authors as the ultimate authorities on what is "right" or "wrong." One of the responses Maribel wrote on the end-of-semester questionnaire confirmed her reliance on the opinions of authority figures. When asked how she felt about my written reactions to her journal, she wrote, "I love to read your responses to my journals because I find the good and bad things." Many times during the interviews, Maribel made it clear that she felt she would progress if she could successfully reproduce what the teacher felt was "right" for her to do.

In responding to the Sydney Harris essay, "What True Education Should Do" (1990), she initially agreed with Harris that knowledge "comes from your mind." But she went on to disclose the important role of memorization in acquiring this knowledge: "I don't think that we memorize something because we have to or because we need to. It is because we want to and we want in the future to be somebody." Maribel sees memorization as the route to social mobility—hardly the notion that Harris had in mind when he wrote of education as drawing on one's mental resources to evaluate, analyze, and synthesize ideas.

According to Belenky, Clinchy, Goldberger, and Tarule (1986), other characteristics of received knowers are their intolerance of ambiguity, their literal-mindedness, their preference for clarity and predictability, and their facility in collecting facts contrasted with their difficulty in developing opinions. Maribel's journal entries and interviews provided numerous examples of all of these qualities, and she, like some of the received learners interviewed for *Women's Ways of Knowing*, had been "quite successful in schools that do not demand a reflective, relativistic stance" (p. 43). However, as she moves ahead into higher level college courses, this stance is likely to become increasingly problematic:

Reliance on authority for a single view of the truth is clearly maladaptive for meeting the requirements of a complex, rapidly changing, pluralistic, egalitarian society and for meeting the requirements of educational institutions, which prepare students for such a world. (1986, p. 43)

How can a teacher help a student like Maribel move from her received-knowing stance to a more sophisticated understanding of her own role in the social construction of knowledge? My confusion about how to respond productively to Maribel's journal and others that I judged to be largely "unreflective" ran like a litany through my field log. In my first letter of response to Maribel, written about 3 weeks into the semester, I praised her "very complete summary" of the assigned reading in A Place for Us and went on to say, "I especially liked your last page, where you pointed out that the mother's dream had come true, but she wasn't there to see it." I tried to encourage more connected knowing by writing: "In the last paragraph you mention that all immigrants face the same experiences. In your next journal, you might want to write about how this book compares with your own experiences."

But Maribel didn't write about the book at all in her next journal submission, which consisted entirely of entries written in class in response to my prompts. She attached a note explaining: "I'm sorry that I would [not] be able to hand in the journal from the book. I have part of it done, but I want to finish it."

When Maribel did submit her writing about the book, there was an indication that she was attempting to respond to my request to "write about how this book compares with your own experiences." She began this entry by stating, "I could say that this book A Place for Us has a lot of things that are similar to my own experience, when I came to New York. But I also could said that Nichola had a lot of problem that I did not have." But she went on, in the next seven pages, to summarize her understanding of the reading without referring in any way to her own opinions or experiences. Only in the last paragraph of this entry did she return to a more personal assessment:

I enjoyed this book, it true that from this book we can learn a lot. Also we can see how a father try to support his family without their mother, and try to give them a good education. They are trying very hard to get success and a better life as all immigrat who came to America. Almost all of us are here for the same reason, better life and a good education.

Why, I often asked myself in frustration, did Maribel resort to such clichés rather than using her own experience as a way of more deeply understanding the issues explored in the book? I continued to puzzle over this question in the field log, and about a month before the end of the course I wrote:

> By not getting personal about the books she reads, is Maribel also ruling out reflection? Do some teachers discourage reflection by insisting that students not respond to their reading in a personal way—for example, not use the first-person pronoun? Teachers do send messages about whether personal responses are appreciated, expected, tolerated. In other semesters I have had the students do their reading journals on xeroxed sheets where a short space is left for summary and a much longer space for personal reactions. Most students get the message and start writing longer personal reaction responses. This semester I probably haven't done enough to squelch the students who like to write very long summaries. Should I? A conversation would probably be the best way to deal with this.

Eventually, during the postsemester interviews, Maribel and I did have this conversation. But it wasn't until many months after the interviews had been completed that I finally came to see that perhaps Maribel herself had provided the key to understanding her reluctance to use the journal for personal reflection. When, in the second interview, I asked her to choose the "one entry that stands out for you in some way, that you remember writing or that was important for you," she quickly selected her final journal entry, one in which she was writing about *Hunger of Memory* by Richard Rodriguez:

> After he [Rodriguez] published his first autobiographical essay seven years ago, his mother wrote him a letter pleading with him never again to write about their family life. She said, "Write about something else in the future. Our family life is private and besides why do you need to tell the gringos about how 'divided' you feel from the family?"
>
> One thing that never has changed in his family is that his parents know the difference between private and public life. And their private society remains only their family. No matter how friendly they were in public.
>
> I think that Richard's mother has all the right to tell Richard not to reveal the things that happened to the family. I believe that as he [his] mother said he could write about something else.
>
> I'm alway saying that something that happened to a family, nobody has to know it. Because is no their problem.

In this passage, which Maribel identified as being the most important in her entire journal, she seems to be telling me why she did not use her journal to connect with her reading in a personal way. To her, this would have felt like telling her family secrets to "the gringos," teachers who in her view had no right to know what happened within her family "because is no their problem."

Initially, the realization that Maribel did not feel comfortable writing about personal subjects in a journal that only I would read made me feel rather defensive. I have worked for many years with students of diverse racial and ethnic backgrounds. And I try hard to be sensitive to their needs and open to their experiences and values. Still, being brought face to face with Maribel's discomfort in writing about personal matters has convinced me of the validity of Ruth Spack's (1997) observation that in analyzing interactions among students, teachers, and texts, the subject position of the teacher cannot be ignored. Moreover, the teacher's identity as a person of a certain age, race, gender, and social class becomes increasingly problematic as students are asked to read "multicultural" texts, which may have been written by members of groups to which they belong while their teacher belongs to another group.

As I considered Maribel's position in my course, I also began to realize how different it was from my own situation in returning to graduate school. For me, the doctoral seminar was a safe place. I could relax and enjoy the chance to "get personal" in my learning logs not only because doing so tapped into my natural tendency toward connected knowing but also because I felt supported by my professors and student partners, most of whom were similar to me in being well-read, middle-class, and middle-aged. Because I was a proficient writer, skilled at making adjustments for different audiences, I was able to monitor my journal writing carefully, making conscious decisions about what to disclose and how to disclose it.

Maribel's situation was very different. She was new to college and forced to take developmental courses because of failing the placement tests. She was repeating the writing course, which she had failed the previous semester. Although she told me she felt more comfortable in the ESL writing class than she had in the class for native speakers, she found herself among students from many different cultures and educational backgrounds, none of whom she had known before entering the class. The whole academic world—which to me was so natural, having been raised by a mother who was a high school teacher and a father who was a college professor—must have felt alien and intimidating to Maribel. In addition, as a nonnative speaker of English, she didn't have the facility in writing that would enable her to monitor and control what she wished to reveal.

When seen in this light, Maribel's need to use her journal primarily for summarizing the book makes a great deal of sense. This was a strategy she had used successfully in high school. Summarizing helped her to understand and remember the reading without putting her in the uncomfortable position of revealing private information about her personal life or family.

I believe, nevertheless, that Maribel needs to develop as a learner by moving beyond simple summaries. In order to succeed as a college writer she needs to practice expressing her own opinions in ways that do not make her feel that she is betraying her family. Although I now understand and respect Maribel's decision not to write about her family in the journal, I am still concerned that she learn to express her opinions on important issues that arise in her college courses.

Toward the end of the semester, I became more forceful in my efforts to push Maribel in this direction. After speculating about the causes for the lack of reflection in her journal, I tried a different tack in my last and longest response letter to Maribel (Entry 3 in Appendix D):

> Thanks for including your journal on *Hunger of Memory*.... Did your [reading] teacher tell you to do a long summary and a short reaction? Actually, I would rather hear a long reaction and a very short summary. For example, I would like to know how you, as a Spanish speaker, feel about Rodriguez' ideas about language. Do you think parents should stop speaking their native language to their children if a teacher tells them to? You say that Richard learned English but he was forgetting his native language. How do you feel about that? If you have children, how will you handle these issues with them? Is it always necessary to give up the first language in order to learn the second one?
>
> In your next journal please write about your own feelings about these ideas. Check with me if you have any questions.

It had taken me practically all semester to figure out that being explicit about how I hoped Maribel would use the journal might be the best approach. She wrote only four pages in her journal after receiving the response letter just quoted. Yet in this final journal there was a different quality to the way in which Maribel engaged with the reading. For example, 1 week before the end of the semester, she wrote:

> Is it always necessary to give up the first language in order to learn the second one?

You asked me this question before, but I never wrote in my journals my feelings about this topic. I wrote some journals about Richard Rodriguez. He learned English but he was forgetting his native one.

I'm not agree with him. I think that you can learn another language without forgetting your native one, I learned English and I didn't forget my first language.

Now [in the United States] there are people who need person that speak more the one language. So learning a second language is very important and is necessary.

In this journal entry Maribel was doing something she had not done earlier—expressing her opinions on an issue of immediate importance in her own life. She was also moving away from her stance as a received knower by disagreeing with Rodriguez, who as a published writer was an authority figure. I saw Maribel's expression of an opinion on an issue of relevance in her own life as a significant step forward. However, Maribel's experience raises the question of whether it is possible for teachers to encourage students to write more reflectively while at the same time respecting their need for privacy. The tension that is always present when teachers attempt to promote change was evident throughout the interviews with Maribel, discussed in the next section.

Entering the Reflective Conversation

Having finally acknowledged Maribel's uneasiness in writing or talking about personal subjects with a teacher, it is easier for me to understand her apprehension during the interviews. As I wrote in the field log shortly after the first interview:

Maribel appeared to be nervous in this interview. She's very friendly and outgoing, but she seemed unsure of why I wanted to talk to her. Probably no teacher has ever expressed an interest in her opinions before. Part of my approach in this interview was trying to get her to relax; I didn't want to push her in ways that made her even more uncomfortable.

In the interviews we spent a lot of time talking about her reactions to *Hunger of Memory*. Early in the first interview, Maribel said that she disagreed with the nun who told Rodriguez' mother that her son should speak only English, both in and out of school. When I asked why she felt that way, she found it painfully difficult to articulate the reasons for her opinion:

Like, you know, [pause] because when she ca-, you know, when the parents, you know, she wants, they, you know, that the sons, you know, her sons, you know, learn the second language, you know, English. I think that they don't have, you know, to, like, to forget. You know, the first, you know, the native language. So, like, you know, they, because it was hard, you know, for them because his parents, they didn't know English at all. So [louder] how can they speak English to him? They, you know, they didn't know. Just because she [the nun] told you because, you know, she told her [Richard's mother]. So I don't, like, in my opinion, I don't know, I wouldn't do it, you know, because I think that he could learn the second language without forgetting, you know, the native one, right. So I don't know why. I disagree with that.

As I listened to Maribel struggling to find the words to express an opinion that seemed so clear in her own mind, I too felt uncomfortable. As the interview progressed, however, the words began to come more easily. For example, when I asked why she thought Rodriguez went on to get a PhD in English literature, she paused for a few seconds and then said:

I think that, like I say before, you know, the guys always talk. They tell him like, you know, to prove some people that he can make it.... Like not only the native speakers could write like that well, and, you know, speak that way.

I found this hypothesis interesting and expanded on what Maribel had said:

So, yeah, maybe it was his pride, like, to prove that he could do it. So he picks the very hardest thing. Not only to learn English well enough to communicate, but to learn it so well he could get his PhD in English. And, you know, in Shakespeare and all the classics of English literature. That's what he studied. So it was like when you said "to prove something." I think maybe that was it. Maybe he felt [pause], he felt *very* sensitive to anybody who was putting down Spanish speakers. But his reaction to that was to prove that he could go further with English even than most people who were born here. So maybe that was it. He was hurt by that, and he was trying to prove he could do it.

During the interview, I wasn't aware of my role in shaping this conversation for educational ends. Only in retrospect, as I analyzed the transcript, did I notice the pedagogical purposes of this exchange. Pleased to see Maribel going beyond the concrete details of the reading to make an inference about Rodriguez' motivation in pursuing doctoral studies in literature, I expanded on her idea that Rodriguez was out "to prove something," modeling the ways that one can develop a simple inference into more sustained discourse. But I also indicated that all such inferences are matters of interpretation and need not be universally accepted when I commented, "So maybe that was it."

As I looked closely at the transcript, I saw signs that, as the interviews progressed, Maribel was loosening up, feeling more comfortable in expressing her opinions to a teacher. I noted my perceptions of this change in the field log:

> Toward the end of the second interview, our talk feels much more relaxed—especially compared to the first interview. Maribel seems really comfortable with me. She is overlapping with my speech at times, supplying more information without being asked. At this point we seem to have gotten past some of the teacher–student dynamics that were so prevalent in our first interview.

Often, while working on this chapter, I have thought of Mike Rose, who, like Maribel, came from a poor, immigrant family and who spent 2 years in his high school's vocational program because of an administrative mistake. Finally, through a teacher's intervention, the mistake was rectified, and Rose began the intellectual odyssey he described in *Lives on the Boundary* (1989). One of the most crucial things he needed to succeed in his studies was talk, lots of it. Fortunately, during his undergraduate education in Loyola University's English department, he encountered a dedicated group of teachers who were willing and able to give him what he needed. He and his mentors spent hours sitting around in the office or at informal backyard barbecues talking and talking and talking about ideas. As Rose pointed out, contrary to the popular myth that in the United States poor but motivated students can move up the educational ladder by means of hard work and determination, students like Maribel cannot make it on their own. As Rose explained:

> You'll need people to guide you into conversations that seem foreign and threatening. You'll need models, lots of them, to show you how to get at what you don't know. You'll need people to help you center yourself in your own developing ideas. (1989, pp. 47–48)

Unfortunately, with students who are operating from positions of silence or received knowledge, schools and teachers often discourage the kind of connected knowing that might allow them to grow intellectually. Two of the basic writers described in Jensen and DiTiberio's study (1989) persisted in writing dry and formulaic essays that excluded any reference to the self. When the composition professor, through written comments, encouraged them to include some personal examples to illustrate their ideas, both students explained that they were only doing what they had been taught in high school. As one of these students explained: "The reason I didn't deal with personal experiences in my essay is because where I went to high school, it was tabu to do so" (1989, pp. 107–109).

With Maribel, however, the challenge for the teacher is to help her learn to express her own opinions in writing without compromising her strong sense of family privacy. Toward the end of the second interview, I asked Maribel if she remembered my end-of-semester request that she write a shorter summary and a longer reaction. She laughed and said she did. I pointed out that her last journal submission did have a longer reaction and asked if she had been influenced by my suggestion. She replied: "I thought that you say that you prefer a longer reaction than a longer summary, so I wrote, you know, a longer one."

Earlier in the interview I had asked Maribel to think about why I had asked for her personal responses to the ideas in the Rodriguez book: "Why would a teacher care about your thoughts? I mean, what's the point of that?" Maribel said that she really wasn't sure, but maybe it had something to do with comparing her thoughts those in the book, or her thoughts on the book to those of other students. I said that I did value comparison and went on to explain:

> Basically I was trying to get you to think more, you know. [Maribel laughs]. Really. Not just summarize the book, but really think about it and analyze it more.... I wanted you to reflect. And for me "reflect" means take the ideas in the book and somehow connect your own ideas to them.... I think that the real learning comes when you grasp onto what you're reading or what you're writing and relate it to your own life in some way that it's gonna become a part of you. Now, Richard Rodriguez, in a way, is a part of you, you know. [MARIBEL: Yeah]. You can always—you'll probably always remember this book.

But now as I look back on Maribel's experience, I wonder if the small signs of change we see here will be lasting. After completing the course, she felt that she had made substantial progress, and her responses on the end-of-term questionnaire were extremely positive. What I had perceived as minor changes seemed major to Maribel. In responding to the questionnaire, she wrote that she saw real signs of progress in her writing and that she had enjoyed her first-ever experience with journal writing because, as she put it, "I liked to share my ideas and feeling with you." She seemed to appreciate my belated suggestions on what to write about: "Sometimes I choose a topic to write in my journal because I found it interesting and also you asked me to write about some specific topic." She wrote a brief note at the bottom of the questionnaire: "I'd like to say thanks for helped me. I will never forget this course. Even though at the beginning I felt like not taking it, I hope to pass it now. Thanks."

Of course, every teacher loves to hear such words of thanks and appreciation. But I realize now that there were several unresolved issues as Maribel completed the course. During my early analysis, the case study of Maribel had seemed simple and straightforward. I saw her as an "unreflective writer" who would naturally become more reflective if she could find a way to connect her personal experience with issues she encountered in her reading. But the longer I spent analyzing this material, the more complex it became. In fact, my scrutiny of Maribel's experience has raised more questions than it has answered. So rather than writing a neat conclusion detailing what I have learned from this case study, I instead end with some of the questions it has raised.

* * *

For much of the semester, I seemed to equate the absence of reflective writing in Maribel's journal with an inability to reflect (mentally) on her reading. How could I have been more successful in encouraging Maribel to use the journal to record the thoughts she had while reading?

Why did it take me so long to recognize that Maribel's reluctance to use her journal to connect with her reading in a personal way was related to her unwillingness to discuss the private life of her family in the public setting of a college course?

What can I do with the knowledge that not all students will share my tendency toward connected knowing or my enthusiasm for using journals to make personal connections with the books they are reading?

Am I correct in assuming that it is important for all students—even those who do not use a connected-knowing approach in their journals—to learn to express personally held opinions on issues they confront in college courses? And if so, how can I work with these students to encourage them to use journal writing as a way of developing opinions while at the same time respecting their privacy?

* * *

I hope that readers will continue to consider these questions as we move into the next chapter, which reinforces the need to resist simple solutions when discussing the complex, human phenomena involved in teaching and learning.

7

Lan and Kiyoko:
Surprising Reactions to Journal Writing

Different students present different phenomena for understanding and action. Each student makes up a universe of one, whose potentials, problems,
and pace of work must be appreciated as the teacher reflects-in-action on the
design of her work. (Schön, 1983, p. 333)

In this chapter I profile two students who outwardly appeared to have a great
deal in common, but whose responses to journal writing could hardly have
been more different. Lan and Kiyoko were Asian women in their mid-20s,
both of whom had received some higher education in their native countries.
Lan had completed a 2-year teacher education program in the People's
Republic of China. In the United States, she was majoring in early childhood
education and planned to teach young children. Kiyoko had finished most
of her university studies in Japan, where she had majored in Japanese
language and literature and had worked as a tutor, teaching Japanese to
Americans. As a college student in the United States, Kiyoko was planning
to major in anthropology and had not decided whether she would return to
Japan after graduation.

Lan had immigrated to the United States with her family 3½ years earlier.
She had not studied English in China and received her first English instruction in a U.S. public high school. Two years later, when Lan enrolled in
college, she was placed in the lowest levels of developmental reading and
writing. By the time I met her she had fulfilled all the developmental
requirements except for the upper level writing course, which she was
struggling to pass. Lan entered my class as a "multiple repeater," forced to
take the course for a third time. As with many repeaters, she was doing
extremely well in her other courses, with a grade point average of 3.72 out
of a possible 4.0. However, she had not yet been able to pass the final exam,

which required her to write a fluent and fairly correct argumentative essay in 50 minutes.

Kiyoko had come to the United States alone 2½ years earlier. At first she lived with Japanese friends and studied English at a language institute. Seeking more opportunities to practice her English, she enrolled in a college in another part of the country and lived in an apartment with native speakers. But after 3 months, she found the surroundings "too boring" and was particularly disturbed that there was no bookstore in the town. She asked me, "They don't read? American people? I mean after they graduate, they don't read books?"

After visiting five or six colleges to find one that met her needs, Kiyoko decided to enroll in the college where I was teaching. Her test scores placed her in the intermediate writing course for bilingual students, which she passed in one semester, and the lower level reading course, which she had to repeat. She then passed both the upper level reading and writing courses during the semester in which this study was conducted, her third semester in the college.

Initially, I had assumed that because these students shared certain outward similarities—both female, both Asian, both in their early 20s, both interested in education—they would also share a common reaction to journal writing. Now, when I look back on this assumption, I wonder why I expected a simple, unified explanation of something as complex as students' responses to journal writing. My years in the writing classroom have taught me that every student is different. Moreover, my reading and experience with hundreds of Asian students have made me well aware that China and Japan have very different cultures. Yet I still grouped Lan and Kiyoko together in my mind and expected them to react similarly to the journals. When they didn't, I began to search for explanations that would help to make sense of my work in the writing classroom. I especially looked for a cultural explanation for Kiyoko's negative reaction to journal writing. I finally came to realize that with Kiyoko, as with most other students, it is impossible to untangle culture from other powerful influences such as personality, educational background, and so on. Indeed, the comparison of Lan's and Kiyoko's experiences with journal writing has convinced me that, as Schön reminded us in the epigraph to this chapter, every student represents "a universe of one," presenting "different phenomena for understanding and action" (1983, p. 333).

LAN: JOURNAL WRITING
AS BREAKTHROUGH EXPERIENCE

Lan enjoyed keeping a journal for my class and felt that it was a significant factor in the improvement in writing that enabled her, finally, to pass the writing exam. Throughout the semester she devised ways to use journal writing in a proactive way, ignoring my instructions and the journal guidelines when they made her uncomfortable or did not seem helpful. The uses Lan found for her journal are summarized in Table 7.1.

Lan used the journal primarily for her own purposes, devoting 32% of it to writing about topics she chose and an additional 26% to her efforts to prepare for the final exam, a very high priority for Lan.

In my three letters of response to Lan, I took my cues from what she had written and responded to her priorities. In the first letter I acknowledged her frustration as a multiple repeater and offered support and encouragement:

> I'm glad you mentioned your negative feelings about repeating this course and being back in the Writing Center. I know how depressing that must feel. But you must have worked very hard to write 20 essays and at least 2 journal entries every day. It's very important for you to remember your own words here [quoted from her journal]: "Even though I failed again, my English improved a great deal. I am keeping working hard and hoping I will pass this semester."

My letters to Lan, though warm and encouraging, focused primarily on the concerns she had raised in her journal and contained few questions for further reflection. But in my response to Lan's next-to-last journal, I posed two questions related to the final exam. After an entry about how the exam is graded, I asked, "Do you think your understanding of these things helped you to write a passing essay on the practice exam?" In another entry she

TABLE 7.1
How Lan Used the Journal

A Place for Us	In-class entries	Her own topics	Final exam	Responses to my questions
12 pp.	18 pp.	23 pp.	19 pp.	0 pp.
17 %	25 %	32 %	26 %	0 %

talked about how hard she had worked during the 3-week intensive writing course she had taken just before my course, and I asked, "Do you think that all the work on English last semester is starting to pay off for you now?" Lan did not answer either of these questions in her last journal, and I realize now that they put her in a double bind. She would either have to "brag" about her own progress by agreeing that her writing had improved or show disrespect by disagreeing with her teacher and saying she had not improved. Seen in this light, her decision not to respond to my questions is not surprising.

Despite the fact that Lan devoted 17% of her journal to writing about *A Place for Us*, she never became fully engaged with the book and, in fact, stopped reading and writing about it at the end of the first month. Lan explained this decision during our final interview:

> I just, when I read up to like chapter 10, something like that, I felt it's too bore. And then I just keep reading it, and then I didn't learn anything. That's why I decide to stop and just write something, whatever I want to write.

Although Lan didn't enjoy the assigned reading for the class, she did like journal writing—so much that she started a second English-language journal in which she could write even more freely and on more personal subjects. During the semester I had no idea that Lan was keeping what she referred to in the first interview as "another freewriting book." She explained, "I wrote some secrets in that book. That's why I don't want to turn it in."

Lan's decision to start a second journal may have been related to her positive experience with journals in the past (see Lucas, 1992). She had kept a diary while she was in high school in China. She also kept a journal, written in Chinese, during her first two years in the United States. Lan had been introduced to freewriting in the 3-week-long intensive writing course she had taken immediately prior to my class and had found it very useful for improving her fluency. Thus, when Lan learned that journal writing would be an important component of her course with me, she eagerly embraced the opportunities it offered. The most important ways in which Lan used her journal were preparing for the final exam, communicating with the teacher, and apologizing.

Preparing for the Final Exam

Lan entered my class disappointed by her inability to pass the writing test. At the end of the intersession writing course, she had failed the exam again, her third failure in less than a year. She expressed her frustration in an early journal entry, written only a week after classes began:

> Today is Tuesday. It is the second day of the second week of this semester. I am still not feeling good about coming back to classes after the long winter vacation. Especially when I come back to the Writing Center again for tutoring. Whenever I remember the moment that I took back the exam paper from [the teacher in the intersession course] and realized that it was a failing score, I feel very upset. Now, I am here, in the same Writing Center again. The difference is that it is a new semester. When my friends ask me, "How are you doing in English," I feel very shame on myself and give them a bitter smiling answer, "Fine, thank you." Anyway, I have to work harder in this semester and try to pass it this time.

Many students who have repeatedly failed this exam are so demoralized that it takes them weeks before they can begin to focus on their writing again in a positive way. But Lan refused to be deterred by her disappointment. She submitted a practice exam essay as part of her first journal.

As Table 7.1 reveals, Lan devoted approximately one quarter of her journal to practice essays and other writing related to her feelings about the final exam and her plans for doing well on it. During our second interview, I asked Lan to look through her journal and choose one entry that had been "meaningful or important" to her. She selected an entry, written about 2 weeks before the end of the semester, in which she developed a plan for passing the final exam:

> I was late for English class yesterday, and I forgot to take back my jourals of last week. However, I got the respons sheet from Ms. R. M. In this week, our journal topics are all about our preparations for the final exam. Well, I think there are many different ways for me to prepare for this exam. Firstward, I will keep writing for my journals and free writings. It really can help me if I keep writing a few times per day, because I am a slow writer. This practice can help me to write fast. Secondly, I am going to look over all the writing works I have done during this semester, and collect all the mistakes which I had made, and correct them all; or I am going to copy the correct form of each of them for at least five times so that I can remember them, and will not make the same erroes again. Finally, I am going to write more extra practice essays, I am going to give me 45 minutes for each essay, then back to 50 minutes for each.

When I asked Lan whether she felt writing this entry actually helped her to pass the exam, she said, "Yeah. Because before I didn't think about how can I avoid some mistakes. Because during the whole semester, I did repeat the same mistakes sometimes." A pattern I have noticed in many journals is that after initially venting strong emotions such as anger, fear, or self-doubt, students then go on to formulate a plan for dealing with the problems they have written about. In preparing for the exam, Lan actually did all the things she listed her journal entry. And for the first time she went into the test feeling confident that she would pass, which she did, receiving a solid 4 rating from both readers.

During our last interview, I too selected an entry from Lan's journal for further discussion, one in which I felt she was using journal writing in a reflective way. The entry I chose, which Lan wrote at home during spring vacation, also focused on the final exam:

> I think I have a very special feeling about this exam. In the past years, I had three experiences for this exam already. However, I kept failing it again and again. On one hand, I felt very disappointed for myself. On the other hand, I am so afraiding to take this exam again that I really want to escap far away from it if I can. Normally, people should feel more confident as he/her takes the exam more times, but how about me? I suppose I am not a normal person. Almost everybody considers that this test is indeed a difficult exam, so do I. The problem is what most difficult for me personally about the test. Well, reviewing the three experiences that I already had, I think they are time pressure and grammar erroes. Usually, I spend too much time to think about the topic, and even though after start writing, I need time to think before I keep on writing. Sometimes I just have enough time to finish the essay, but I don't have even one minute to check the grammar. I think this is the major problem that I have.

This passage provides an intriguing insight into the role of journal writing in stimulating reflection. In this entry, written on April 21, Lan identified a problem: she often had no time left to proofread her essays for grammatical correctness. In the entry quoted earlier but actually written later in the course, she formulated a solution for this problem: She would force herself to write faster by allowing only 45 minutes for practice essays. In fact, this solution appeared to work. Lan surprised even herself when she found that she could complete an essay in 45 minutes. Then when she went back to the 50-minute time limit, she had 5 minutes left for proofreading. She stated enthusiastically, "it really helped."

It must have been gratifying for Lan that this technique of limiting the time for writing helped her to solve a major problem she had experienced with the timed essay exam. What is even more relevant for readers of this book is the journal's role in helping Lan to develop a new writing strategy.

In the first entry she stated a problem. Then in a later entry, she devised a possible solution. I don't know whether Lan was conscious of the connection between the two entries. But delineating the problem in writing in the journal of April 21 served a crucial metacognitive function, enabling Lan later to develop a workable solution.

That the journal played a role in stimulating reflection on a problem of great concern to this student is significant. It seems likely that by carefully selecting questions for students to write about in their journals, teachers can encourage important metacognitive activity. While this type of teacher-prompted reflection may be especially helpful for students who do not generally use their journals to explore ideas, it may also be necessary to encourage reflection on painful but important subjects. If left to choose all their own journal topics, most students would avoid unpleasant or threatening subjects like the writing competence exam; however, teachers can stimulate meaningful thinking by asking students to write on such topics.

Of course, there can also be disadvantages when teachers attempt to guide their students' journal writing in certain directions. I realized, for example, that asking the students to write about the final exam would lead to a certain amount of discomfort and that airing negative feelings might do more harm than good. Most students admitted that they found this writing uncomfortable. As Lan said, in explaining her feelings about writing the entry of April 21:

> It's, like, *scary* because as you failed more times, and then you felt shame....
> And what the people saw is not you. You work hard. They think you just *lazy*
> *person*. They didn't know you work hard for it. And I think I am a hard-work-
> ing person. But I still failed, and that's why I felt really, really bad and was
> very upset.

I asked Lan whether she thought that writing about the exam had been worthwhile even though it had caused some uneasiness. As I put it in the interview, "Was it worth the pain or not?" She replied:

> Maybe on one hand, maybe that can force students to think more things, like
> more wide, more broader. Yeah, broader. Because if you just let people do
> whatever they want, maybe they just go one direction and ignore the other
> things.... *Honestly*, I don't like it when you give us topic and then have to do
> that topic. But after I do it, I learn it, and then I have to think more about
> the topic, what I am going to write. If you don't give us the topic and just let
> us write whatever, I can write some easy things and without thinking, right.
> But if you give the topic, I have to think, maybe.

As we continued to explore this idea, I told Lan that I had felt a conflict between my wish to encourage students to write whatever they wanted in the journals and the desire to stimulate reflection on particular subjects by giving prompts for journal writing:

> I felt torn between wanting the journals to just be for you, to do whatever you wanted, and my feeling that I could encourage some thinking that might be useful. And with the final exam I was trying to do that. I feel that on this kind of an exam, which is so different from any other exam that you ever have to take that it's very important to have a strategy, and how you're gonna do your best. So I wanted people to use the journal to become aware. And I was sort of pushy about that. I wanted it to happen.

Lan's growth as a writer in English had been a gradual process, occurring over several semesters. However, by her own account, journal writing played an important role in this growth. And perhaps my encouragement to use the journal to reflect on strategies for passing the final exam was also a factor in Lan's increasing confidence and ability as a test taker and a writer of English.

Communicating With the Teacher

Another way in which Lan used her journal was as a line of communication with me. About 2 months into the course she addressed me directly for the first time in the journal: "Also, I would like to ask you one question—the one I also want to discuss with you in next Tuesday's appointment time in your office." This question turned out to be about another course Lan was taking, sociology. She had enrolled in six courses and was finding it impossible to keep her grades up in sociology; she wondered whether she should drop the course. In this journal entry she carefully laid out all the factors involved in the decision, and addressed me again in closing:

> I am really upset about this problem. Would you please help me to work it out? I don't know if I can ask you about the questions of my other courses, but thank you anyway and we will discuss [in our conference] on Tuesday.

Some teachers might feel this was an inappropriate way for Lan to use her journal. Yet I felt that Lan's confusion about whether to drop sociology, like Roberto's exploration of his relationship with his father, was an important issue for her and constituted a valid use for the journal. During our conference we discussed Lan's options thoroughly, and she eventually decided to drop the course.

But what was more significant, in my mind, than the ultimate decision Lan made was the way she used the journal to develop a more personal relationship with me. We talked about this during our second interview. I asked Lan, who was preparing to be a teacher of young children, whether she thought it was important for teachers and students to know each other. "Yeah," she said, "I think if the teacher is more like a friend to students, it's more helpful than we just, like, we have a limit here, 'You're a teacher, and I am a student.'"

After this comment I asked Lan if she felt the journals "became a way to develop friendships between the teacher and the students." She thought they did and explained that this evolving friendship was related to the responses I wrote to each student, "If somebody asks you a question, you feel that means the person feels *comfortable* with you."

Quite a few students, including several other Chinese women, used the journal to cultivate a personal relationship with me. For example, one young woman, who had arrived from Hong Kong only about 6 months before the course began, wrote a journal entry about a month into the semester entitled "The Best Way to Communicate":

[Writing] is the best way to communicate with classmates, friends and especially my teachers. I remember when I was still in high school. Every week I had to hand in writings to my Chinese subject teacher. I could write on any topics for at least two pages. Many of my classmates would write on some common things, liked the Swimming Gala, ... Sports Day or any other events concerning our school. Yet I never wrote these as I did not want to waste my chance to communicate with my teacher.

Ever since there is education, there are teachers and pupils. Even though the teachers may be very kind and friendly, there are still a distance between them and their students. Being a student, I clearly know that there is something I will not talk about it with my teacher directly in class. Yet what can I do in order to know my teacher's opinion? The only way is to write.

We could talk about things that everyone said yes but I said no. We could talk about the policy of the school or even the way I felt about his teaching. In return, I was given a long piece of comments and now I still kept them in good order. I really enjoyed the relationship between me and my teacher. We were not only teacher & student but also good friends.

Having started my college life, I found that there was a great difference in relationship between the teachers and the students. Whenever I have questions, I have to make appointment with my teacher so as to see him or her. Sometimes, it is even impossible to meet them because of my schedule of classes clashes with their office hours. I am very disappointed and I miss my teachers in Hong Kong.

> However, I liked my English course. It is the only one class that I can talk
> to my teacher directly and even through writing.... The most important thing
> is that I can have my teacher's comment after I handed in my writings. I am
> looking forward to receiving the comment of this little piece of writing.
> Thank you so much! My friend.

Besides providing a natural way for students to communicate more
directly with me, the journals also helped me get to know my students better.
Before I began to use journals, there were always a few students who came
to class regularly but rarely spoke up or attracted my attention. Soon after
I began asking my students to keep journals, I found that I got to know every
student on a much deeper level. The journals provided the possibility of
enhanced communication between student and teacher.

Apologizing

Besides using her journal to communicate directly with me, Lan often used
her journal to apologize for her perceived shortcomings as a student. In this
respect, her journal was markedly different from Roberto's journal, which
was often used for self-validation. Partly this may reflect gender differences,
for as Deborah Tannen has noted, women spend much more time apologizing—at least in the middle-class American conversations on which her
research is based—than men do (1990). In Lan's case, cultural factors may
have been involved as well because Chinese students—both males and
females—are very concerned with politeness and, instead of attempting
one-upmanship, put a great deal of effort into maintaining what Tannen
called a "one-down" position (1990, p. 24).

Whatever the reasons, Lan frequently used her journal to apologize for
her failings as a student. These apologies began on the first page ("Untill
last semester after I failed English, I realized that my laziness influenced me
so much") and extended through page 64, where she described meeting a
classmate from the winter session with whom she shared a common bond
(" ... we are both lazier during this semester than in the winter section").
In the entry where she introduced her problem with the sociology class, she
began by apologizing:

> Well, what should I say in today's journal? Excuse words! Of course—except
> the excuse words, I don't think I have anything else to say because you can
> see—I only have two pages of the previous journals this time.

In actuality, Lan was anything but lazy. This was the student who wrote practice essays from the beginning of the semester, attended regular tutoring sessions at the Writing Center, kept not one, but two English-language journals, and—toward the end of the semester—corrected every one of her grammatical errors five times.

In the rush of the semester, I interpreted Lan's apologies at face value as signs of self-doubt and perceived inadequacies. However, near the end of our last interview, Lan expressed her real feelings on the question of whether or not she was a lazy student. In discussing all the language-learning strategies she used in her efforts to pass the final exam, I said, "Not everybody has the will power that you have. That's what was rare.... Even though it was disappointing and painful, you didn't give up, you know. You never gave up." Lan agreed and elaborated:

> Sometimes I really want to give up, but I have to *do* it. I tell myself I cannot give up. Just like I am attending college, right. So for the other people, they think it's like impossible for me. Just like knew no English and come here for two years and then enter college. They think it's impossible. Sometimes, I try *very* hard, and didn't get anything. That's why I really want to give up. But I told myself, "I can *not* give up."

I remember vividly the intensity in Lan's voice as she spoke of her hard work and determination to succeed in college. The pattern of apology that ran through her journal was undoubtedly influenced by self-doubts caused by her repeated failure on the writing exam and may also have reflected expectations of deference in speaking with teachers. But what seems most important for teachers like myself to realize is that there is often a disjunction between our students' formulaic expressions of politeness and what they really think and do. Although Lan often apologized in her journal, she was an extremely resourceful writer and language learner. In order to teach her effectively, I needed to disregard some of the surface meanings of Lan's journal entries to better understand who she was as a student. Fortunately, the interviews enabled me to do this.

Connected Knowing: A Minor Theme

Lan's journal contained some examples of connected knowing. For example, in the four entries Lan wrote about A *Place for Us*, she sometimes engaged in connected knowing as she compared her own life to that of Nicholas Gage. But she did not use the journal to shuttle back and forth between events in the book and her own experiences. Moreover, her journal was not marked by expressions of empathy and identification with people and ideas in the reading.

One type of connected knowing that recurred in Lan's journal was related to her tendency to formulate the moral, or lesson, of the stories she told. These morals, which occurred four times in her 72-page journal, suggested Lan's belief that knowledge is derived from personal experience. Lan expressed this idea in her journal, "In our life, we have experienced a lot of things which gave us good lessons and benefit so that we could remember some of them. If we want to write them down on papers, I am sure it is a pretty easy thing to do." An example of Lan doing exactly this occurred in an early journal entry where she explained that the story of the young Nick Gage being punished for stealing money from his father's wallet reminded her of the experiences of her cousin in China. Never punished for his minor crimes as a child, he continued his misdeeds and was eventually sentenced to 3 years in jail for stealing a car. According to Lan, the cousin emerged from prison "another person." She concluded, "… a suitable punishment can renew a person as well."

Similarly, she found a moral in her own decision to drop the sociology course, "From this story, I learned a very good lesson that I have to think it very carefully before I regerster for the courses of next semester. Otherwise, I will waste both time and money." Lan's penchant for finding morals in personal experience—her own and other people's—is an example of one of the forms that connected knowing may take.

Freewriting for Fluency

Lan wrote in her last journal entry for the semester, "I like to write journals because I can write whatever I want to write, and write without thinking." For Lan, journal writing and essay writing were very different, and she welcomed the journal's freedom. When I gave the students specific prompts for journal writing, Lan was not pleased: "Sometimes you gave us topics, and I don't like topic journals. I just want to write something. I just want to write *something*."

Because Lan was so convinced of the benefits of writing freely in English, a few weeks after the beginning of the semester she decided to start a second English journal, in which she would have even more freedom. She found this private journal "more helpful" than the journal I had assigned to the class "because I can write more freely." Lan described the writing process she used for this personal journal, "And sometimes I just write, and it's nonsense, you know. And sometimes I just start like this: 'I'm sitting here and writing, but I don't know what I'm going to write at this sentence.'"

Lan reveled in the increased freedom she found in her personal journal, and to protect herself from the embarrassment of having others read it, she employed a simple solution. She kept this second journal completely to herself. When Lan told me about her private journal during the first interview, I asked if she would show me one or two entries so that I could compare them to the entries she had written for the course. She politely but firmly declined. This journal was for her eyes only.

One of the major benefits Lan felt she derived from her extensive journal writing was that her fluency, as evidenced by her writing speed, increased dramatically. She explained:

> Before I write very slowly. Slowly. And then, after the journal, I used to write whatever I like. And I write whatever comes up from my mind, and I just keep doing it. Even though it's nonsense words and the same sentence. I just want to keep writing it, and want to write fast.

Lan's perception of the journal's role in helping her to become more fluent supports the view of Mayher, Lester, and Pradl (1983) that beginning first-language writers develop fluency by attempting to express meaningful ideas rather than focusing initially on matters of clarity or correctness. In my 15 years of working with second-language writers, I have come to believe that this principle applies to them as well. Lan's progress in English, which she attributed to freewriting, suggests that this approach worked well for her.

A large part of Lan's increasing fluency in English was related to her recently acquired ability to think in English. When I asked whether she translated most of her ideas from Chinese into English, she replied, "Yes, before I do, but now I think in English because it takes a long time to translate from Chinese into English." Lan explained that this change had happened during her semester with me and specified that it "really happened when I start to do freewriting or journals." Lan felt the great improvement in the grammatical correctness of her writing, which I too had noticed, was related to her increased ability to think in English, which usually eliminated the need to translate.

Not all of the students, however, were as enthusiastic about freewriting as Lan was. The case study that follows suggests some of the reasons why journal writing is not universally popular or successful for second-language learners.

KIYOKO: DOUBTS ABOUT JOURNAL WRITING

I chose to interview Kiyoko because I judged her to be one of the more reflective writers based on her journals and essays. The extract that follows, in which she pondered the meaning of *A Place for Us*, gives some idea of the quality I found so appealing in her journal writing:

> [In the book] Christos [the father] becomes an old person so quickly (at least I felt so, because I had to read quickly). So I had to face the sadness because I felt that Christos became old and so fragile and poor in health. I was reading the great saga of the Greek family. It made me sorrowful and uncomfortable because their lapse of time passed so quickly. I saw their history, struggles, and their sorrows. I saw the lifelong story of the clan and had a glimpse of their life in such a short time. As if their profound sighs and murmurs reach my ears. So my thoughts and the mixed emotions could not catch up with my reading speed.

Not only was I impressed by the poetic, reflective quality of Kiyoko's journal writing, but I also sensed that her fluency and comfort with English had increased tremendously during the semester. I thought journal writing might have been a factor in that improvement. So it came as a surprise when Kiyoko told me during the first interview that she did not believe her writing had improved and that she had negative feelings about the journal.

This revelation was just the beginning of a challenging experience in student–teacher communication. Sometimes the strain was related to language difficulties. During the interviews I often had to slow my speech considerably, and even then I sometimes had to rephrase questions two or three times. Despite these communication difficulties, however, I respected Kiyoko's diligence as a student and valued her seriousness and honesty as an interview participant.

When I mentioned to Kiyoko in the first interview that I thought her fluency had improved tremendously, she broke in to say, "You say my writing had been improved, but I don't think so." I was surprised by this statement since she knew by then that she had passed the final exam. Kiyoko did not have her journal with her for this interview, but I asked her to bring it the next time so we could examine it more closely for signs of writing development. In fact, within the space of a few minutes I asked her five times to bring her journal to our next interview. This is how I put it the fourth time around:

It's interesting that I had the sense that your writing changed more than almost anyone else. But you weren't conscious of it. So it'll be interesting to see why I thought your writing improved so much. And the only way we can do that is to look at your journal.

I also asked her to bring some of the essays she had written for other courses.

Two weeks later, when Kiyoko arrived for the second interview, I was astonished when she told me that she had thrown away her entire journal while cleaning her apartment. She had, however, brought along some of the essays she had written for content classes and two essays from my class. I will never fully understand why Kiyoko, a serious student and a conscientious research participant, knowingly destroyed valuable data. But I suspect that because her conception of what writing should be was very different from my own, she felt seriously compromised by the journal and wanted to put it behind her as quickly as possible.

Although I do not have Kiyoko's complete journal to analyze—I had made copies of several entries such as the one included before—her frustration has caused me to face the realization that journal writing was not a satisfying experience for all of my students.

Frustration With Freewriting

There were many indications in the interviews that, for Kiyoko, keeping a journal had been a frustrating experience in which she felt compelled to follow my instructions even when they clashed with her own ideas about "good" writing. When Kiyoko voiced her dissatisfaction with my requirement to write at least five pages a week in the journal, I apologized for not having emphasized quality more than quantity and said that perhaps I gave "the wrong impression" about how to use a journal. Kiyoko went on to explain that having to do an assignment just to satisfy a teacher was not a new experience for her: "It's usual in Japan, in school system in Japan."

In spite of her doubts about journal writing, Kiyoko spent about 2 hours a week producing the required five pages and submitted her journal dutifully throughout the semester. For the first 2 months, she wrote about her reactions to A Place for Us. As she explained, "For me it was easy to describe about the book than personal things." When the class finished the book, Kiyoko again took my suggestion and used the journal to describe her feelings about and preparations for the final exam. She was quite clear in explaining how she decided what to write about: "I followed the directions which you gave me [referring to the letter to students I distributed before spring vacation].... The direction said: 'Write like this.'" When I inquired how she felt about being asked to write about the final exam, she said, "I didn't mind. But just I said, 'I *have* to follow the directions.'"

The following excerpt from the second interview gives an indication of Kiyoko's negative feelings about journal writing:

> **Kiyoko:** But even if I didn't have any ideas, I have to write. So I don't have, good mem-, I don't know how to say, about journals. I don't have any comfortable memory of [laughs]/
>
> **Rebecca:** /Uh-huh, [echoing] comfortable memory.
>
> **Kiyoko:** Because I *have to*, *I had to write*. Continue to write so I didn't think of ideas or anything. Just too casual.

Perhaps one reason for Kiyoko's discomfort with journal writing was that she was not able to build on positive experiences with journal writing in the past as Lan had done. When I asked whether she had ever kept a journal, either in English or Japanese, she said she had tried keeping a diary once while she was still in Japan but abandoned her efforts after 2 or 3 days because it was "too boring."

In Kiyoko's view, a major problem of journal writing was its lack of formality. She explained:

> Sometimes, journals can be, I don't know [pause], too casual.... So I didn't care so much to think.... Maybe it depends on each person. But for me, if I get title on more formal essay, I feel, I don't know, I feel I have to try hard, harder. Because formal writing, I don't know, maybe it's better for me. If I want to write good writing.

This comment sheds light on two of the problems Kiyoko was facing. First of all, she felt constrained to follow the advice I had given on the day I introduced the concept of freewriting. The transcript of this class session reveals that I had said to the students:

> So that's the practice we'll be using for all the journal writing—freewriting. You don't have to get all bogged down about making it perfect, having it correct. Just write a lot. Get your ideas out of your head, onto the paper.

Looking back at these words, I realize that I was sending conflicting messages, essentially "forcing" the students to be "free" and implying that only one writing technique could be used for the journals. Luckily, most students felt free to disregard this advice when they found that freewriting didn't work for them. Roberto, for example, made lists of subjects he might like to write about in his journal and thought about each topic carefully before he put pen to paper. When Lan found that she was writing some things she didn't want to share, she started a private journal that no one else would read. And when Maribel had trouble deciding what to write about for my class, she turned in journals written for her reading class instead. Kiyoko, on the other hand, was in a frustrating double bind: She felt obligated to follow my original instructions exactly, but she didn't like freewriting and didn't believe it would lead to improvement in her writing. During an interview she admitted that she postponed doing the journal until all her other work was completed, and often didn't give it her full attention: "Sometimes, I [laughing], I feel sorry for you, but sometimes I was writing with watching TV. So maybe the quality of my journals wasn't good."

What seemed to bother Kiyoko most about freewriting was the lack of a clear focus or, as she referred to it several times in the interviews, a "title." As she explained in the second interview:

> **Kiyoko:** If I have to write some essay, I think with title … so maybe I organize. But journal is like a draft.
> **Rebecca:** Right. Not even like a draft, even looser than a draft.
> **Kiyoko:** It's kind of draft so I don't have to pay attention about anything.

In order to see if I was understanding Kiyoko correctly, I echoed what I heard her saying:

> **Rebecca:** It seemed to be that it bothered you that there was really no focus for the journals.
> **Kiyoko:** Yes, yes.
> **Rebecca:** Like a title. That you were just sort of wandering, aimlessly, wandering around in your writing.
> **Kiyoko:** Yes. Exactly.
> **Rebecca:** And you wanted to put it into some sort of a form.
> **Kiyoko:** Yes.

Kiyoko confirmed that the freedom to choose topics and to pay minimal attention to organization, which Roberto and Lan had found liberating, was threatening to her.

In explaining why she didn't feel journal writing had helped her, Kiyoko focused on its "freedom": "When I write journals, I don't know how to say it, anyway, I write freely." Of course, this is exactly what I had hoped the students would do, and perhaps one of the reasons I had liked Kiyoko's journal so much. But for her, this freedom was disturbing: "Because in writing [journals], ... I don't pay attention grammar, anything. Just I continue to write." If I were to look at this comment out of context, I would see it as an important validation of the freewriting process. I was hoping that the students would develop their English fluency by writing more freely in their journals, temporarily suspending the "monitor" (Krashen, 1981) that often inhibits second language acquisition. But for Kiyoko this supposed freedom represented a serious conflict with her own views about how writing should be done.

Differing Concepts of "Good Writing"

Although I was disappointed that Kiyoko had not found journal writing rewarding and that she had not felt free to modify my original instructions for freewriting, I also learned during the interviews that in other ways she had been one of the most active and independent learners in the class. Throughout the semester Kiyoko had been consciously trying to assimilate new attitudes toward her own education, and particularly toward herself as a writer of English. In fact, she had been one of the most resourceful students in the class in trying to understand what kind of writing was rewarded in my class and analyzing how this writing differed from the writing she had done for other U.S. college courses. These active efforts provided a striking contrast to the more conformist side of her, depicted earlier in this chapter.

Kiyoko's attempts to understand the varying types of writing she was encountering as a U.S. college student centered on two major questions: How does writing for the developmental English courses differ from writing required in the content areas? And how do American writers deal with issues of complexity or ambiguity?

In trying to answer the first question, Kiyoko adopted a proactive strategy I wouldn't have expected from a student who rarely spoke in class and who felt obliged to follow my directions for journal writing precisely. Fairly early in the semester Kiyoko began to borrow and photocopy the papers of other students in the class. This led to an important discovery. From reading these papers and studying my comments, she concluded that the type of writing that I, and the evaluators of the final exam, were looking for was what she termed "spoken English" as opposed to the "written English" she had been using in papers for the content courses.

In trying to understand what the terms "spoken English" and "written English" meant to Kiyoko, I asked her about the rather strict levels of formality that exist in the Japanese language. As she explained, "Writing has to be *formal*. Not spoken Japanese. Written Japanese has to be written Japanese and formal." In fact, Japanese has several different levels of formality, sometimes even with different vocabulary. According to Kiyoko, most of the writing she did for my course was comparable to the "spoken-style" language she would use for writing personal letters in Japanese, a type of language she would never choose for a school assignment. Not surprisingly, Kiyoko was more comfortable with the "written-style" language that was considered appropriate in content courses such as anthropology and sociology, and she was pleased with the grades she received, usually As and Bs. Her pride in these essays was demonstrated by her decision to save them and bring them along as samples of her writing to the same interview during which she told me she had thrown her journal away.

The second question about writing that Kiyoko investigated was how American writers deal with complexity and ambiguity, or as she expressed it, the "gray" areas. In her last journal entry of the semester, she addressed this issue:

> I'm beginning to understand how I should try [to write on the] writing test. And I think there are something special skills to pass the exam as well as our abilities. If we know the skills, we may pass. For example, writing in English seems so different from my native language. So I should forget about Japanese way of writing. In English, it has to be everything so clear, sometimes too clear, while Japanese way of writing prefers some shading of things. In the beginning it was too confusing to me. But now I'm beginning to understand that. Probably there is a perception gap between the two cultures. And it comes from perhaps the different sense of value between the cultures.

Kiyoko's active interest in this issue of shading was apparent in the interviews, where she interrupted to ask questions regarding American concepts of good writing. As she posed the question in our first interview, "In Japan we can choose gray, between black and white. But how about in this country? We must choose black or white?"

I quickly answered, "No," and went on to illustrate how I would approach an essay on the question of whether the home or the school should be responsible for sex education. I explained that I would probably qualify my thesis: "Given the reality of the situation, it's important that sex education be the responsibility of both the home and the school." I asked Kiyoko, "So, would you call that gray?" She said, "Yes ... cause it's controversial."

Kiyoko was concerned about what she perceived as the American tendency to oversimplify complex ideas: "I thought American people must choose A or B, black or white." When I explained that it was possible to admit complexity, to write from the gray area, she seemed relieved: "I'm glad."

What impresses me as I look back at Kiyoko's experience in the course is her early recognition that she was dealing with varying concepts of "good writing" and her efforts to learn more by questioning her classmates and later her teacher. In this active exploration, Kiyoko was learning not only about American writing styles but also about cultural expectations. She expressed this idea in her final journal entry for the semester, "It is also interesting to know and learn how to write in another language besides our native language. From writing experience I can learn the values of this culture as well."

Changing Attitudes Toward Writing in English

According to Kiyoko, near the end of the semester she began to feel more positive about writing in English. Initially, she had felt ambivalent about being in the ESL writing course. When I asked students to write about their feelings on being in the class about 3 weeks into the course, Kiyoko explained:

> Actually I do not like or I should not say like this in front of you (my professor) but I am not good at writing. The first day of the class, I felt so tired because I realized that from now on I have to write in great deals. But the class was fine and the atmosphere was nice. And the professor did not intimidate us about writing. I felt rather free in the class. Actually I do not dislike writing. I'm just not good at it.

Then near the end of the semester, she described how her attitude had changed:

> Before I took this course, I actually wanted to avoid taking writing courses if possible. But during this semester, we have been writing in great deals and we write about various kinds of subjects. So I think I could familiarize my self with writing by taking this course. And perhaps I came to like writing.
>
> And I believe that the enthusiasm of the professor for teaching is the most important. I believe that the value of the class would depend greatly on the professor's attitude. And I like to read the professor's reaction about my writing because I can know how I did on my writing and [written in later] for the

correction of my grammar & spelling mistakes. So I appreciate your attitude because you write the reactions of our writing everytime and even give us long type written reactions for the journals. And you often pay attention to each individual person & writing and have short meeting with us....

So I wanted to express my gratitude to you in this journal. It is really amazing because I came to like writing in English. I used to like writing in Japanese but not in English before.

Given all the difficulties Kiyoko had experienced, particularly with the journal, I found this changed attitude toward writing surprising. When I asked her what she felt led to the change, she said: "We wrote papers in great deal, so maybe I don't have to translate so frequently."

What she said about her increased ease in writing and her need to translate less frequently led me back to the journals:

> Rebecca: The journals, do you think that just writing in those journals, even if you weren't interested in it, might have helped you get that way or not?
>
> Kiyoko: But I think I didn't spend much time for journals. I think more for essay or/
>
> Rebecca: /Right. You didn't spend much time. What I'm wondering is whether just doing it even if you weren't very interested, even if the television was on, whether just doing it might have been one factor in English becoming easier. [pause]
>
> Kiyoko: By writing journal, I think, I mean, by taking your class, I think it becomes easier. Not only journal.
>
> Rebecca: Right. Journal was one part of it. We can't/
>
> Kiyoko: /Maybe/
>
> Rebecca: We don't know how important it was. Because added together all the other writing/
>
> Kiyoko: /I think, I think I should agree with you. It's a part, part of writing. [more softly] Journal's a part of writing.
>
> Rebecca: But you did a lot of other writing too besides the journals, and maybe if we had it all here/
>
> Kiyoko: /I think I agree with you. [laughs]

In this exchange from our final interview, Kiyoko and I are holding on to our deeply felt positions in a kind of verbal tug of war. Of course, I can see my face-work to protect the student's self-image ("You did a lot of other writing besides the journals") as well as Kiyoko's need to respect her teacher's opinion ("I think I should agree with you"). Nevertheless, our positions are fairly clear. I thought the journal helped Kiyoko to become more fluent in English, and she did not. There is no definitive way to prove either of our positions.

But Kiyoko's frustrating experience with the journal has taught me several important lessons. The most significant one is the need for teachers to keep the lines of communication open by encouraging students to talk or write about their reactions to newly introduced pedagogical techniques such as freewriting. Had I known earlier about Kiyoko's problems with this approach, we could have worked together to adapt the journal to accommodate her preferred writing and learning styles. Despite Kiyoko's lack of enthusiasm for journal writing, however, it is still possible that regular freewriting played a significant role in her improved fluency in English, an improvement that both of us had noticed.

About the same time that Kiyoko felt that writing in English was becoming easier, I also perceived a tremendous growth in her fluency. As I expressed it in the interview:

> That might help to explain what I was seeing because especially in the last month, all of a sudden your writing seemed so different. And I think probably I was seeing the real you that I would see if I could read Japanese. You know, I was seeing your ideas, your real ideas. Somehow, [more softly] I think that might be important.

Of course, another possibility is that Kiyoko had simply learned to present her ideas in a way that was more in keeping with my own preferences. What I do find significant, however, is that Kiyoko said she began to enjoy writing in English although she couldn't really explain why.

THE VALUE OF CASES
FOR REFLECTIVE PRACTICE

Before the interviews I never would have predicted that Lan and Kiyoko would have such different reactions to and experiences with journal writing. When I learned of their differences, I wanted to know why. I was especially curious about Kiyoko's discomfort with journal writing and searched for a cultural explanation. Maybe, I reasoned, Japanese students are not comfortable with informal writing. Initially, I suspected that the journal might be an alien form for Japanese writers.[1] I wondered if Japanese students might be

---

[1] I later learned that diaries, in the form of "pillow books," were kept by Japanese women in the 10th century, hundreds of years before diaries or journals originated in the West (Lowenstein, 1987).

uncomfortable with freewriting because they have been trained in Japan to regard correctness as more important than content.

After consulting the scholarly literature, I found sources to support most of these generalizations. And yet the transcript of my interviews with Kiyoko and my past experience with other Japanese students who had enjoyed journal writing didn't support such a simplistic solution. Surely, Kiyoko's acculturation and previous education in Japan were important influences on her attitude toward journal writing, but many other forces were at work here as well—forces to which I as a teacher and even as an ethnographic interviewer did not have access. In an article on culturally influenced approaches to reading, Parry (1996) cautioned against the simplistic assumption of culture as causality:

> Although knowing about central tendencies within cultural groups is useful, it is dangerous if it leads teachers to characterize groups and individuals in terms of easy dichotomies; it may lead teachers to assume that they understand the students in their classes without looking at them as individuals. (p. 667)

Finally, after months of puzzling over the case study of Kiyoko, I realize that the difficulty was not Kiyoko's dislike of journal writing but rather my quest for solutions. I have now come to realize that in order to be useful to other teachers and researchers, the problems posed by Kiyoko and the other students described in this book do not have to be solved once and for all. Ironically, it is really the problems that are useful, not some attempts at all-purpose solutions. The moral of this story, one that teachers always need to keep in mind, is that in teaching we should expect the unexpected. We can never predict exactly how a given student will respond to a particular teaching technique, but we *can* expect that students will not all respond in the same way. This is true whether the students were all born and educated in the same country or in many different countries.

Studies like this one are helpful not because they provide solutions that can be applied without further thought; instead their usefulness lies in the problems they raise and in the thick descriptions of student and teacher behavior that increase the experiential database from which teachers can operate as reflective practitioners (Schön, 1983).

In their influential book on teacher research, Cochran-Smith and Lytle explained the need for "rich classroom cases," which they feel "are often more powerful and memorable influences on decision making than are conventional research findings in the form of rules and generalizations"

(1993, p. 20). Certainly, the case studies of Lan and Kiyoko do not yield a set of neat rules or generalizations. What they do very effectively, however, is to remind us of the complexities inherent in every teacher's daily decision making.

In the next chapter I discuss what I have learned from the experiences of the five students described in this book. I also show how some of my initial interpretations and responses—often based on commonly accepted assumptions about writing and learning—turned out to be wrong or at least overly simplistic. As we move into the final chapter, I encourage readers to engage in the analytic process along with me, making their own connections and reflecting on their own practice.

8

The Conversation Continues

There is neither a first nor a last word and there are no limits to the dialogic context (it extends into the boundless past and the boundless future). Even *past* meanings, that is, those born in the dialogue of past centuries, can never be stable (finalized, ended once and for all)—they will always change (be renewed) in the process of subsequent future development of the dialogue. (Bakhtin, 1986)

As I begin to write the final chapter, I wish I could meet again with Roberto, Cliff, Maribel, Lan, and Kiyoko. I'd like to talk to them about their experiences in college and in life, to ask whether they think any lasting changes resulted from the journals they kept for my course. As often happens in teachers' lives, however, the students have slipped out of reach. Several years ago as I was completing the initial research report, I was able to contact Roberto, Maribel, and Lan by phone. In those brief conversations I asked about their college life in the year following the interviews.

Because of financial problems, Roberto had taken a full-time job and was attending classes at night. As a result of his busy schedule, his grades had slipped, and he was eagerly anticipating the fall semester, when he intended to enroll again in college as a full-time student. Journal writing had continued to play an important though inconstant role in his life in the intervening months. Sometimes he had felt the need to write about personal problems, and he had worked out a way to do this during his lunch hours in the office where he worked. He wrote freely on one of the office computers and then, feeling relieved after expressing his thoughts in writing, deleted the file to preserve his privacy.

Maribel was still enrolled in college full time but was having problems in some of her courses. She was especially worried about her communications course because she had failed the midterm exam. She told me that she had difficulty with the course reading. The assignments were long, and she had trouble sorting the main ideas from the details so that she could effectively review for tests. After learning the results of the midterm, she scheduled an appointment with her professor and asked his advice. According to Maribel, he tried to be supportive but wasn't able to provide the individualized tutoring she needed because of the large size of the class, which included more than 60 students. When I asked Maribel whether she had continued to write in her journal, she said she hadn't.

Lan was the third student I was able to contact. Having finally passed the writing exam, she was free to take courses in her major, early childhood education. She was enjoying these courses immensely and consistently getting As in them. In the past two semesters Lan had discovered that by using English to communicate in speech and writing about her area of interest, the education of young children, her proficiency in the language was increasing dramatically. As I talked with her on the phone, I was struck by her increased self-confidence and the improved clarity of her speech. When I asked whether she had continued to keep a journal, she laughed and told me that although she didn't write regularly, she still had her "private English journal," in which she occasionally recorded her thoughts and feelings.

Unfortunately, I wasn't able to locate Cliff and Kiyoko. And now, several years later, I have lost contact with the other three students as well. But even though I am no longer in touch with the students, my conversations with them are far from over. On the contrary, during the period in which I have been analyzing and interpreting their journals and interviews, it is as if we have been engaged in an ongoing dialogue. My experience in this lengthy conversation confirms a phenomenon that qualitative researchers are fond of citing as a characteristic of this type of research: the data have continued to talk to me (Ely et al., 1991). As a result of this continuing conversation, my understanding has evolved—often complicating and sometimes contradicting my initial interpretations, and occasionally challenging commonly held assumptions about writing and learning.

QUESTIONABLE ASSUMPTIONS

I would like to begin this section by talking about stereotypes, for in each of the points discussed later, I reveal how my initial assumptions—in most cases assumptions based on my understanding of current research—proved, upon close analysis of specific cases, to be overly simplistic. This discussion underscores just how difficult it is for teachers to go beyond stereotypes in dealing with the daily problems of teaching, as most such generalizations have their basis in cumulative experience. Having expectations is an important part of how we survive in the world, and in the classroom. And more often than not we draw upon these expectations consciously or unconsciously in deciding how to handle a particular student in a particular situation. What I have learned from looking closely at the experiences of the five students described in this book is not to dismiss all preconceptions—that would clearly be disastrous—but rather to recognize situations where the stereotypes don't apply, where they impede our ability to solve problems.

In the sections that follow I discuss five of my initial assumptions that later proved inadequate for explaining the data in this study. I hope that readers will use this discussion not as the basis for a new set of stereotypes, but rather as a reminder of the complexity of our work as teachers.

Personal Writing Comes More Naturally to Women Than to Men

It is generally accepted by writing teachers and by the public at large that female students are more likely than their male counterparts to be comfortable writing about highly personal or emotional subjects. One doesn't have to look far to find examples of this assumption in casual conversations among teachers or in articles in professional publications. Consider, for example, this quotation from a recent article in *College English*:

> Throughout history, women's worlds have been considered the personal and interpersonal, emotion and relationship, sociality and self-development, and though feminism has allowed women to transcend these personal worlds it has never encouraged leaving them or ignoring their importance. Young men, on the other hand, are seldom encouraged to consider the personal worlds of feeling and relationship in any except the most narrowly focused ways. (Connors, 1996, p. 146)

Like Robert Connors, a respected figure in the field of composition, I expected that female students would be more likely to use their journals to explore personal issues and that male students would shy away from these areas. But after reading the students' journal entries, I realized that this bipolar distinction along gender lines was overly simplified. While some women did use their journals for personal and expressive writing, some of the men did as well.

Among the five students I interviewed, it was the two young men who most often included personal writing in their journals. Roberto and Cliff seemed eager to share stories about personal struggles, stories that were often deeply emotional. Roberto's writing about his problematic relationship with his father and Cliff's narratives dealing with his illness were highly personalized accounts of emotional themes in their lives.

It is intriguing that none of the three women engaged in personal writing to this extent. Maribel carefully guarded her thoughts and opinions, perhaps because to write about them in a journal that would be read by a teacher violated her strong sense of family privacy. Lan was more comfortable with personal subject matter, using her journal to communicate directly with me about issues that affected her life as a student. But when she began to write about her life outside of school, she started a "private English journal," where she felt she could express herself more freely. Kiyoko's negative reaction to journal writing was complex, and I don't pretend to understand it fully. But I am sure that her decision to throw the journal away while cleaning her apartment a few weeks after the course ended was not solely a matter of housekeeping. It was a sign that she was deeply conflicted about the writing she had done in this journal. Some of her discomfort derived from the personal aspect of journal writing, which she described as "spoken English." In her native Japan, she explained during an interview, it would not have been proper to use the spoken form of the language in writing submitted to a teacher. For this reason, she was more comfortable with the traditional academic writing she had done for other college courses, which she described as "written English" and "formal." For Kiyoko, the personal and informal aspects of the journal were sources of deep dissatisfaction.

As I reflect on the reasons for the students' differing views on the appropriateness of including personal writing in a school journal, I can see the oversimplified nature of my initial assumption that personal writing is a female form. In making this assumption, I was categorizing as personal writing not only my students' compositions and journals but also personal diaries and letters, forms that are not done for school but rather for the writer himself or herself or for communication with a specific correspondent one knows well. The changed audience for personal writing when it is done for a school assignment changes many other things as well.

In my sample of five second-language writers, the interviews revealed that the men and women had a different sense of the teacher as audience and that Roberto and Cliff felt free to use their journals in ways that Maribel, Lan, and Kiyoko did not. Often these ways had to do with an unspoken belief that their personal stories mattered and would be of interest to their teacher/reader. In their journals Roberto and Cliff presented themselves as protagonists of their own life stories. And I as the reader (and a woman) welcomed this heroic voice from the two young men and encouraged it with enthusiastic comments in my letters of response.

In considering the different ways in which the students used their journals, we cannot ignore the distinction between public and private. Although I had not conceived of the journals as public documents, the students never lost sight of the fact that they were required for a college course and would be read by a teacher. Seen in this way, it may not have been an anomaly that the two young men felt most free to relate their personal sagas. As Jane Miller (1996) has pointed out, despite the assumption by most teachers that women are more comfortable with autobiographical writing than men are, most published autobiographies are written by male authors and often follow a prescribed form in which the protagonist overcomes various obstacles before emerging victorious. The personal narratives with which Roberto and Cliff began their journals conformed to the requirements of this genre. Later entries in Roberto's journal were undoubtedly influenced by the autobiographical style of the assigned course reading, in which Nicholas Gage told the classic story of an immigrant boy's success in his new country.

Carolyn Heilbrun (1988) reminded us that female students do not have a similar tradition, although there have been significant stirrings of change since 1970. As Heilbrun pointed out, "Anonymity, we have long believed, is the proper condition of woman" (p. 12), a condition she described as "storyless" (p. 12). This lack of story was, in her view, related to power relations between the sexes. Because women (and men) have been conditioned to believe that the quest for power is unwomanly, "women have been deprived of the narratives, or the texts, plots, or examples, by which they might assume power over—take control of—their own lives" (p. 17). I don't think it was an accident that among the five students in this study, only the two young men asserted the right to "author" stories in which they were the heroes.

The commonly accepted view that men are not comfortable with personal or emotional writing was subjected to closer scrutiny by Kathleen Dixon in an essay entitled "Gendering the 'Personal.'" Dixon problematized gender stereotypes related to personal writing, pointing out ways in which the public and the personal often merge when men tell their stories:

> Despite our claims to objective, distanced knowledge, emotions do not go unexpressed in (masculine, middle-class) academe; indeed, academe and the larger polis are constructed so as to give voice to emotions that are expressed in masculine terms, and by masculine conventions. Pain that is the result of

masculine and/or class competition that is borne heroically (emphasizing the independence of the male subject, his ability to stand alone and distinguish himself from others)—pain so inscribed may be expressed in the most dramatic ways. (Dixon, 1995, p. 273)

This description accurately characterizes the style and subject matter of the stories Cliff and Roberto told in their journals. And in hindsight, I realize that my reactions as a teacher were conditioned by gender expectations as well. My effusive response letters to Roberto and Cliff demonstrate without a doubt that I enjoyed the way these young men used the journal to validate themselves in the traditional epic form. Would I have been as open to similar validation stories coming from female students? I certainly hope so. I wish I could say that gender plays no role in how I respond to student writing. But after looking closely at my written and spoken responses to the students in this study, I doubt whether I have transcended the unconscious ways that gender influences my expectations and reactions as a teacher. As this study and many others have made clear, there is nothing simple or simplistic about the ways in which gender intersects with authorship and with readers' interpretations of texts. Teachers' unwitting ways of reinforcing gender stereotypes are subtle but pervasive as revealed by a recent study of how the writer's gender (or even imagined gender) influences teachers' reactions to student writing (Haswell & Haswell, 1995).

What I learned from my own study is not to ignore gender but rather to attempt to look beyond the stereotypes and to encourage my students to do the same as they explore the different ways journal writing can be useful to them. Heilbrun (1988), in concurring with the ideas presented in an essay by Jehlen (1984), asserted that only by learning to act in "the public domain" will a woman achieve "the right to her own story" (p. 17). If Heilbrun and Jehlen are correct, and I suspect they are, then encouraging all students—women as well as men—to tell their stories in the public setting of a college class is a worthy goal.

Native Culture Is the Most Important Determinant of How Second-Language Students Respond to Different Types of Writing

The previous section called attention to the ways in which teachers often fall prey to unsubstantiated assumptions about the effect of gender on student writing. Of course, the same could be said of culture, which may be an even more powerful construct than gender among teachers of second-language students. How often have I heard myself (and other ESL teachers) say things like "Russian students don't like small-group work" or "Chinese students won't talk in the large group" or "Haitian students love to engage in heated discussions"? With the challenges posed by an increasingly diverse student population, the tendency for teachers to make generalizations about students from different cultures is understandable. There is usually some validity at the core of such stereotypes, and they sometimes provide a useful first step in enabling teachers to adapt their teaching to meet the needs of culturally diverse students.[1]

If, however, generalized assumptions about different cultural groups are relied on exclusively without further thought, they can lead to a dangerous oversimplification of the complexities of intercultural teaching and learning. A further problem with basing explanations students' learning styles solely on their native culture is that students from other countries who are attending U.S. colleges and universities can no longer be regarded as monocultural. As Ruth Spack (1996) pointed out in a book review entitled "Teaching Across Cultures," "Students who literally and figuratively crisscross borders are not just products of culture; they are creators of culture" (p. 596). Thus, Spack cautioned teachers "to avoid simplistic generalizations about groups of writers and what they are likely to do as a result of their language or cultural background" (p. 596).

My attempt to explain Lan's and Kiyoko's reactions to journal writing as culturally determined illustrates some of the pitfalls of this approach. At first, I categorized Lan and Kiyoko as Asian women and was therefore surprised when their reactions to journal writing turned out to be so different. Yet the more I analyzed the cases, the more I realized that the ways in which these two students differed were far more significant than the ways in which they were similar. Starting with the obvious fact that Japan and China are different countries with very different cultures, I proceeded to more ephemeral differences between Lan and Kiyoko.

Finally, I realized that whereas Kiyoko's reaction to journal writing was certainly influenced by attitudes she had developed in her native Japan, her cultural background was only one piece of a much more complicated puzzle. My error, and I suspect one that other teachers make as well, was in

---

[1]As an example of the ways in which heightened cultural awareness can lead to improvements in instruction, I cite two articles that have influenced my teaching of reading to second-language students (Parry, 1996; Song, 1995). Both articles make a strong case for the powerful ways in which students' native cultures may influence their approaches to reading. Not only have these articles provided me with valuable background information, but I have sometimes shared them with students, who found them extremely useful.

mistaking one piece for the whole picture, thereby reducing a complex teaching problem to a study in black and white, as Kiyoko herself might have put it. In falling back on cultural determinism, I had erased the gray areas, where learning usually occurs.

Speaking from a practical point of view, even if Kiyoko's resistance to journal writing had derived solely from her cultural background, that knowledge would not have been terribly useful to me as a teacher. What was needed was not so much an explanation of where Kiyoko's problems with journal writing had originated, but rather a way of working with her to discover how she might use the journal as a constructive force in her learning.

Freewriting Is the Most Appropriate Technique for Journal Writing

In introducing journal writing to my students, I urged them to use the technique of freewriting, to just "think on paper" without stopping to edit their work. After the initial demonstration of freewriting during class, I didn't say much more about this technique, although I regularly gave the students prompts for in-class freewriting and asked them to include these pieces in their journals.

During the interviews I learned, much to my surprise, that the only one of the five students who had practiced true freewriting in the journal was Kiyoko, who felt bound to follow my instructions about how to write even though she found this approach unsettling. Roberto, whose journal appeared to me to be a pure stream of consciousness, actually took notes on his reading and spent hours planning what he would write for each week's journal. There was no pretense of freewriting in Cliff's journal because he often typed his entries on a computer and included earlier drafts, which he had edited and corrected. During an interview he told me that he needed to think about what he was going to write and that he often needed time for his ideas to "come into memory." Maribel's writing usually consisted of summaries of her reading, and she stopped to consult the text as she wrote. Lan actually did use freewriting but only in her private notebook. In an interview excerpt quoted earlier, she explained the writing process she used for her personal journal: "And sometimes I just write, and it's nonsense, you know. And sometimes I just start like this: 'I'm sitting here and writing, but I don't know what I'm going to write at this sentence.'" Lan told me that she felt this private journal helped her more than the "official" journal she turned in to me. But she didn't feel comfortable letting me read her uncensored freewriting.

As I considered the ways in which these students had adapted freewriting for use in their journals, I had to admit that, while freewriting has been an extremely helpful technique in my own writing, I too consciously modify the process to suit my own purposes. Sometimes, if I'm stuck in my writing, I will write freely for 5 or 10 minutes to get the ideas flowing again. But this was not the primary approach I used in the learning logs I wrote for graduate school. I usually took a lot of time to think before beginning to write and often edited my writing for substance and style.

By acknowledging the limitations of freewriting, I don't mean to imply that it is not a valuable writing strategy. For second-language students, writing quickly without being concerned about correctness often serves to suspend the monitor that may inhibit the development of fluency (Krashen, 1981). Moreover, in my own writing I have found that freewriting sometimes unleashes thoughts and words that otherwise remain locked inside.

It's important to point out that Peter Elbow (1973) intended freewriting to be a recursive process occurring over long periods as writers refine and shape their initial thoughts into polished prose. Problems occur, however, when a writer's first words on a subject also become the last. Perhaps this is what bothered students like Roberto and Cliff and probably Kiyoko as well. They knew they wouldn't return to revise what they had written in their journals. In addition, they felt that I would judge them as writers based on the quality of their journal writing. Roberto stated that he wanted to express his ideas in the journal "in a way that it's gonna look nice on paper." Cliff echoed this sentiment when he said, "I want to write it nicely." It was understandable that most students felt uncomfortable showing their raw writing to a teacher who had in effect been designated by the college as the arbiter of their writing competence. It's not a mere coincidence, therefore, that Elbow presented his theory of freewriting in a book entitled *Writing Without Teachers* (1973), for only in a teacherless writing class such as the one Elbow proposed will students feel liberated from the fear of being judged on the basis of their written words.

Returning to my study, what we see is a gap between what I said in class—to keep writing, without pausing to edit or correct—and what I and most of the students actually did—to experiment with our own techniques, using freewriting as one method in a larger repertoire. Obviously, the applicability of many strategies to journal writing is a subject I should have explored more openly with the students throughout the course. Asking them to talk and write about the methods they found most useful for their journals would have provided a valuable focus for small-group discussions. And it would have been a good idea to encourage the students to experiment with a variety of techniques, gradually discovering their own preferred approaches to journal writing.

Journal Writing Encourages Students to Engage in Connected Knowing

When I first encountered the concept of connected knowing in *Women's Ways of Knowing* (Belenky et al., 1986), it struck me with the force of revelation. I was convinced I had discovered the key to explaining why the learning logs I kept as part of my doctoral studies felt so much more rewarding to me as a writer and thinker than the academic papers I had written previously.

The sense of liberation I experienced when writing the learning logs was related primarily to the freedom from the demands of objectivity. In these informal learning journals, I no longer felt compelled to detach myself from my learning as I had when my writing was judged by the traditional standards of the academy, standards derived from separate knowing: "Separate knowers' procedures for making meaning are strictly impersonal. Feelings and personal beliefs are rigorously excluded" (Belenky et al., 1986, p. 109). In the learning logs, I welcomed the opportunity to draw on all my resources, invoking the private as well as the public, the emotional as well as the intellectual.

My affinity for connected knowing helped to explain my enthusiastic reception of the journal writing of Roberto, a young man who not only empathized with the characters in *A Place for Us* but also traveled across space and time to connect with concepts he encountered in his classics course. Roberto's journal provided the most dramatic and sustained example of the use of connected knowing, but many other students used this approach as well. I soon noticed, however, that not all students drew upon connected knowing in their journals. Students like Roberto, who were already connected knowers, saw journal writing as an opportunity to employ a preferred epistemological perspective. However, simply asking students to keep a journal didn't in itself transform students into connected knowers.

Partly because of my own epistemological preference, I had difficulty responding in helpful ways to journals in which students mainly summarized their reading rather than engaging with it in active ways. My discomfort, I later came to realize, resulted from a contradiction between my hope that students would use the journals to relate to their reading in a personal way and my professed aim, stated many times in the field log, that I wanted them to find *their own ways* to use the journal productively.

The issue I was grappling with is an important one for teachers. Do we have the right to use our considerable power to encourage students to adopt (or pretend to adopt) our own epistemological stances? This is an extremely difficult question and one that teachers must ultimately answer for themselves. I think it's unrealistic, however, to pretend that we can totally disguise our own stances toward learning. Most students are adept at figuring out where teachers are coming from and giving them what they want.

In my case, I have decided that the best approach is to be open about my values as a thinker and writer, without putting undue pressure on students to adopt these views—a difficult balancing act, to be sure. I will illustrate what I have in mind by referring to Linda, a student from the Dominican Republic whom I did not interview but often discussed in the field log. After reading Linda's first journal entry, in which she wrote about *A Place for Us*, I felt she would get more out of her reading and journal writing if she engaged with the book in a more direct way. In responding to her journal I wrote:

> I was especially interested in the part where you described Nicholas confronting his father. You said you thought this was a little "unfair." Think some more about why you feel this way. Do children have the right to confront their parents? Try to examine your own beliefs on this subject. (Note: I'm not criticizing your statement; I'd just like you to think about why you feel the way you do.)

Linda didn't answer this question in her next journal, which like the previous one consisted largely of a summary of her reading. But by the end of the semester I sensed the beginnings of epistemological change in Linda. She too was aware of a change. In her last journal she wrote:

> When I first started this class I didn't have motivation to write and read. I just used to do what the teachers assigned me to do. But now I woke up a desire in reading and writing about what matters are important to me and what is happening in our society nowadays.

Further proof of Linda's intellectual awakening was provided in another journal entry where she told of making a special trip to the library to look up the newspaper for the day she was born. Linda, it seemed, was becoming a more active learner while at the same time becoming aware of her own place in history. She might not have experienced this change without my intervention, and I think it was an important one in her intellectual development.

Another teacher who encourages students to engage with their learning in a personal way is Dan Morgan (1993), who described his pedagogical approach in an article entitled "Connecting Literature to Students' Lives." Although Morgan did not use the term *connected knowing* (see my commentary on his article in Mlynarczyk, 1994), he clearly advocated this approach in his community college literature classes. Morgan's hope is to empower students "to draw conclusions, comment, disagree, genuinely respond to the literature studied," and he measures his success "by whether they make thoughtful connections to their own lives and concerns" (p. 495). Not surprisingly, he requires his students to keep reading response journals, and in his article he quoted from a journal entry in which a student explained how the course had changed her attitude toward reading:

> As I was saying, every story, every poem, every book has related to my life in some way, sometimes happily, and sometimes sadly. As corny as it may sound, each one has given me more insight into my life. For a person like me who hates to read, you've given me the knowledge of how important and rewarding it can be. (p. 500)

These words suggest something I observed among my students as well—that making personal connections with academic material is an important part of the reflective process. In analyzing the thought processes of ESL students, Tarvin and Al-Arishi (1991) stated "… the value of reflection is personal; it brings an inner satisfaction that one has done one's best to confront an extraordinary situation" (p. 17). These authors believe that if students engage first in an inner reflective process of "intrapersonal testing," they will subsequently "approach the valuable public negotiation of meaning with greater confidence" (p. 17). The data from my study of student journal writing lend further support to the idea that there is often a personal element in reflection as students bring their own experiences to bear on the ideas they are encountering in school.

Student Journal Writing Is Private and Therefore Does Not Require an Outside Reader

In a presentation at the 1997 Conference on College Composition and Communication, Toby Fulwiler, editor of a widely read collection of essays on journal writing (1987), stated that in contrast with letters, which have the potential to become reflective dialogues, journals are essentially private notebooks. He went on to say that when he reads a student's journal, he feels as if he is looking over the writer's shoulder rather than participating in a conversation.

Although Fulwiler has done a great deal to promote the use of journals in academic settings, his position that journals are private has sometimes been interpreted in a way that is problematic. For example, some teachers have used this position to justify their decision not to comment on—or in some cases even to read—the journals they require for their courses. A case in point was described by Ann Johnstone (1994) in a study of journal writing in a college geology course. The professor in Johnstone's study required every student to keep a journal consisting of one entry for each day the class met, but he did not collect or read the journals during the course. He justified this pedagogical decision by referring to writing theory as it had been presented at a writing-across-the-curriculum workshop he had attended a few years earlier:

> I have consciously made the decision that I didn't want to interfere in the journals. I didn't want to say something that would indicate to the student or make the student think that I was thinking this is right, this is wrong. I think I should stay out of the journals. I justify my laziness—or, I interpret this on the basis of what … Toby Fulwiler … [said]: he said a piano teacher doesn't have to sit and listen to a student practice. You can assign writing without having to grade it or even having to read it …. This is an assignment for them to do for learning, not a grade, and certainly not my opinions on their opinions. (quoted in Johnstone, 1994, pp. 158–159)

The results of this nonintervention policy were disappointing. By providing no audience for the students' writing, the geology professor in Johnstone's study had ruled out the communicative element. Most of his students, sensing that they were writing in a conversational vacuum, abandoned the problem-posing approach the teacher had advocated, instead using their journals to summarize the reading or to recapitulate information presented in lectures. After classes ended, the professor gave the journals a cursory reading, but he wrote no comments and counted the journals as part of the students' grades only in borderline cases. Like the professor, the students assigned a low priority to these required journals. Very few of them bothered to pick up the journals from the professor's office after the course had ended.

By eliminating the communicative element, the professor had also eliminated the factor that motivates most students to invest time and energy in their journal writing. In actuality, it is the dialogic aspect of journal writing that, for most writers, accounts for its power and distinguishes it from the more monologic style of writing (sometimes recommended for school essays) in which ideas are presented as fixed and immutable. The experiences of the students in my study indicate the importance of this communicative element. They also strongly suggest that students write most reflectively when they conceive of their writing as part of an ongoing dialogue. There are, however, many forms that this reflective dialogue may assume.

Roberto, for example, was unusual in that the dialogue in his journal was primarily an introspective one, a conversation within his own mind. In his first journal entry, quoted as the epigraph for chapter 4, he invoked the image of the journal as listener: "No one will listen to you as a notebook can. No one will listen [to] your thoughts about politics, problems, love, faith as a good diary can. A piece of paper never lets you down." Although Roberto was comfortable having me read his journal, he neither needed nor wanted my suggestions for possible journal topics. While writing in the journal, he explained during an interview, "I don't really think about the reader. I really think about what I want to say." In the interviews Roberto revealed that in his mind, journal writing was a kind of inner debate. As he explained, "It makes you decide where you really are standing." Roberto's tendency to "talk to himself" has been noted in chapter 4, confirming his use of the journal as a kind of internal conversation conducted in the language of inner speech (Vygotsky, 1986). However, Roberto stated that he wouldn't have kept the journal if I hadn't required it, and he also made it clear that he was validated by my enthusiastic letters of response. He certainly wouldn't have spent so much time and effort on his journal if I had decided not to read and respond to it during the course.

Like Roberto, Cliff was a highly reflective writer with a habit of "talking to himself." But he required the comments of an interested reader to sustain his interest in and commitment to journal writing. As I read Cliff's journal, I felt that I was being invited into a conversation, and I responded with long, personalized letters. Cliff's responsiveness to the questions I asked in these letters is not surprising because his major concern, as expressed many times in his journal and interviews, was communicating effectively with his reader. At the end of the final interview when I asked Cliff if he thought he would continue writing in his journal after the course ended, his reply confirmed his strong need for reader response: "I don't think I'll do it if it is for myself. If I'm doing it for somebody else, I probably will do it. I want a response, personally. I need somebody else to read it and tell me what they think."

Lan actively managed her journal writing in a way that enabled her to get the best of two dialogic worlds. In her private journal she pursued an introspective dialogue, writing only for herself. Here she could relax and write secrets and nonsense words, freed from the delicate balancing act that always occurs when students write for teachers. In her class journal, on the other hand, she wrote directly to the teacher, frequently addressing me personally and consulting me about problems that affected her life as a student. Lan said that she was encouraged by the individualized responses I wrote. As she explained during the interviews, "If somebody asks you a question, you feel that means the person feels comfortable with you." Lan herself was clearly comfortable with the idea of using her journal to establish a relationship with me, seeking my advice as a trusted mentor in her academic decision making.

Kiyoko, however, was not comfortable using the journal for a written dialogue with me. The informal nature of journal writing and the notion that, in this type of writing, communication was more important than correctness contradicted her internalized notions of what college writing was supposed to be. However, although Kiyoko was discomfited by journal writing, she said she liked my written responses to her writing. On the end-of-semester questionnaire she attributed her changed attitude toward writing in English to this aspect of the course: "I appreciate your attitude because you write the reactions of our writing everytime and even give us long type written reactions for the journals. And you often pay attention to each individual person & writing and have short meeting with us." Although Kiyoko did not use her journal to address me in a personal way, she did value my individualized responses to her writing. Hence, even for Kiyoko it was the dialogic use of language that she identified as a positive force in her learning.

For Maribel, the communicative aspects of the journal and my responses were problematic. In her mind, writing done for school was different from writing done outside of school. As she expressed it in her first journal entry (used as the epigraph for chapter 6), she enjoyed writing in her native language as part of a meaningful dialogue with a correspondent she knew well: "When I recived letters from my friends, I love to answer them as soon as posible." But writing for school was much more threatening to Maribel. Not only was it done in her second language, but she thought of it as a formal exercise on which she would be assessed: "When I'm writing I'm always afraid to write something wrong, or write something that doesn't relate with the topic." Maribel's anxiety was understandable given that she perceived writing done for school not as communication with a reader, but as the basis for an evaluation (usually negative) of her work. And because she also felt uncomfortable writing about personal matters in the public context of school, it is not surprising that she did not see the journal as a chance to engage in a dialogue, either within her own mind or with me.

The absence of dialogue in Maribel's journal made it difficult for me to write meaningful letters of response. Throughout the semester I often used the field log to recount my frustration with journals like Maribel's that I described as unreflective. For example, about a month into the course I noted:

> When students just write summaries of the reading, it's hard for me to write a response. There's not a conversation. I try to ask some questions to encourage more reflection. But it's really hard, doesn't come naturally, and I often feel stuck.

I see now that my unconscious choice of metaphors was appropriate, as it was precisely the lack of reflective dialogue in such journal entries that made it difficult for me to respond.

At some level I was grappling with the same issue as the geology professor Johnstone's study (1994): I was unsure how much I should interfere in the students' journal writing processes. Based on my past teaching experience, I firmly believed that my responses were crucial in sustaining the students' motivation to keep writing; in my own classes and those of colleagues, I had seen that when teachers did not collect and respond to student journals, most students stopped writing. However, I was conflicted about how directive I should be in my letters of response. In the field log I kept repeating the idea that I wanted the students to have a sense of ownership of their journals and that they would know best how to use them. But eventually my frustration with what I perceived as the unreflective quality of certain students' journals forced me to take a more active role in determining how and what the students wrote. My first three letters of response to Maribel were written before I reached this decision, and consequently these letters were uninspired and only about half as long as the ones I wrote to Roberto and Cliff (see Appendixes B, C, and D for samples of these letters). Often I ended up praising Maribel's complete summaries rather than being more honest and suggesting ways I felt she could use her journal more productively.

When I finally decided to give Maribel more candid feedback about how I hoped she would use the journal by suggesting questions for her to address, she began to write more reflectively. Later, while analyzing her entire journal, I made another significant discovery. When I posed questions for in-class freewriting—for example, by asking the students to write about their definition of history or their own theories of education—Maribel's writing was much more reflective than when she devised her own topics for writing.

If the task was simply to write about her reading, Maribel fell back on the pattern she had used for her high school book reports, in which she summarized the reading and concluded with a general and undeveloped personal response. But when I supplied a direct question asking her to take a stand, she responded reflectively.

This suggests that different students may benefit from different instructions for journal writing. Open-ended journals work beautifully for students like Roberto and Cliff, who already conceive of writing as part of a dialogue. For such students, the freedom to choose their own topics is often empowering. But for students like Maribel, whose concept of school writing is much more limited, the provision of specific questions for journal writing may encourage written reflection that would not occur otherwise. Writing in response to a teacher's prompt often has a sense of dialogue built into it because the student is answering questions or discussing topics that the teacher has presented in order to promote reflection. When students respond to such questions, they engage in an important kind of learning by doing. And as they become accustomed to writing reflectively in their journals, they may begin to apply this approach in other areas of their education as well.

Recognizing the role of dialogue in student journal writing leads naturally to questions about the appropriate audience for such writing, for very few students will be motivated to write regularly if they do not have a responsive conversational partner. In the study described in this book, I devoted a lot of time and energy to writing individual letters of response. And the students' answers on the end-of-semester questionnaire indicated that they appreciated these letters. As one student wrote, "Always when I received my journals, I would read the letters from you first, like most students did. Sometimes I forgot what I had wrote. After I got my journal back, I was surprised that you mentioned my journals with your own feeling and encouragement."

It is not reasonable, however, to expect all teachers to respond at such length to their students' journals, and, in fact, I have had to modify my way of responding since completing this study. As a recently hired professor working toward tenure and promotion, I find that the uninterrupted hours I once spent writing individualized responses to student journals are now taken up with committee work, grant-funded activities, and writing for publication. So in my present teaching, I respond to student journals by writing comments in the margins of their papers.

There have been gains as well as losses in this new way of responding. Realizing that the students needed more response than I alone was able to supply, I have broadened the audience for journal writing. I explain to the students I currently teach, most of whom are recent immigrants to the United States, that they will be sharing their journals in peer response groups. The students meet once a week in groups of four or five to read their journals aloud and discuss them with classmates before turning them in to me. Although sharing the journals with peers may cause some students to write less freely, other students, especially those who have not kept journals in the past, are helped by seeing a range of possible approaches. In addition to heightening the social, communicative aspects of journal writing, asking the students to read their journals to classmates has enabled me to make them a more integral part of the curriculum, as students write about the books we are reading and explore important issues related to the course content.

Another way of encouraging students to use journals for written dialogues, and one that I have used successfully, is to set up journal exchanges between students in different classes. I also sometimes ask students to choose their own books to read and share their reading journals with a small group of classmates who are reading the same book (see Mlynarczyk, 1991b). In classes where students are reading several different books, journals provide an important means of communicating about these books, creating a dialogue among students as well as between teacher and student. E-mail journals also have great potential for enabling students to experience writing as communication (see Tillyer, 1993, 1994), although I haven't yet tried this technique in my own teaching.

To return to the assumption stated at the beginning of this section, I now believe that conceiving of journals as private is a serious oversimplification that may lead teachers not to utilize journals to their fullest potential as meaningful contributions to an ongoing conversation about ideas. Among the students described in this book, journals were most successful—and most reflective—when they were part of a continuing dialogue. Sometimes this dialogue was external, between interested partners; sometimes it was internal, an animated conversation within the writer's mind. But in both situations, the use of language was fluid and meaning-centered, as spoken conversations are at their most satisfying.

The possibility for meaningful dialogue is, of course, always inherent in language. But journal writing with its freedom from rules and restrictions is, for many writers, especially conducive to a reflective dialogue. Thus, the key to understanding the power of this multifaceted genre lies, it seems to me, in recognizing its roots in speech and writing. For while journals have the potential to approach the freshness of speech, they also benefit from the qualities inherent in writing—the permanence on the page that captures thought for later reflection and revision.

This was more or less the idea I expressed at the end of my final interview with Lan as we spoke of how writing can sometimes cause us to see past experiences in a new light:

> That's the thing about reflection. You keep looking back on your past. But somehow as you look back on things from a long time ago, you see them in a slightly different way; you see more connections. So it's really a process that lasts your whole life long, and I somehow feel that writing can be an important part of that process.

Throughout this study, as I periodically reviewed my field log, I was struck by the number of times I referred to student journals as conversations or dialogues. In retrospect, I also see that the dialogic nature of reflection was a recurring theme in much of the theoretical material that informed my analysis. Britton (1982) drew attention to the speechlike qualities of expressive writing. Cognitive researchers often describe reflection as similar to the turn-taking of speakers in a conversation (see, e.g., Scardamalia et al., 1984). And Belenky, Clinchy, Goldberger, and Tarule (1986) emphasized the dialogic, personally involved nature of connected knowing. The prevalence of the metaphor of dialogue in all of these theories suggests that human thought is patterned on the dynamics of speech, as Vygotsky (1986) surmised when he proposed that inner speech, or verbal thought, evolves from our earlier experience with social speech.

Just as dialogue is an important signal of reflection in student journal writing, so too it is an essential component of reflective teaching. According to Schön (1983), reflective teachers constantly monitor their teaching as they listen to the situation talking back to them: "The unique and uncertain situation comes to be understood through the attempt to change it, and changed through the attempt to understand it" (p. 132).

Since the completion of the interviews, I have noticed this phenomenon more than once. As I continue to reflect on the students and their journals, new questions constantly arise, causing my understandings to change and evolve. Often these questions emerge in conversations with colleagues. Several years ago, for example, I conducted a workshop at a professional conference in which the participants read excerpts from the students' journals and discussed their differing approaches to writing. A few days later, one of the workshop participants came up to me in a hallway. "I keep thinking about Maribel," she said. "I have so many students like her who don't really know what to write in journals. I keep wondering what we can do to help them use writing to develop their thinking." Obviously, Maribel was continuing to talk back to this teacher as she has to me in the 5 years since she was a student in my class.

The ways in which the conversations begun in the students' journals and interviews have continued in subsequent years is in keeping with Schön's (1983) idea of reflective practice in teaching. He spoke of "reflecting in action," and skilled teachers are adept at responding instantaneously to challenging situations that arise in working with students. But what I have done in writing this book is to "reflect *on* action," another process that Schön recommended, which in my case was greatly enhanced because I was working with written materials. By keeping a field log in which I recorded the fleeting moments of classroom life as well as my own thoughts about the students in my classes, I captured valuable data for later analysis. Because I had copies of the students' journals and interview transcripts, I was able to consult and reconsult them in a way that would not have been possible without these written records. In an article on her work with adolescent students in England, Jenifer Smith (1991) emphasized the benefits of recording the ephemera of classroom life in a teaching journal: "Once I had fixed something on the page I could return to think about it at leisure. The writing became an important part of my thinking about what was happening in the classroom. Writing was a part of change" (p. 77). I hope that, through reading this book, other teachers will be convinced of the possibility and desirability of undertaking studies of important issues in their classrooms. Those who don't wish to undertake a full-fledged research study can still gain much from spending an hour or two each week writing about their work in a teaching journal.

As I come to the end of this book, I ask myself what other teachers and researchers will gain from reading it. Recently, a subscriber to an e-mail list to which I belong raised questions about the usefulness of educational research:

> Do articles about how to teach writing solve problems? Do postings on this list solve problems? Can you recall specific postings/threads which significantly aided you in your teaching/research? What has been the role of educational research in your ongoing personal development as a teacher/researcher?

These questions gave me pause. After 5 years of study and analysis, I have raised more questions about student journal writing than I have answered.

Rather than supporting commonly accepted assumptions about writing and learning, my study has revealed these assumptions to be overly simplistic and inadequate for explaining the experiences of the students whose journals I analyzed. Will my findings be of use for other teachers and researchers and, if so, in what ways?

After giving serious consideration to these questions, I realized that studies like this one—qualitative research that looks closely at the experiences of real students and teachers—are crucial to the development of a literature of reflective practice. Elliot Eisner explained the rationale for scholarship that attempts to capture the rich complexity of problems in the social sciences:

> Research studies, even in related areas in the same field, create their own interpretive universe. Connections have to be built by readers, who must also make generalizations by analogy and extrapolation, not by a water-tight logic applied to a common language. Problems in the social sciences are more complex than putting the pieces of the puzzle together to create a single, unified picture. (1991, p. 210)

The contribution this book will make is not to solve teaching problems, but rather to heighten readers' sensitivity to and appreciation for the unexpected situations that occur in teaching—for example, the strong statement Kiyoko made when she threw away her journal or Lan's active decision to keep a private English journal so that she could write more freely. Schön spoke of "back-talk" as taking "the form of unanticipated meanings, problems, and dilemmas" (1983, p. 347). And it is really these complex and unanticipated occurrences, not a set of simple solutions, that make the work we do as teachers so rewarding and intellectually challenging. I hope that the case studies of Roberto, Cliff, Maribel, Lan, and Kiyoko will resonate for readers as they return to their own classrooms and consider how best to handle the complex problems that arise there.

Appendix A

Response Letters to Entire Class

April 30, 1992

Dear Students,

I didn't have time to write a separate letter to each one of you about your journals (although I did record which students turned the journals in to me). Instead, I thought I would respond in a letter to the whole class including a few quotes from what you said.

On the Interviewing Process: "It is totally not as easy as I thought about the interview: It is just preparing a list of questions then starting listening a story while making a few notes if it is necessary. In fact, a satisfactory interview may also require skill. For example, how to 'draw' the information from an interviewee. As the process of fishing, an interviewer might need to know how long a 'line' is proper to be thrown, when to draw it back in order to catch a big fish.... I have learnt that an interview should not only depend on the questions that I already had; it is important to note and ask the spontaneous questions from the information I get during the interview. As pushing the boat along with the current is for making use of an opportunity to gain its end."

On Finishing A Place for Us: "I have become an addict to books. Once I have finished the book, I try to read some other books in order to keep on my practice in reading. This is a good beginning. As far as I am concerned, I love and enjoy reading. I hope my desire for reading will never end."

Against Racism, Especially Important in Light of Recent News Events (the Los Angeles riots following the Rodney King verdict): "I learn here that we should love every person as a human being or individual not as a race or nationality. I love people; I don't have differences toward people. I accept all kind of human beings regardless their races, nationalities, sex or religions. I believe God has made all equal. We are brothers and sisters in God's eyes. We should love each other despite our differences."

How the Final Is Graded: "The final exam are graded from 1 to 6, 6 being the highest grade and 4 is passing. All the ESL teachers grade the exam. I don't know how long but I think it's about 20 min. [Actually about 2 minutes]. They're looking for basic understanding of how to write an essay—the standard essay form, right use of punctuation, paragraphs, sentences, etc. Maybe they are also looking for if you can use some outside source to combine in your essay. But whatever they're looking for, they should first give us extra credit for going through that 50 minutes of terror."

As usual, I was fascinated by all the different things you wrote about in your journals—the coming of spring, things that are happening at work and in your other classes, thoughts about your interviews and the upcoming final exam.

Have a good weekend, and enjoy reading these excerpts from the last set of journals.

Rebecca

May 19, 1992

Dear Students,

Your last journals for this course were so interesting that I wanted to share some of the ideas that were expressed. This letter contains quotations from the journals written in both sections of the course.

Several students used the journal to write about the tragic and historic events that have occurred in this country recently.

On the Los Angeles Riots: "I don't believe somebody can use someone's misery as an excuse to steal and murder. This is what is called fighting fire with fire. This shows no concern at all. Instead, it shows the ignorance of some animals. This is not about races. We were all mad about the jurors' decision. But we can't just go out killing people and damaging the business that cost them a life time of hard work and dedication. This is not the way to demonstrate anger...."

"I don't know what to say about the policemen who punched the guy. They are even worse than the so called 'demonstrators.' They hid in their uniforms to do the same garbage that today I condemned....

"The jurors have no pardon. Justice was given to them, i.e., the power to do justice. They should be locked up with the 'demonstrators' and the 'guardians of the law.' They shouldn't be part of our future."

Another Perspective on the Riots: "I do not agree about the Rodney King verdict. There was obvious evidence which was video tape and everyone in the United States saw it and felt terrible about it.... I believe that the police can not beat anyone as long as they do not do anything against the police. I still wonder why these police are innocent. Besides, because of this wrong verdict, LA was hell for several days and this rebellion affected many people, especially a lot of Korean's business, badly. Their businesses were burned out and some Koreans were killed. I do not know why Koreans were involved in this tragedy. I am not defending Koreans because I am a Korean. They are innocent, hard working, and peaceful people.... But Koreans were the first target of rebellion and they lost everything within several days. All of their property was changed to smoke and it has gone with the wind."

Since I had requested it, lots of you wrote entries related to the final exam. Here are some of your comments:

Cultural Differences in Writing: "I'm beginning to understand how I should try on the writing test. And I think there are some special skills to pass the exam as well as our abilities. If we know the skills, we may pass. For example, writing in English seems so different from my native language. So I should forget about the Japanese way of writing. In English, it has to be everything so clear, sometimes too clear, while Japanese way of writing prefers some shading of things. In the beginning it was too confusing to me. But now I'm beginning to understand that. Probably there is a perception gap between the two cultures. And it comes from perhaps the different sense of value between the cultures."

Being Aware of Your Own Progress: "The courses of English reading and writing are different from the courses of science and others because learning language takes time to build up the foundation, especially for the foreign students who have different backgrounds of English. If a student couldn't pass the final exam, it doesn't mean that he has not learned and gotten improvement from the course, but he might need more time to practice."

Last-Minute Preparations: "If I say that I am not afraid of taking this examination, nobody believes me. In the meantime, my concentration is to improve my writing and try to avoid the unnecessary careless mistakes. I have made many mistakes in both my essays and journals. However, it is not easy to correct them all in a sudden, especially within a few months time. No miracle can be found!

"... After three months hard working, it is time for me to slow down a little bit. Let the pressure inside me reduce to zero. Therefore, I take time to watch television, read the magazine and newspaper and talk with my friends in English. Of course, I am still doing my assignments. If I have enough sleep the night before the examination and my mind is sound with good health, I will definitely do it better."

I think this is very good advice. You have all worked very hard this semester, and your writing skills will come through for you on the day of the final.

Best of luck to you on Thursday and in the days ahead!

Rebecca

Appendix B

Selected Entries From Roberto's Journal and Teacher's Response Letters

1. Out-of-Class Journal Writing

2/9/92

I felt very familiar with the book *A Place for Us*. There wasn't a single thing that the little guy lived that I didn't, or, at least, similarly. The first thing that shocked me was the sacrifice that his mom Eleni did for him. Although my parents didn't have to give their lives for me, they left a culture where they were always welcomed to a place where nobody would know if you die. My dad gave up his lifetime savings to buy all the plain tickets, he gave up having his own business and here he can't get a job. All that my parents have in their mind is our future and they really push me into not giving up my dreams. The support I get from my mom is unbelievable. I can't think of loosing her, let me die before I have to see them leave, I couldn't handle it. I know my mom would give everything for me just as Eleni did. I also know I would too.

Another parallel is when he sees the american kids and feels kind of rudimentary because he wears decent and humbl clothes. You think they are not normal and are a bunch of jerks. Personally, I felt much more mature than them. The things that they did were childish I thought, and out of reason. I never saw kids beating up a weak little guy. I know exactly how the boy felt. Knowing that you had felt more pain than any of them could imagine makes you not fit in, not until you find someone with similar experiences. And not being able to afford their taste of clothes in that moment makes you stay away from them. Not knowing what they are saying makes you look at them defiantly. This is exactly how I felt towards my american cousins, they were born here and because of the ignorance of some parents, they didn't or I would say weren't allow to learn something about the old culture and who their grandparents, uncles, and even their parents' past. But I know how much they are missing because even if they got american last names to hide their background, they will never be able to hide their mothers. They (mothers) sure don't look american at all. I hate them for forgetting who they were....

Another stage was the one which we end chapter two. People bragging about america and how practical the people are. In the beginning you are shocked, later I found a big dissapointment. My uncle, when he went to Colombia, he convinced us that america was heaven. I have to be gratefull. I made [it] here but america is not all that great. Money is not that easy to get. I won't say that the system is unfair but I will say that people don't give a penny about each other. There is not sense of nationalism or such thing as feeling sorry for your american brother. If the men see a chance to hit on his brother's or best friend's wife, he'll do it. They won't feel sorry for you if your tonge was sticking out in christmas. My uncle never told us about south bronx, Harlem, drugs, murders, assaults etc. All he had to say was America has all the problems of a third world country but there is a chance to scape from them and not every one succeeds.

I'm sorry I got off the track. Most of the time I feel how Nichola [the narrator of *A Place for Us*] felt at Pulerma. He's thankful that he's scaping calamity and poverty when he sees little boys his age crying for food. I feel just like that when I get letters from Bogatá. My friends graduated with high grades from high school. After that: No jobs, university if you had the money and the right crowd and the anguish of being nothing. I, instead, have been working a part time job for over a year and went to college right after high school. I'm still a nobody but at least I keep my self busy and have not time to think about it. So far, I'm doing just fine.

To end, I have to say that Nichola is the best example of an immigrant. It's the best approach in describing an immigrant I ever read or watched. This is one of the few books I ever got along with.

2. In-Class Freewriting

2/14/92

I think what we read [the essay about education by Sydney Harris, 1990] is very true. The best math teachers that I've had consider that the best way to understand math was by playing with it. They would show us an example, give us some notes and the rest were exercises for us to play. They would get harder and harder but if you saw it as a game within you, you'll work them as if that was your life. Some other teachers would just make us memorize theorems or whatever, they would just give you more and more concepts that at the end weren't good for anything. But the practice and the game in your own were the keys for good understanding.

I wouldn't go to a doctor with two hundred degrees in medicine concepts. I'd go to the one who spend his life playing with dead bodies and animals. He's the real doctor.

I once read that we only use 15% of our real capability of our minds. There was necessary a good teacher to explore the rest. I believed it. We all have the same capabilities, it's just that one uses more of it than others. I think you never stop getting knowledge from yourself. You'll always need to explore yourself because there is always something in there to develop or to bring up. That's why I admire the old folks that come to college with us to audit classes. They know that you are never to old to explore all the knowledge within you. That will be with you until you die. Our mind is the biggest and more effective computer. We have thousands of programs in it. We just have to run those programs.

3. Teacher's Response Letter

Dear Roberto,

I was really impressed with your ideas about education. I like your idea that you learn math or other subjects by "playing with it." Now that I think of it, this is the only way I learn anything; for example, this is how I learned to use a computer. I like this section from your journal: "Some other teachers would just make us memorize theorems or whatever, they would just give you more and more concepts that at the end weren't good for anything. But the practice and the game in your own were the keys for good understanding." I also liked the part about which doctor you would choose.

You do a great job of explaining how you identified with the boy Nick in sentences like: "I know exactly how the boy felt. Knowing that you had felt more pain than any of them could imagine makes you not fit in, not until you find someone with similar experiences."

Reading your journal was like reading a good novel. I couldn't put it down. Have you ever done this kind of writing before? Next time, could you tell me a little bit about how you learned to write this way?

Oh, I see! You answered my question on the last page of your journal: "Writing how you feel can make you realize many things. You can develop a lot of knowledge and open mind thinking. No one will listen to you as a notebook can." Did you always feel this way about writing? What was your experience with writing when you were still living in Colombia?

Rebecca

4. In-Class Freewriting
(Based on Small-Group Discussions of the Meaning of History)

3/27/92

The records of what man has achieved and destroy through time is how I would define history. What's his name wrote "Those who didn't learn history are condemn to repeat it." It's sort of a study of men in time. Because of history we understand the present (Copyright Linda R. 12:10 3/27/92) and are able to calculate and change the future (Copyright Roberto S. 12:15 3/27/92).

The beautiful thing about history is that is not only found in writings but can be found in the inspiration of many artists whose work tell the stories better than the best historian could put them into words. In writings we find causes and consequences, but in the work of art the moment of action is recorded, and the undescribable emotion is then possible to understand.

5. At-Home Journal Writing

4/1/92

I can only think of one thing and that is my car. I know I should be thinking about finals but just the thought of being close to buy my first car makes me shake, not about the cost of insurance but about all the things I'm going to do. I see myself in two months on the beach, looking at the hot body of my car. "DON'T TOUCH IT. STAY AWAY FROM IT, DON'T SIT ON THE

HOOD," I'll say. I'm stuck: run, ruuuun I'm blank run, ruuun. CRASH! Oh! no! I'm in trouble.

6. At-Home Journal Writing

A WORD ABOUT WHAT HAPPENED IN L.A.

I don't believe somebody can use someones misery as an excuse to steal and murder. This is what is called fighting fire with fire. This shows no concern at all. Instead, it shows ignorance of some animals. This is not about races. We were all mad for the jurors decission. But we can't just go out killing people and damaging the businesses that cost them a life time of hard work and dedication. This is not the way to demostrate unger [anger]. Three days after now. I ask myself and everyone: What did they accomplish? The hatred and repugnance of all people who can think rationally and whom their hands will shape the best of our future. What will happen to us in the years to come if we are not able to put reason above evil passions? All our cities will look like the damaged part of L.A. There won't be more meaning to justice and peace because they won't exist anymore. We will run out of tears and our feelings for others will become hatred. Why can't we work together, and if it's too much, why don't we leave each other alone if we can't be together? This people weren't showing their unger. They were being themselves: irrational animals, rebells without cause, and with no crops or green plants. They called bitting [beating] a person up to death justice. Also, the violation of private property rights they called a demonstration. The real name to all is Barbarism.

I don't know what to say about this policemen who punched this guy. They were even worse than the so called "demonstrators." They hid in their uniforms to do the same garbage that today I condemned. They used the name of justice even worse than the "demonstrators." I don't see any excuse in this one. They should have been guilty. The punishment should have been heavier than normal just for the fact they were supposed to protect his rights as american citizens or guardians of law.

The jurors have no pardon. Justice was given to them, i.e. the power to do justice. They should be locked up with the "demonstrators" and the "guardians of the law." They shouldn't be part of our future.

Appendix C

Selected Entries From Cliff's Journal and Teacher's Response Letters

1. In-Class Freewriting
(Written in Response to Sydney Harris' 1990 Essay on Education)

2/14/92

Education can and should be different from place to place. In the story that we read, Socrates teached students by making them conciously aware of their talent and talking about it. I think this is a good way or methed that can be used to educate people in general, but not to all students. That is because in my opinion it is time taking and hard to get quick results.

2. Teacher's Response Letter

2/20/92

Dear Cliff,

It is clear that writing is important in your life. I really loved the way you expressed your ideas about writing: "When I think about writing, the first thing that comes in my mind are words full of expressions and meaningful thoughts. Writing has been very helpful to me especially since it has power over me, that lets out the unspoken words and thoughts from the deepest part of my mind." That is beautifully expressed. In your next journal, could you write a little bit about certain pieces of writing that were especially meaningful to you?

Yes, the book is about "the American dream," a very complicated subject. We'll be writing more about it.

Thanks for sharing your ideas.

Rebecca

3. In-Class Freewriting
(later typed and revised)

2/25/92

I am very proud of this class. Even though it is considered a developmental course, I feel it is a bridge that connects the future me to the presant one. I am learning new ideas which can be helpful, and improve my writing ability. For example, knowing how to write as a famous author with words of sound and picture that are interesting for the reader. I am also very sure that by the end of the semester, I will acquire all the skills expected of me. I feel great knowing that I am in this educational class which has already placed me and my fellow students in the right track, becoming excepted writers.

I really enjoy having to talk and exchange information about our essay with one another. Because this shows me where my mistakes are and I am not understood by the reader. Clearly, if I improve this skills with the help of this class, one day I will become the greatest writer ever lived.

All these dreams can come true with the support of this class only. No one else!!!!

4. Out-of-Class Journal Writing

3/9/92

The Other World!

All of a sudden, with or without acknoledgment, a pathetic soul is lured into "the Other World!" In the eyes of pathetic the real world seems unreal and fragile. The people around him have no communication with him while he is in his isolating world. Even if they try to talk or show any recognition of him in his unknown world, he gets filled up with anger, and hate. What kind of world is this where one can't build a bridge, link, between his puzzling world and the real world? Why is it oppressive to realize this is "the other world?"

This poor soul was like everyone else, agile, bright, and can understand his environment. But why is it he becomes so slow, dumb and strange. As if like a person, lost in big place. Is it may be because he is in "the Other World." He can't figure it out. One way or another until he is out from his possesser, "the other World."

3/10/92

This person doesn't eat much. He feels uneasy when he eats a lot. That is when he starts his journey to "the Other World." Which is caused, by an "insulin reaction," a high concentration of insulin in his blood and low concentration of glucose. At this time, this person loses contact with the real world. He feels good and at ease. Since his blood glucose is low but near normal. He thinks he dosn't have to eat. Finally, after an hour or so, he completely blanks out, in "the Other World."

3/12/92

I'm this person who struggles to keep a stable life. Since I have this desire, I most often fall into, as doctors call it, "insulin reaction." Sometimes I feel it coming. And other times I'm inside of it, wondering without knowing it. I call it "the Other World" because I feel different from what I feel when there is no reaction. For example, all of my senses lead me to believe it would be alright, say if I jump off from a cliff or if I break everything that is in front of me. I wouldn't do all these things if only I have had the right mind. So this world exists between real me and me under the influence.

5. Teacher's Response Letter

3-15-92

Dear Cliff,

I'm glad you feel good about being in this class. I think attitude has a lot to do with success.

Your piece about friendship taught me a lot about your native culture. I loved the sentence: "This friendship will go up to death if that is what it takes to return the favor."

The entry about finding out about the diabetes was really powerful. Through your writing you showed me what a tremendous change this marked in your life. I was furious with the doctor for just telling you to come back in 2 months! They should have helped you learn how to adjust to this big change and how to cope with all these complicated procedures.

It sounds as if you have been coping very well, though. I have several friends who have had diabetes since childhood. They have followed all the procedures, and have had no complications even though they are now middle aged.

I've never heard anyone describe the insulin reaction the way you do. It must be very frightening.

Your writing is really amazing. You draw the reader right in to what you are writing about. In your next journal could you tell me more about your past history as a writer? What is your native language? Did you do much writing in your native language? In English? Where did you learn to write? Have you ever kept a journal just for yourself?

Rebecca

6. Out-of-Class Journal Writing

3-17-92

MY PAST HISTORY AS A WRITER

Writing was the most boring and difficult subjece that I had throughout my high school from grade Six-Twelve. Well, from the beginning, I wasn't motivated to write about anything. Except the fact that I was forced to write without any desire towards to what I was writing. This made it so boring up to the point that I couldn't be force to write.

I started writing when I was in grade Six in my country, Ethiopia. I don't remember all the details of what I wrote. But most of the time, I wrote about an event that happened or simply describe what I know about my environment, like how many kinds trees there are, their name and so on. I had difficulty describing these things because I didn't know how to give adequate information about the subject. This had gotten me a bad repetitions from my teachers. They said, "This is not good. Work at it. It isn't enough," no matter how hard I tried. Finally, I concluded that I am not good in writing so I better not waste my time doing effort less work. I went on like this throughout Seventh and Eighth grade.

I didn't even keep a diary, like my sisters. All of my sisters wrote, in the daily bases, what they did and what exciting thing happened to them before going to bed. I sometimes get curious as to what they wrote about and sneak in their room and read. I personally found it exciting seeing how words can give a powerful meaning and reveal our deepest emotions. Most significantly, they wrote about things they don't usually say out loud, which helped them to communicate with their inner thoughts and express it in words. Unfortunately, I didn't see it work for me.

In American high school, similarly, I didn't achieve, or let's say, I hadn't obtain new and important skills. Since my arrival, I was in the ESL class, English as Second Language class. Basically, it involved having to describe what I learned and what I seen in the form of essay, Introduction, Body, and Conclusion.

When I enter college, my attitude toward writing changed. I started in [the intermediate level] class. At first, I didn't like the professor. She seemed strict and uncommunicable. I said to myself, "Here you go again," expecting rejection, like in the past. But to my surprise, she was open and encouraging towards writing. Her ability to make direct communication enable me to write more until I achieved basic skills in writing, Punctuation, Dependent and Independent clauses, Etc.... I still thank her for the change she helped me obtain towards writing. If it hadn't been for her, I would be still the old me who hates writing.

Now I am in this class learning and enjoying the world of writing which I took for granted in the past.

7. Out-of-Class Journal Writing

5/12/92

Why Now!

During the end of each semester I study as hard as I could to get good grades. But now it seems that everything is trying to make me not achieve my goal without going through a hard time.

When I had one day left from taking my most important math test, I got sick and had to be hospitalized. That day I missed important lesson that was big part in the math test. From A average went to B because of one test. I asked myself, "Why this kind of things happen when I want to get A at the end of the term." But I couldn't find the answer for my question.

I usually study with TV or radio on. When I get home I turn the TV on and do my home works or studies.

Two weeks ago something unexpected happened. Right after I finished my English class, I went straight home. When I got there, the apartment's door was open. I didn't think nothing of it since couple of times before I found the door unlocked and partly open. I walked in without any thought going through my mind. To my surprise, the TV, radio, VCR all were gone, like someone told them to do it that day so I couldn't study. I ask myself once more, "Why can't they wait until I finish my final examinations or even come when I don't have any thing to do. And why didn't they take the other things in the apartment, or is it so I won't do well in my class without the things they took."

Almost everything I worked for in school and at work, the answer was, "No." Why is it everything seems negative when I want to get and do well.

I fail to see why things happen the way that they do. I wish I knew so that I could ignore it when it happened.

Appendix D

Selected Entries From Maribel's Journal and Teacher's Response Letters

1. Out-of-Class Journal Writing

2/12/92

Journal

On the story Going to America [in *A Place for Us*] is about a family who exeles feed on dreams of hope on having freedom and a successful life. Seeking for a place where they wuld be safe and freedom for four young kids, three girls and a boy whom could follow there mothers dream.

They left their home country Greece because the communist guerrillas occupying it had began gathering children to send them to an indoctrination camps behind the iron curtain. They left their mother and their sister Glykeria, fifteen, was missing behind the iron curtain, where they had been imprisoned, tortured and finally executed by the escape. The four travelers set sail to america on March 3, 1949. They passage on the Marine Carp. Their absentee father's American citizenship waited for them in American, whom believed that he's family should stay in Greece because America life is to dangerous specially for teenagers girls.

While traveling to America Olga was seasick. As the only man in the family, he [Nicholas] felt personally responsible for Olga's safety. Nichola met this lady whom was Greek and was married an Ameria soldiers stationed in Greece, her name was christina. She learned English in school. She was willing to teach Nichola English everyday after breakfast while waiting to arrive to America. They founded difficult to learn the English language. Nichola and his sisters found the American food terrible, but as day went by, he learned the English language. It seem kind of hard for them to adopt themselves to the American way of living but they got acustom to America way.

193

The ship approached New York harbor whe[n] Nichola felt an ache of disappointment, New York wasn't the way he pictured it. It was so different from Greece. At the same time he looked over the crowd of people waiting on the land, trying to recognize the Father he had never seen as they found his father shaded in tears of happiness.

[Maribel goes on in this vein for several pages before concluding with the following two paragraphs.]

Their father gave them a tour in their new home in which they were totally amuse in seeing different things. They saw how technology was so advance in America from Greece. Olga was shocked when she was brought to her room, it was diffently from Greece because they would have to share rooms with one and others. In America they had chance to have their own privacy.

Their father wanted to take them shopping so they culd get into the America style, but Olga refused to buy any clothing that wasn't black because she was in mourning for her mother, when she stated she would wear black for five years. Olga and her brother and sisters were still living their mother's death. Remembring their mother dreams "Coming to America" which they had made it come true but their mother isn't there to see. Now they have the father to provide all the love and affection that all four children need at the absentee of their mother.

In my opinion I enjoy reading the story "A Place for Us" because all of us immigrant face the same struggle to form a better future.

2. Teacher's Response Letter

Dear Maribel,

I can understand your feelings about writing [see epigraph at beginning of chapter 6]. It's the assigned essays that are difficult. I hope that you will begin to feel more confident about essay writing by the end of the semester.

You wrote a very complete summary of the chapters in A Place for Us. I especially liked your last page, where you pointed out that the mother's dream had come true, but she wasn't there to see it. In the last paragraph you mention that all immigrants face the same experiences. In your next journal, you might want to write about how this book compares with your experiences.

Rebecca

3. Teacher's Response Letter

April 12, 1992

Dear Maribel,

I like your thoughts on history, for example, when you say, "We can say that people make history. For instance everything that we do everyday, that's history."

Thanks for including your journal on *Hunger of Memory.* Are you keeping this journal for your reading class? Did your reading teacher tell you to do a long summary and a short reaction? Actually, I would rather hear a long reaction and a very short summary. For example, I would like to know how you, as a Spanish speaker, feel about Rodriguez' ideas about language. Do you think parents should stop speaking their native language to their children if a teacher tells them to? You say that Richard learned English but he was forgetting his native language. How do you feel about that? If you have children, how will you handle these issues with them? Is it always necessary to give up the first language in order to learn the second one?

In your next journal please write more about your own feelings about these ideas. Check with me if you have any questions.

Have a nice vacation!

Rebecca

4. Out-of-Class Journal Writing

4/30/92

Hunger of Memory
The Education of Richard Rodriguez

Rodriguez called this chapter Mr. Secrets. In this chapter, he talked about things that his mother has asked him not to reveal. After he published his first autobiographical essay seven years ago, his mother wrote him a letter pleading with him never again to write about their family life. She said "Write about something else in the future. Our family life is private and besides why do you need to tell the gringos about how 'divided' you feel from the family?"

One thing that never has changed in his family is that his parents know the difference between private and public life. And their private society remains only their family. No matter how friendly they were in public.

I think that Richard's mother has all the right to tell Richard not to reveal the things that happened to the family. I believe that as he [his] mother said he could write about something else.

I'm alway saying that something that happened to a family nobody has to know it. Because is no their problem. Another thing that I learned is that if something embarrest happened in a classroom, the other classroom don't have to know it. Is something that have to be between those four walls.

5. Out-of-Class Journal Writing

5/8/92

I don't think that parents should stop speaking their native language to their children. Parents are the first one whom I believe that they have to teach their children the first language.

A native language is part of a culture. That is something that you feel proud of it. When I get married and I have children, I'm going to teach spanish. They have to learn it, because no all of my family speak English. And also when we go back visit my native country, Dominican Republic, my children will be able to communicate with other people.

I think that the best age for anyone to learn any language is when you are little. When you are a child.

6. Out-of-Class Journal Writing

Is it always necessary to give up the first language in order to learn the second one?

You asked me this question before, but I never wrote in my journals my feelings about this topic. I wrote some journals about Richard Rodriguez. He learned English but he was forgetting his native one.

I'm not agree with him. I think that you can learn another language without forgetting your native one. I learned English and I didn't forget my first language.

Now [in the United States] there are people who need person that speak more the one language. So learning a second language is very important and is necessary.

Appendix E

Selected Entries From Lan's Journal and Teacher's Response Letters

1. In-Class Freewriting

Free Writing

2/7/92

As I have heard by one of the examples that Ms. Mlynarczyk read for us, I have a mix feeling about my attitude of writing. Sometime I find out that I have a lot of words in my mind that I would like to write them down on a piece of paper, it is very hard to explain all of them by writing, especially writing in English. May be that is because my English is still very poor and I know too few of English words. On the other hand, because it is hard for me to write in English, therefore, I write nothing besides the assignment that the teachers give me in school. Untill last semester after I failed [the writing course], I tried to write more often in English such as daily and journals. While this winter section, I wrote twenty essays and at least two free-writing or journals each day. Even though I failed again, my English improved a great deal. I am keeping working hard and hoping I will pass this semester.

2. Out-of-Class Journal Writing

2/8/92

During the class, Ms. Mlynarczyk asked us to buy the book *A Place for Us* and assigned the first two chapters for us to read during the weekend. I brought it immediately right after the class and began to read in the train on my way home. Honestly, I did not crazy for the book because I almost fell in asleep while I was reading it. May be I felt tired or may be there were some words which I did not understand so that I felt boring of reading it.

In the first chapter, the author, Mr. Nicholas described he and his three sisters left his own country after the murder of their mother and the last of one of their sisters to move to America as immigrants, and to meet their father in the United States.

I remembered that the same sad feeling which happened to me when I left my country, China and came to the United States. On one hand, I was luckier than Mr. Nicholas because both my parents were alive and came with me together. On the other hand he was more fortunate than me because by the time he came, he was ten years old and learned some English on the ship while he was on the way traveling to America. Futhermore, he was still a child and he would catch up a new language fast. However, I was twenty when I came and knew nothing of English. My pressure was much than his. Anyway, thanks God, I am here reading Mr. Nicholas' book. Even though my English was still poor and I am still taking Bilingual course [actually an ESL course], I have full of confident that one day I will become as good as Mr. Nicholas at the level of writing and reading in English.

3. Out-of-Class Journal Writing

2/8/92

It must be something wrong with me today. Otherwise, I shouldn't feel so sleepy today. May be it is because I did not sleep enough last night. However, I went to bed at 12:30 Am and got up at 7:15 Am this morning. That means I slept almost seven hours and It seemed enough for a person. Then why did I feel so sleepy today? Perhapes I need eight hours for sleep a day because I slept so much during the winter vacation. Yet it is the first day of the week. May be I just still not feel comfortable for back to school after the long vacation. Anyway, I have to face myself get used to it. I am taking six courses this semeser and I need a lot of energy for my hard working. I should not fall in asleep any more during the classes. I ought to use the time wisely and concentrate at every lectures in school. Even though I will have a very hard time this semester, I have to try my best, especially in Anthropology, Sociology, and Geogograph.

4. Teacher's Response Letter

Dear Lan,

I'm glad you mentioned your negative feelings about repeating this course and being back in the Writing Center. I know how depressing that must feel. But you must have worked very hard to write 20 essays and at least 2 journal entries every day. It's very important for you to remember your own words here: "Even though I failed again, my English improved a great deal. I am keeping working hard and hoping I will pass this semester."

I can see the evidence of the improvement you have already made. Your writing seems quite good to me, and it is realistic to expect that you will pass this semester if you keep working hard. I'm glad to see you writing the practice essays. You can keep putting these in your journal if you would like. The content of this essay is good, especially the example about your brother. There are some grammar errors here. See if you can go over the grammar with your tutor.

Good luck to you.

Rebecca

5. In-Class Freewriting

2/25/92

"How do you feel about being in this class?" When Ms. Mlynarczyk asked this question in class, I answered it without any hesitation: "I hate it, I hate it very much!" It is not that I hate to study, especially writing. It is that I just don't like this education system of the [name of the university]. It takes me so long to stay in this class and cannot move foreward. In other word, it waste both my time and money.

However, as a foreign who studies English as a second language in the United States, I should glad that I have the opportunity to repeat this class again. Last time, I didn't pass this course. That means I was not in the level of progression. I had to take it one more time to improve my writing of English.

In fact, I should never complained about anything, but working hard all the time I should practice more essays and keep writing journals in this semester so that I can pass this time.

6. In-Class Freewriting
(Prompt: What does history mean to you?)

"What is history means to you?"

"History," whenever this word comes into my mind, I feel have a kind of headack because I think about when I study history, there are a lot of things which I requirt to remember, and the names of the famous people and the events always give me a big headack. However, I like history because from (through) history, I learn a lot of knowledge about my culture, my country and the whole world.

7. Out-of-Class Journal Writing

I didn't write my personal daily journals for a long time. That's why I am feeling strange when I peck up my pen and try to write something. There is a saying which is very suitable for this situation, "When you used to do something, you do it fast." Otherwise, you do it slowly still. Even worse, you will gradually forget it at all if you don't do it again. However, I am glad that I am holding my pen now so that I remember to write something—even-thought they are some nonsense words.

8. Teacher's Response Letter

April 13, 1992

Dear Lan,

When I was in college and high school, I didn't like history either. But now I have a sense that all of us are really making history through our own lives. How was history revealed when you did your interview?

Thanks for telling me what you finally decided to do about sociology. I think you made a wise decision, and I don't really think the W [for withdrawal] will be seen as something negative. It's certainly much better than a D or an F.

I read your anthropology paper before I read your journal, so it was nice to learn your feelings about writing this paper. I really liked the way you included an analysis of your own family structure along with the two cultures in the assignment. I liked your paper very much and also learned from reading it.

Your last entry [number 7 in this appendix] made me laugh. I agree that one quickly loses one's writing ability if one doesn't practice. That's one of the main reasons why I require these journals.

Thanks for sharing your thoughts.

Rebecca

9. Out-of-Class Journal Writing

4/29/92

Wednesday: It is a day that I always feel terrible with. Actually, during the dean's hour, we have a Chinese Christian Fellowship which meets today. On the other hand, the dancing club is opening in the same time. I am a Christian and I am a secretary of this CCF. I should go to the meeting every time. However, I am taking Modern Dance this semester and I am crazy for dance. It would be a lot of help for me if I go to the dancing club every week. Sometimes it is very hard to decide where I should go better. Today I had no idea again. Finally, I prayed before the hour came, and I went to Fellowship.

References

Bakhtin, M. M. (1986). *Speech genres and other late essays.* C. Emerson & M. Holquist (Eds.). Austin, TX: University of Texas Press.

Baldwin, C. (1977). *One to one: Self-understanding through journal writing.* New York: M. Evans.

Belenky, M., Clinchy, B., Goldberger, N., & Tarule, J. (1986). *Women's ways of knowing: The development of self, voice, and mind.* New York: Basic Books.

Bereiter, C., & Scardamalia, M. (1983). Does learning to write have to be so difficult? In A. Freedman, I. Pringle, & J. Yalden (Eds.), *Learning to write: First language, second language.* London: Longman.

Bereiter, C., & Scardamalia, M. (1985). Cognitive coping strategies and the problem of "inert knowledge." In S. F. Chipman, J. W. Segal, & R. Glaser (Eds.), *Thinking and learning skills: Vol. 2. Research and open questions* (pp. 65–80). Hillsdale, NJ: Lawrence Erlbaum Associates.

Bordo, S. (1986). The Cartesian masculinization of thought. *Signs: Journal of Women in Culture and Society, 11*(3), 439–456.

Britton, J. (1970). *Language and learning: The importance of speech in children's development.* London: Penguin.

Britton, J. (1982). *Prospect and retrospect: Selected essays of James Britton* (G. M. Pradl, Ed.). Montclair, NJ: Boynton Cook.

Brookes, G. (1987). *Promising practices in the teaching of writing.* Unpublished doctoral dissertation, Teachers College, Columbia University, New York.

Bruner, J. (1985). On teaching thinking: An afterthought. In S. F. Chipman, J. W. Segal, & R. Glaser (Eds.), *Thinking and learning skills: Vol. 2. Research and open questions* (pp. 597–608). Hillsdale, NJ: Lawrence Erlbaum Associates.

Burtis, P. J., Bereiter, C., Scardamalia, M., & Tetroe, J. (1983). The development of planning in writing. In C. G. Wells & B. Kroll (Eds.), *Exploration of children's development in writing.* Chichester, England: Wiley.

Calkins, L. M. (1983). *Lessons from a child: On the teaching and learning of writing.* Exeter, NH: Heinemann.

Cochran-Smith, M., & Lytle, S. L. (1993). *Inside outside: Teacher research and knowledge.* New York: Teachers College Press.

Coles, R. (1989). *The call of stories: Teaching and the moral imagination.* Boston: Houghton Mifflin.

Collins, A., & Gentner, D. (1980). A framework for a cognitive theory of writing. In L. W. Gregg & E. Steinberg (Eds.), *Cognitive processes in writing: An interdisciplinary approach.* Hillsdale, NJ: Lawrence Erlbaum Associates.

Connors, R. J. (1996). Teaching and learning as a man. *College English, 58*(2), 137–157.

Cruickshank, D. R. (1987). *Reflective teaching: The preparation of students of teaching.* Reston, VA: Association of Teacher Educators.

Cumming, A. (1989). Writing expertise and second language proficiency. *Language Learning, 39*(1), 81–141.

Cummings, M. C. (1988). *What we talk about when we talk about writing.* Unpublished doctoral dissertation, Teachers College, Columbia University, New York.

Derber, C. (1979). *The pursuit of attention: Power and individualism in everyday life.* New York: Oxford.

Dewey, J. (1933). *How we think: A restatement of the relation of reflective thinking to the educative process.* Boston: Heath.

Dixon, K. (1995). Gendering the "personal." *College Composition and Communication, 46*(2), 255–275.

Eisner, E. (1991). *The enlightened eye.* New York: Macmillan.

Elbow, P. (1973). *Writing without teachers.* New York: Oxford University Press.

Ely, M., Anzul, M., Friedman, T., Gardner, D., & Steinmetz, A. (1991). *Doing qualitative research: Circles within circles.* New York: Falmer Press.

Emig, J. (1971). *The composing processes of twelfth graders.* Urbana, IL: NCTE.

Erickson, F. (1993). Foreword. In M. Cochran-Smith & S. L. Lytle (Eds.), *Inside outside: Teacher research and knowledge* (pp. vii–ix). New York: Teachers College Press.

Flower, L., & Hayes, J. R. (1980). The cognition of discovery: Defining a rhetorical problem. *College Composition and Communication, 31,* 221–232.

Flower, L., & Hayes, J. R. (1981). The pregnant pause: An inquiry into the nature of planning. *Research in the Teaching of English, 15,* 229–244.

Fulwiler, T. (Ed.). (1987). *The journal book.* Portsmouth, NH: Boynton Cook.

Gage, N. (1989). *A place for us.* New York: Simon & Schuster.

Gannett, C. (1992). *Gender and the journal: Diaries and academic discourse.* Albany: State University of New York Press.

Gardner, H. (1983). *Frames of mind: The theory of multiple intelligences.* New York: Basic Books.

Geertz, C. (1973). *The interpretation of cultures.* New York: Basic Books.

Gere, A. (Ed.). (1985). *Roots in the sawdust: Writing to learn across the disciplines.* Urbana, IL: NCTE.

Gilligan, C. (1982). *In a different voice: Psychological theory and women's development.* Cambridge, MA: Harvard University Press.

Goetz, J. P., & LeCompte, M. D. (1984). *Ethnography and qualitative design in educational research.* Orlando, FL: Academic Press.

Graves, D. (1983). *Writing: Teachers and children at work.* Exeter, NH: Heinemann.

Harris, S. (1990). What true education should do. In R. Spack (Ed.), *Guidelines: A cross-cultural reading/writing text* (pp. 9–10). New York: St. Martin's.

Haswell, J., & Haswell, R. H. (1995). Gendership and the miswriting of students. *College Composition and Communication, 46*(2), 223–254.

Heilbrun, C. G. (1988). *Writing a woman's life.* New York: Ballantine.

Helle, A. P. (1991). Reading women's autobiographies: A map of reconstructed knowing. In C. Witherell & N. Noddings (Eds.), *Stories lives tell: Narrative and dialogue in education* (pp. 48–66). New York: Teachers College Press.

Higgins, L., Flower, L., & Petraglia, J. (1992). Planning text together: The role of critical reflection in student collaboration. *Written Communication, 9*(1), 48–84.

Hycner, R. H. (1985). Some guidelines for the phenomenological analysis of interview data. *Human Studies, 8,* 279–303.

Jehlen, M. (1984). Archimedes and the paradox of feminist criticism. *Signs*, 6(4), 575–601.

Jensen, G. H., & DiTiberio, J. K. (1989). *Personality and the teaching of composition*. Norwood, NJ: Ablex.

Johnstone, A. C. (1994). *Uses for journal keeping: An ethnography of writing in a university science class* (Rev. ed; B. Johnstone & V. Balester, Eds.). Norwood, NJ: Ablex.

Joos, M. (1961). *The five clocks*. New York: Harcourt Brace & World.

Krashen, S. (1981). The monitor model for second language acquisition. In R. Gingras (Ed.), *Second language acquisition and foreign language learning* (pp. 1–26). Washington, DC: Center for Applied Linguistics.

Krashen, S. (1982). *Principles and practice in second language acquisition*. Oxford: Pergamon Press.

Larsen-Freeman, D. (1991). Second language acquisition research: Staking out the territory. *TESOL Quarterly*, 25(2), 315–350.

Leki, I. (1992). *Understanding ESL writers: A guide for teachers*. Portsmouth, NH: Boynton Cook.

Lincoln, Y., & Guba, E. (1985). *Naturalistic inquiry*. Beverly Hills, CA: Sage.

Lofland, J., & Lofland, L. H. (1984). *Analyzing social settings: A guide to qualitative observation and analysis* (2nd ed.). Belmont, CA: Wadsworth.

Lowenstein, S. (1987). A brief history of journal keeping. In T. Fulwiler (Ed.), *The journal book*. Portsmouth, NH: Boynton Cook.

Lucas, T. (1992). Diversity among individuals: Eight students making sense of classroom journal writing. In D. E. Murray (Ed.), *Diversity as resource: Redefining cultural literacy*. Alexandria, VA: TESOL.

Luria, A. R. (1982). *Language and cognition* (J. V. Wertsch, Ed.). New York: Wiley.

Lyons, N. (1983). Two perspectives: On self, relationships and morality. *Harvard Educational Review*, 53, 125–145.

Mayher, J. (1990). *Uncommon sense*. Portsmouth, NH: Boynton Cook.

Mayher, J. S., Lester, N., & Pradl, G. M. (1983). *Learning to write/writing to learn*. Portsmouth, NH: Boynton Cook.

McCarthy, L. P., & Fishman, S. M. (1991). Boundary conversations: Conflicting ways of knowing in philosophy and interdisciplinary research. *Research in the Teaching of English*, 25(4), 419–468.

Miller, J. (1996). *School for women*. London: Virago.

Mlynarczyk, R. (1991a). Is there a difference between personal and academic writing? *TESOL Journal*, 1(1), 17–20.

Mlynarczyk, R. (1991b). Student choice: An alternative to teacher-selected reading materials. *College ESL*, 1(2), 1–8.

Mlynarczyk, R. (1994). A comment on "Connecting literature to students' lives." *College English*, 56(6), 710–712.

Mlynarczyk, R., & Haber, S. (1996). *In our own words: A guide with readings for student writers* (2nd ed.). New York: St. Martin's.

Moi, T. (1985). *Sexual/textual politics: Feminist literary theory*. London: Methuen.

Morgan, D. (1993). Connecting literature to students' lives. *College English*, 55(5), 491–500.

Newell, A. (1980). Reasoning, problem solving, and decision processes: The problem space as a fundamental category. In R. S. Nickerson (Ed.), *Attention and performance VIII*. Hillsdale, NJ: Lawrence Erlbaum Associates.

Noddings, N. (1984). *Caring: A feminine approach to ethics and moral education*. Los Angeles: University of California Press.

North, S. N. (1987). *The making of knowledge in composition: Portrait of an emerging field.* Portsmouth, NH: Boynton Cook.

Oxford, R. (1993). Language learning strategies in a nutshell: Update and ESL suggestions. *TESOL Journal, 2*(2), 18–22.

Parry, K. (1996). Culture, literacy, and L2 reading. *TESOL Quarterly, 30*(4), 665–692.

Perkins, D. N. (1985). General cognitive skills: Why not? In S. F. Chipman, J. W. Segal, & R. Glaser (Eds.), *Thinking and learning skills: Vol. 2. Research and open questions* (pp. 339–363). Hillsdale, NJ: Lawrence Erlbaum Associates.

Perl, S. (1975). *Five writers writing: The composing processes of unskilled college writers.* Unpublished doctoral dissertation, New York University.

Perry, W. G. (1970). *Forms of intellectual and ethical development in the college years.* New York: Holt, Rinehart & Winston.

Peyton, J. K. (Ed.). (1990). *Students and teachers writing together: Perspectives on journal writing.* Alexandria, VA: TESOL.

Peyton, J. K., & Staton, J. (1993). *Dialogue journals in the multinational classroom: Building language fluency and writing skills through written interaction.* Norwood, NJ: Ablex.

Peyton, J. K., & Staton, J. (Eds.). (1996). *Writing our lives: Reflections on dialogue journal writing with adults learning English.* McHenry, IL: Center for Applied Linguistics and Delta Systems.

Pianko, S. (1979). Reflection: A critical component of the composing process. *College Composition and Communication, 30*(3), 275–278.

Polanyi, M. (1958a). *Personal knowledge.* Chicago: University of Chicago Press.

Polanyi, M. (1958b). *The study of man: The Lindsay memorial lectures.* London: Routledge & Kegan Paul.

Progoff, I. (1975). *At a journal workshop.* New York: Dialogue House.

Raimes, A. (1983). Anguish as a second language? Remedies for composition teachers. In A. Freedman, I. Pringle, & J. Yalden (Eds.), *Learning to write: First language/second language* (pp. 258–272). London: Longman.

Raimes, A. (1985). What unskilled ESL students do as they write: A classroom study of composing. *TESOL Quarterly, 19*(2), 229–258.

Raimes, A. (1991). Out of the woods: Emerging traditions in the teaching of writing. *TESOL Quarterly, 26*(3), 407–430.

Rainer, T. (1978). *The new diary: How to use a journal for self-guidance and expanded creativity.* Los Angeles: J. P. Tarcher.

Rodriguez, R. (1982). *Hunger of memory.* New York: Bantam.

Root, C. B. (1979). The use of personal journals in the teaching of English to speakers of other languages. *TESL Reporter, 12*(2), 3–5.

Rose, M. (1989). *Lives on the boundary: The struggles and achievements of America's underprepared.* New York: Penguin.

Rosenblatt, L. M. (1968). *Literature as exploration.* New York: Appleton Century. (Original work published 1938)

Rosenblatt, L. M. (1978). *The reader, the text, the poem: The transactional theory of the literary work.* Carbondale: Southern Illinois University Press.

Rowe, D. (1978). *Choosing not losing: The experience of depression.* London: Wiley.

Savignon, S. (1991). Communicative language teaching: State of the art. *TESOL Quarterly, 25*(2), 261–277.

Scardamalia, M., & Bereiter, C. (1985). Fostering the development of self-regulation in children's knowledge processing. In S. F. Chipman, J. W. Segal, & R. Glaser (Eds.),

Thinking and learning skills: Volume 2: Research and open questions (pp. 563–577). Hillsdale, NJ: Lawrence Erlbaum Associates.

Scardamalia, M., Bereiter, C., & Steinbach, R. (1984). Teachability of reflective processes in written composition. *Cognitive Science, 8*(2), 173–190.

Schlafly, P. (Ed.). (1984). *Child abuse in the classroom.* Alton, IL: Pere Marquette Press.

Schön, D. A. (1983). *The reflective practitioner: How professionals think in action.* New York: Basic Books.

Schön, D. A. (1987). *Educating the reflective practitioner.* San Francisco: Jossey-Bass.

Schön, D. A. (Ed.). (1991). *The reflective turn: Case studies in and on educational practice.* New York: Teachers College Press.

Shuy, R. W. (1988). The oral language basis for dialogue journals. In J. Staton, R. W. Shuy, J. K. Peyton, & L. Reed (Eds.), *Dialogue Journal communication: Classroom, linguistic, social, and cognitive views.* Norwood, NJ: Ablex.

Smith, F. (1991). *To think.* New York: Teachers College Press.

Smith, J. (1991). Setting the cat among the pigeons: A not so sentimental journey to the heart of teaching. *English Education, 23*(2), 68–126.

Sommers, N. (1979). *Revision in the composing process: A case study of college freshmen and experienced adult writers.* Doctoral dissertation, Boston University, 1978. (University Microfilms No. 7905022).

Song, B. (1995). What does reading mean for East Asian students? *College ESL, 5*(2), 35–48.

Spack, R. (1990). *Guidelines: A cross-cultural reading/writing text.* New York: St. Martin's.

Spack, R. (1996). Teaching across cultures. *College English, 58*(5), 592–597.

Spack, R. (1997). The (in)visibility of the person(al) in academe. *College English, 59*(1), 9–31.

Spack, R., & Sadow, C. (1983). Student-teacher working journals in ESL freshman composition. *TESOL Quarterly, 17*(4), 575–593.

Spradley, J. (1979). *The ethnographic interview.* New York: Holt, Rinehart & Winston.

Staton, J. (1980). Writing and counseling: Using a dialogue journal. *Language Arts, 57*(5), 514–518.

Staton, J. (1988). An introduction to dialogue journal communication. In J. Staton, R. W. Shuy, J. K. Peyton, & L. Reed (Eds.), *Dialogue journal communication: Classroom, linguistic, social, and cognitive views.* Norwood, NJ: Ablex.

Staton, J., Shuy, R., & Kreeft, J. (1982). *Analysis of dialogue journal writing as a communicative event: Vol. 1. Final report to the National Institute of Education.* Washington, DC: Center for Applied Linguistics.

Staton, J., Shuy, R. W., Peyton, J. K., & Reed, L. (Eds.). (1988). *Dialogue journal communication: Classroom, linguistic, social and cognitive views.* Norwood, NJ: Ablex.

Sternglass, M. S. (1988). *The presence of thought: Introspective accounts of reading and writing.* Norwood, NJ: Ablex.

Swain, M. (1985). Communicative competence: Some roles of comprehensible input and comprehensible output in its development. In S. Gass & C. Madden (Eds.), *Input in second language acquisition* (pp. 235–253). Rowley, MA: Newbury House.

Tannen, D. (1990). *You just don't understand: Women and men in conversation.* New York: Ballantine.

Tarvin, W. L., & Al-Arishi, A. Y. (1991). Rethinking communicative language teaching: Reflection and the EFL classroom. *TESOL Quarterly, 25*(1), 9–27.

Tesch, R. (1990). *Qualitative research: Analysis types and software tools.* New York: Falmer Press.

Tillyer, D. (1993, March). World peace and natural writing through Email. *Collegiate Microcomputer, 11*(2).

Tillyer, D. (1994, Spring). High tech/Low monitor: An ESL writing course at City College of New York meets multicultural needs with E-mail. *APEX-J (Electronic Journal of the Asian/Pacific Exchange Electronic List)*.

Valdes, G. (1992). Bilingual minorities and language issues in writing: Toward professionwide responses to a new challenge. *Written Communication, 9*(1), 85–136.

Vygotsky, L. (1978). *Mind in society: The development of higher psychological processes* (M. Cole, V. John-Steiner, S. Scribner, & E. Souberman, Eds.). Cambridge, MA: Harvard University Press.

Vygotsky, L. (1986). *Thought and language* (A. Kozulin, Ed.). Cambridge, MA: MIT Press. (Original work published in English, 1962)

Zamel, V. (1976). Teaching composition in the ESL classroom: What we can learn from research in the teaching of English. *TESOL Quarterly, 10*(1), 67–76.

Zamel, V. (1983). The composing processes of advanced ESL students: Six case studies. *TESOL Quarterly, 17*(2), 165–187.

Zamel, V. (1991). Acquiring language, literacy, and academic discourse: Entering ever new conversations. *ESL College, 1*(1), 10–18.

Zamel, V. (1992). Writing one's way into reading. *TESOL Quarterly, 26*(3), 463–485.

Author Index

Subject Index

A

Assessment of writing ability, effects of, 39–41, 67, 71–73, 96–98, 126, 137

Attitudes toward reading and writing, 38, 44, 52, 67–69, 84, 85–89, 92, 152–154
  influence of family on, 85–86, 94–95
  influence of schools and teachers on, 85–89, 94–95, 103–108, 131–132, 152–154, 171

Audience for journal writing, *see* Journal writing, communication with readers

C

Connected knowing, 25–28, 80, 101–102, 126, 132, 166–168
  as an analytic framework, 30–32
  in Cliff's journal, 102–103
  connection with other theories of education, 28–30
  definition, 25–28
  empathy and identification in, 26–27, 61–63, 70
  internal dialogue in, 59–60, 99–101, 175

in Lan's journal, 143–144
  recognition of temporal flux and change in, 59
  in Roberto's journal, 56–63
  role of emotion in, 58–59
  role of the personal in, 28–30, 63, 101–102, 124–128

Constructed knowledge
  definition, 32
  in Roberto's journal, 77–83
  in Cliff's journal, 103

Cultural expectations for writing, 150–152, 162–164

D

Dialogue, *see* Reflection, social dialogue in; Reflection, internal dialogue in; Reflective practice, dialogic quality

Dialogue journals, 14–17

Diaries, 85–86, 136, 148, 154, 160

E

Epistemological perspectives, 31–32

Essay assignments, list of, 38

Ethnography, 3, 5, 9–10

Expressive language, 19–21, 24, 175